SCAPEGOAT

Scapegoat

The Impact of Death-Fear on an American Family

Eric Bermann

Ann Arbor
THE UNIVERSITY OF MICHIGAN PRESS

Here at a center is a creature: it would be our business to show how through every instant of every day of every year of his existence alive he is from all sides streamed inward upon, bombarded, pierced, destroyed by that enormous sleeting of all objects forms and ghosts how great how small no matter, which surround and whom his senses take: in as great and perfect and exact particularity as we can name them:

This would be our business, to show them each thus transfixed as between the stars' trillions of javelins and of each the transfixions: but it is beyond my human power to do. The most I can do—the most I can hope to do—is to make a number of physical entities as plain and vivid as possible, and to make a few guesses, a few conjectures; and to leave to you much of the burden of realizing in each of them what I have wanted to make clear of them as a whole: how each is itself; and how each is a shapener.

—*James Agee*

Preface

Because of its ubiquity and its sheer potential for terrorizing, death would seem among the more deserving topics for social scientific inquiry. Certainly, few phenomena, either in their anticipation or in their wake, can so devastate the fabric of social bondedness and interaction, so blight the growth of intellectual and emotional consciousness, and so fundamentally alter one's perception and one's tacit conviction about the "goodness" or "meaningfulness" of events in this world. Yet, the truth is that few topics have been more neglected.

The aversion of behavioral scientists and mental health professionals to the study of death and death-related behavior is both understandable and lamentable. It is understandable if only from the point of view that the mental health professional and clinical researcher are themselves products of a death-denying culture. They thereby share the public's antipathy toward a subject that has been consensually deemed a social taboo. It is lamentable insofar as the antipathy has resulted in a severe imbalance in our accumulated knowledge of human behavior; the entire field is peculiarly atrophied in some regards and hypertrophied in others. By extension, our explanations for behavior are decidedly circumscribed. We presume to know a great deal about how man learns to live and about the ways in which he adapts to changed environs; we know next to nothing about how he learns to die, or how he daily contends with the inevitable prospect of death, or, in some instances, adapts to its imminent occurrence. Until the former concerns are informed by knowledge of the latter we may reasonably wonder what we truly know about either.

Death, of course, is by no means the only topic in social science to have been badly neglected. It is, by virtue of its ubiquity, merely one of the more glaring examples of neglect. Another, equally prominent in its own strange way, is the study of family interaction. As a social institution, the family may be one of the most researched features of the human condition, yet our knowledge of it remains oddly empty, externally derived, and devoid of intimacy. The reason is simple enough. Except for rare instances, the Western and especially the middle-American family have not been studied from the inside in their natural habitat—the home. The home remains a privileged sanctuary protected by privacy. The ultrarespect accorded family privacy has enforced data collection and research techniques that are presumed to be less intrusive to family function than naturalistic methods or participant-observation methods. Experimental laboratory techniques, office interviews, or survey research data have been almost exclusively relied on, producing a field of study remarkable for its disjunctive qualities. We know a great deal about family structure, form, and function, at least as publicly presented or reported by family members, but we know virtually nothing about the routines of day-to-day family interactions in the home, or the moment-to-moment dynamisms that guide a family's private adaptations to stressful events.

This book seeks to intrude into both these neglected territories, and it attempts, among other things, to come to grips with the sources of the neglect and its ramifying effects. Quite explicitly, the book is about death and a family. It presents a close-up view of a single American family enmeshed in an extended deathwatch. It is concerned with the impact of both latent and imminent death-fears on the daily functioning of seven persons as observed over a period of time in the familiar surroundings of their own home. The method of data collection employed is that of naturalistic observation. Because the book is centered about these concerns and this method, it is, inevitably, about more as well.

To the extent that it is a book about a middle-American family, it is, in the broadest conception, about American culture, values, and life-styles, replete with their inherent inconsistencies and strains. It is, of course, also about American attitudes toward death and dying, impotence and mastery, and about those coping techniques most preferred by middle-American families when they are transfixed by dread.

To the extent that it is a book about a single family observed in the home, it is a book about the advantages and disadvantages of "N of 1" research, and, perforce, about the
virtues and liabilities implicit in the naturalistic method; relatedly and importantly, it is about the ethics and imperatives of
social and personal privacy in our society today.

To the extent that it is a book about a family that is officially, if not spiritually, enrolled in our mental health care system, it is a book about that system, and about the frustrations
of wrongheaded help-giving, and about the biases that permeate our theories and methods, and about the all too frequent co-optation of our good purposes and hopeful commitments.

Ultimately, however, in the focused, particularized view,
this book is about a family's reaction to stress and then to crisis. It is about shifting role function and reordered group
alignments in the interests of individual defense and interpersonal adaptation. It is about saving some things and some persons, and sacrificing others. It is about the numbing of human
sensibilities and the destruction of children, and the far-reaching, wholesale effects of frightening and sad moments. Quite
literally, it is about the high cost of dying, tallied not in mone-
tary but in psychological terms.

It would be highly misleading, however, to leave the impression that this book was, in the beginning, and by deliberate preconception, about any of these things. It was not. It had
its origins in the immediacies of clinical work and diagnostic
confusion. The knowledge that mental health research had
tread lightly on the subjects of death and the family played no
part in its early phases. It was only much later that the con-
tours of the mental health field began to influence the shaping
of the book.

The book evolved from simple but vivid images that kept
recurring long after the period of observations had come to an
end. Some of these were physical images—of household, of objects, of furnishings and possessions—of inside things: uphol-
stered couches worn at the seams; kitchen appliances spotted
by chipped enamel; grey light, diffuse and weak, filtered
through small, screened windows; and darkened rooms lit only

by the flickerings of television. Outside, there was bright sunshine, and polished motorcycles with glinting chrome, and grass and space—lots of grass and lots of space.

Other images were of people—sometimes of children seemingly lost and wandering in their own home; sometimes of faces haggard, and drawn and impassive, fatigued beyond their years; occasionally of faces hardened and soured before their time; but, mostly there were images of vacant-eyed strangers who, though in the confines of the same room, seemed to glide by each other, very rarely touching.

Still other images were of moments—moments decisive for their cavernous silences, defaulted opportunities, embarrassed abdications, belittlements and petty recriminations, and futility.

Such memories have an indelible tone and a persistence that made them easy to redintegrate and hard to resist. In them lay the wellsprings for the book.

Acknowledgments

First and foremost I must acknowledge my indebtedness to Daniel R. Miller of Brunel University, London, upon whose intellectual resources I have drawn most heavily in putting together this book. He has been both teacher and colleague, and I esteem him among the more creative social scientists I have encountered. Frankly, I have internalized a great deal of his orientation to social and psychological analysis, with the consequence that I can seldom ascertain any longer where or when I have "borrowed" his conceptualizations or terminologies. I can say with certainty that it was Daniel Miller who first alerted me to the value of home observation as a method for the diagnostic study of family, but, beyond that, the task of giving him credit for what is properly his in this book becomes difficult. Suffice it to say that the book is throughout imbued with his thinking.

I am also deeply grateful to Albert C. Cain whose patient encouragement never seemed to get in the way of his critical eye. He is a man who has the rare knack for bringing out the best in people. He has been instrumental and integral to the development of this book every step of the way.

For advice on structure and organization of materials, manner of presentation and sequencing of chapters, I owe much to the efforts of Robert Kastenbaum.

Jane Drotos and Pauline Newby were most helpful in the typing and preparation of the manuscript. Their personal interest and comments proved both useful and cogent.

My wife and my four children have been of invaluable assistance from the outset. With characteristic joie de vivre they peppered me with encouragements and votes of confidence. They displayed patience and understanding for my absences and preoccupations, and did so with good humor. They have a tendency to make every effort, whether large or small, meaningful and worthwhile, and for this I thank them.

Above all, however, I recognize my gratitude to the family described in this book—the A.'s. Their identities and rights to privacy have been protected through the use of pseudonyms, but I express my indebtedness to them for granting me the privilege of entering their home and lives. They have greatly increased my understanding of human transactions, and it is to them that this book is dedicated.

Contents

Introduction   1

I. CLINICAL PROBLEM AND RESEARCH METHOD

1. Roscoe A. and His Parents   17
2. The Home Visit   33

II. CONFIGURATIONS

3. Interaction Frequencies in Behavior Exchange   47
4. Pairs   60

III. DEATH-TERROR

5. Fear as an Organizing Theme   95

IV. SOME DEFENSES AGAINST
"KNOWING" AND "FEELING"

6. Thanatophobic Countermeasures   109
7. Time Out of Mind   124
8. Cognitive Dysfunction as Family Style   135

V. THE FATE AND DISSIPATION OF ANGER

9. Father Absence   143
10. The Uses of Scapegoating   159

VI. SEQUELAE

11. The Immediate Aftermath   201
12. Recent History   215

VII. CONCLUSIONS AND FURTHER THOUGHTS

13. Clinical Research and Death   235
14. Clinical Research and the Family   262

Appendix   327

Selected Bibliography   341

Index   355

Introduction

Several years ago in his book *Culture Against Man* Jules Henry observed:

> There are many roads to insanity and our culture has probably trod them all. It is difficult to find in any other society a form of madness, or a pathway to it, that cannot be duplicated by us. The opposite is not true: that all cultures have developed as many forms of psychosis or found as many ways to attain it as we. In this we are secure in our riches. We are as highly developed in psychopathology as in technology (Henry, 1963, p. 322).

The paragraph provides the title for Henry's last book—*Pathways to Madness* (1971), and in both works Henry proceeds to demonstrate his assertion most convincingly. Among other things, he recounts direct observations made in the homes of families having a psychotic child. Along with his sardonic incisiveness, he displays a talent for illuminating the true magnitude and meaning of the small gesture, the unremarkable phrase, the ignored circumstance, the casual encounter, the audible silence. He also manages to write with a poignancy devoid of bathos, and in a language that is at once understated and charged with moral outrage. In all, his accounts of daily family routine achieve some measure of the cogent pungency of Chekov vignettes; they render, in a modest way, a piece of the surface of American experience, and the tragedy of that surface. Henry's accounts of day-to-day family existence more than sustain his central thesis—"culture is a unified whole even unto psychosis and death" (Henry, 1963, p. 323).

This thesis is not unique to Henry.[1] But one tends to believe it more readily coming from him than from others. The

1. See, for example, E. H. Erikson, 1946, 1950; Florence Kluckhohn, 1956; D. R. Miller and M. Hutt, 1949; M. Opler, 1956; J. Spiegel, 1957.

reason lies, perhaps, in his narrative style. But not entirely. Much resides in the data he offers—material derived from direct observation of families in situ. Just how very different these data are from those usually offered will be a matter elaborated later. For the present, suffice it to say that data of this type are still relatively sparse in the social science literature concerned with our own society. In clinical psychological and psychiatric literature they are all but absent. Henry's reports highlight the value of such data, and give the lie to facile argument—that it is mundane information and therefore of limited interest and small consequence for study—that might cause one to undervalue this kind of material. Indeed, just as psychoanalysis has required that we attend to the real significance of seemingly mundane errors—the parapraxes—of everyday mental functioning, so Henry's observations would suggest that we need to attend to the sociological significance of commonplace, everyday, family interactions as they occur in the home—only by attending to such nuances can we fully appreciate the nature of psychopathology and properly understand its sources and contexts. Such a view represents no fundamental change in existing dynamic conceptions of psychopathology; quite the contrary, it holds forth the promise of adding new dimension to traditional theories and approaches —filling them out through meaningful imbrication of the cultural context.

The foregoing serves to outline in good part the task undertaken in this book. Though somewhat different in topic, independently inspired, and differently conceived and developed, this study is also aimed at affirming Henry's premise—"culture is a unified whole even unto psychosis and death" (1963, p. 323). However, while Henry concentrates on sustaining his thesis in relation to psychosis and family interaction, this work is addressed primarily to the topics of death anticipation and family interaction.[2] It looks more particularly at family reaction to impending crisis. But in most respects, this study lays claim to the same philosophical and methodological principles exemplified by Henry's work. It derives from

2. Inevitably, psychosis too is considered, if somewhat more peripherally. Death, however, remains the primary ingredient.

an orientation that is simultaneously clinical, sociologic, and anthropologic.

General Orientation

This orientation views emotional disturbance as too often the "outcome of all that is wrong with a culture" (Henry, 1963, p. 386), and deems much psychopathology as the "extreme expression of the cultural configuration" (Henry, 1963, p. 386)—the ultimate excrescence of social ill and attitude. Indeed, in the instance to be described, we have construed emotional disturbance as a partial consequence of cultural stresses engendered by some of the very technologies that dominate our contemporary society.

Coordinately, this view recognizes that "madness" can be the result of the "confluence in the child of lethal cultural influences mediated to . . . [him] . . . through his parents" (Henry, 1963, p. 386). Because the parents are themselves products of the culture, they are often blinded by and to their own disorientations, fears, and irrationalities. But they are certainly not the only ones so afflicted.

This study suggests that the very specialists who, by training and role definition, are the presumedly sighted individuals in the society, may prove as unseeing as the parents who solicit their insight and help. Clinicians and social scientists are, like most of us, children of their culture. Helping agents, despite the pronouncements of professional societies, are not always immune. They too can be so immersed in their societal context as to be blinded to their own annular scotoma. In this regard, it is interesting to note that Henry (1963) closes his section on "Pathways to Madness" with the observation that only one parent among the families he has visited is seeing a psychiatrist. He concludes, "They all should." There may be wisdom to his wish, but, from our vantage point, there is also room for a large measure of doubt. Our greater pessimism is predicated on an understanding of the mental health worker as fallible in the face of his own social biases. In this sense we extend the "culturally deterministic" approach a step further than does Henry. We include ourselves as mental health workers and social scientists, and do not confine our premises to those we observe or seek to treat.

Finally, we are underwriting an orientation that at least suggests we look to anthropological methods, particularly those that include direct observation of behavior in its natural setting. It is our hope to lend needed perspective to the study of areas of experience that have heretofore been ignored; these are at the same time areas of undeniable significance in our society, and the fact that they have been much neglected by social scientists, we take to be a reflection of certain inhibitory cultural attitudes. The study of interactions between family members in the home is one such area. Henry (1963, 1971), of course, is among those who have pioneered some excellent beginnings in the use of naturalistic methods for observing families. In the report that follows we will attempt to extend the method by demonstrating its general utility. We will, as well, seek to elaborate it in specific directions. It will become evident that our endeavor differs from prior attempts, such as that of Henry's, in its application of more formalized means for categorizing and summarizing interactive processes. Henry's approach may be characterized as intensely cross-sectional, and centrally focused in its observations—in depth analyses of a few families in their homes over brief spans of time; the research to be described here contains a greater longitudinal aspect and, on occasion, reaches outside the home setting in order to draw on relevant clinical and historical data.

Some Particular Goals

This report has two foci—death and the family. It is an attempt to describe from observational data based on more than twenty home visits how a family of seven deals with the prospective and highly probable death of one of its members—the father. The twenty visits are spaced within a year, and extend from November to the following October.

Death does not, in fact, actually occur in this family. This is a nonevent of no small circumstance. Still the presence of death is no less felt. The reasons for this are various, but related and interlocking.

First, the family to be described here shares with millions of other families some culture-wide attitudes about death. It is a matter of their misfortune that the theme of death comes to confront them so barefacedly and causes them to call those death-connected attitudes into exaggerated and destructive play. Not unexpectedly they suffer pitifully under the handicap.

Second, and perhaps no less expected, is the fact that the very clinicians assigned to assist the family fail badly to do so. Despite the best of therapeutic intentions, the mental health workers themselves do not, until quite late, locate the real problem. Instead, they prove all but oblivious to the central role that fear of death plays in this family's dynamics. Thus, the clinicians show that they can be as culture bound as those they want to assist. Great irony attaches to the realization that both help-giver and help-seeker succumb to psychological diversions before the real issue is joined. Hand-in-hand, they succumb in mutual ignorance before the proper enemy has even been identified.

Lastly, and aside from attitudinal dispositions and implicit cultural dicta, the harsh reality has its effects. The family whose daily life is portrayed in the following pages has lived for some years in unspoken—and virtually secret—terror. They have existed beneath the Damoclean sword of the father's precarious physical condition. Though itself "hidden" from view, the sword casts an array of far-reaching, multifaceted shadows. In brief, the aura of death in this family seems so pervasive and so unmistakably real as to constitute a palpable condition of family existence, a condition that affects virtually every area of its functioning. And yet a conspiracy of silence is maintained around it. It is a circumstance that illustrates only too well the role culture can play in compounding and consolidating emotional disturbance once its foundation has been laid. A major purpose of this book then is to illustrate the circumstance.

But there are other subsidiary purposes as well. These are itemized below. The fact that they are stated in discrete form should not mislead the reader. They are highly interdependent items, and their separation for expository purposes is admittedly artificial. Nonetheless, they are offered in an attempt to convey a sense of some of the many intents of this report. They are all dealt with explicitly or implicitly, at length or in brief, in the pages that follow. Their treatment there is less particularized, since it is guided by the material itself. The reader may have to extract from the gestalt, information relevant to any or all of the enunciated purposes. The list below, then, is offered as a guide but not as an organizational outline.

Some Goals Related to the Psycho-social Interior

Handel (1967) has defined the psycho-social interior of the family as "that region of the universe where the members of a family meet and make a life together. . . . [It is] . . . what the family is to and for itself and its members rather than what it is to and for the larger society" (p. 1). Within the framework of this definition we have set ourselves a number of goals. For example, considerable effort will be made to trace the impact of a father's precarious health and potential death on the tempo and quality of his family's home life. This includes consideration of its consequences for (a) all family members, especially as regards the myriad ways in which identities, both those "established" and those "developing," can be affected; (b) the expression of "pathology," not to mention the definition of "pathology," with its attendant implications for the psychological development and status of the family's children; (c) the interaction patterns of family members, together with the ramifications such patterns have for the fabric of interdependent role relationships; (d) the nature and fit of individual, collusive, and collective defensive or adaptive maneuvers employed within the family by its various members; and (e) the construction and use of "time" as a dimension by the family, and its relation to the family's responsiveness to anticipatable fluctuations in stress level.

Some Goals Related to the Family's Interface with Society

The foregoing goals are constructed from a view of the family as a relatively closed social system. They are contingent upon conceptualizing the "family's corporate structure as a product of its members' individuality," independent of the larger culture and social structure (Handel, 1967). Depending on one's purposes, this is not necessarily a limiting perspective. As we will have occasion to point out, most clinically oriented research on the family adopts this frame of reference. However, it is but a partial view, and an artificial one if maintained as the only one. The psycho-social interior of the family is not an isolated domain. It is an integral portion of a larger world, and it articulates with that world all the time. In this sense, and certainly for many purposes, the family may be better construed as a "semi-open" system. While families have their own corporate structure, they participate at the same time in the surrounding social context. The interface between inner and outer is signified by a "legitimized" social boundary. This boundary can serve as a barrier but it is of varying elasticity and varying premeability. It can be extended to include certain persons or groups, or it can be contracted to exclude them. Similarly, it can permit or deny the flow of certain information, or ideas, or attitudes into or out of the family. It is a barrier whose attributes the family can to some extent monitor, but it is also regulated in part by external social agencies and society at large. The boundary embodies the family's "semi-open" character.

Additional objectives for this report emanate from this recognition of the "semi-open" quality of family life. For instance, it becomes virtually mandatory that we attempt to relate the plight of our research family to the ways in which it makes contact with external agencies and components of the larger culture. This entails an analysis of the flow of cultural values and belief systems, and an assessment of the family's interactions with a host of community institutions including (*a*) close analysis of the interdigitation of basic value orientations with family life-styles and attitudes toward death, and, for that matter, with attitudes toward life; (*b*) scrutiny of the relation between occupation, avocation, and school on the one side, and family crisis and family interaction patterns on the other, especially as they pertain to the assignment of responsibility, the assumption of risk-taking, and the experience of mastery and failure in the face of potential death; (*c*) articulation of the reciprocity, or lack thereof, between the activities and dilemmas of family life and the activities and dilemmas of life in a mental health clinic. Some of the difficulties of working clinically with given members of a family in the throes of a death-watch will, perforce, be touched on here; and (*d*) studied consideration of situational variation and behavioral change. Phrased more specifically, to what extent are behaviors within the home congruent with family members' behaviors in extra-familial environs or circumstances? And, irrespective of congruency, to what extent are they predictive of behaviors outside the family?

Goals Related to the Socio-history of Clinical Research

A book devoted to the clinical investigation of a family's reaction to impending death within its ranks should, at a minimum, evoke a double set of theoretical and research questions —one set bearing on the field of family study, the other on the clinical study of death and death-connected attitudes. Both domains have full, if brief and circumscribed, clinical research traditions. It seems reasonable that we try to relate our observations, methods, and findings to each of these traditions if we are to evaluate properly the nature of our research contribution to them.

In so doing, we will undertake a brief review of the salient literature in both fields, and attempt an assessment not only of our efforts, but of each research tradition. Why this is necessary may be readily apprehended. There are few more ubiquitous or age-old phenomena than death and the family. Clinical research traditions in both fields of study are merely fifteen years old.

Why were death and the family not topics of earlier psychological study? Why study them now? The answers to these questions can help one understand why research in these areas has taken particular forms; why certain avenues have been pursued and others not. Concomitantly, they have salience for how and where one might conduct future inquiries into these two topics. A review of the literature in each field, and of the research that has and has not been done, will, therefore, lead to certain conclusions. By way of anticipation, we can say what some of these are.

Ludicrously simple as it may seem, we shall advance the premise that these topics were not studied earlier because they were not problematic from a cultural and psychic standpoint. Past circumstances did not create the need. By the same token, death and the family are studied today because, as mental health professionals, we are given to studying that which has become dysfunctional over the years, and, worse yet, expensively dysfunctional. Wholesale avoidance of death and reliance on nuclear family structure are sources of exorbitant strain in today's culture. They have become topics worthy of study.

These interpretations are admittedly pieces of socio-economic, socio-historic determinism. As such, they are consistent with an orientation that guides much of what is formulated in this book. Their validity, however, is contingent on the evidence marshaled on their behalf. Some may not agree that the evidence warrants the conclusions. This, of course, encourages much needed dialogue. It is yet another purpose of this book to advance the investigation of why we study what we do, when we do, in the way we do. Why, in the course of a study, are we prompted to make certain research decisions and not others? We hope to use the research on death and on the family to illustrate and document some of the circumstances.

In the concluding chapters of this book, therefore, it will be our express purpose to evaluate this study in the light of other efforts and existing theory, and, in short, try to place what we have done in some meaningful context.

Goals Related to the Documentation of Middle-American Existence

Oscar Lewis (1959) once remarked:

> Traditionally, anthropologists have been students and spokesmen of primitive and preliterate peoples who live in remote corners of the world and have little influence upon our civilization. It is ironic that many Americans, thanks to anthropologists, know more about the culture of some isolated tribe of New Guinea, with a total population of 500 souls, than about the way of life of millions of villagers in India or Mexico. . . . (1959, p. 1)

Lewis's observation is noteworthy not only because it is true, but because it points up the social scientist's penchant for doing naturalistic studies of cultures remote from his own. He is inclined to study his own culture in the artificial circumstances of the laboratory or at the arm's length of survey statistics. Lewis succeeded in moving the naturalistic method a step closer to home. The poor villagers of Mexico are, after all, Western and urban. They are, nonetheless, scarcely middle-class Americans of Lewis's generation.

Writing about research on middle-class American families at almost the same point in time, Kaspar Naegle (1960) comments:

> . . . one searches in vain for . . . systematic accounts of the way in which families achieve their specific solidarities, allow or do not allow for privacy or even secretiveness, allot time for sharing information on the day's event, sustain or combat gaps of communication between various members of the family, casually welcome outsiders or keep them remote, encourage dependency or loneliness, or adjust to a name that once meant less or more than now. (p. 418)

Naegle's comments have not gone unheeded. As indicated earlier, Jules Henry (1963, 1971) was among the first to fulfill Naegle's hopes and attempt naturalistic study of his own culture of origin. Still, Henry does so from a particular vantage point. He assumes that psychopathology is the "*extreme* expression of the cultural configuration" (1963, p. 386). We have already embraced this view and seek to demonstrate it with the material in this book. However, we are open to a further possibility. It is a possibility that Henry does not entertain; namely, that there is really nothing very "extreme" or rare in the phenomenon of psychopathology or crisis. We may all be more afflicted than we are willing to acknowledge publicly. There may be a difference only in our adaptiveness. Many of us may suffer our psychopathology more quietly than others. The point is highly moot because it is almost totally unresearched.

It is hoped that this book will be viewed as an attempt to provide an intimate portrait of the routine, day-to-day life of a middle-American family. Its largest purpose remains that of contributing to the comprehension of contemporary middle-class culture in this country. In this regard, it is responsive to Naegle's implicit wishes and faithful to Henry's premise and beginning efforts. Whether the phenomena it describes are commonplace or rare "extremes" is a matter of conjecture, albeit one of utmost significance. For the moment, judgment on this issue must be suspended. Currently, it can only be a function of the reader's willingness to accept a fundamental assumption: the research family depicted in this book is as truly representative of their time and place as a family one would select at random. Some may protest that this cannot be and cite the father's illness and the son's emotional disturbance as invalidating reasons. There is, to be sure, some basis for doubt.

On the other hand, there is ample reason to believe that this family's crisis, while unique in the details of its tragedy, differs little in kind and even less in quality or quantity from that experienced by any of its neighbors. It is conceivable that each family on the same block resides in comparable pain and with consuming guilt, and that each is secure in the unshaken conviction that their hell is a special and lonely private hell. If ultimately this proves to be the case, then this book, ostensibly about death and the family, will have been about far more. It will have been about a variety of common and fully realized perversities inherent in the middle-American cultural skew. It will have been about "deviancies" presumed rare but actually frequent; deviancies that, if something less than the rule, may nonetheless be considerably more than exceptions. The whole topic is in desperate need of empirical documentation. It is hoped that this report may be a contribution to that documentation. More, it is hoped that it offers a beginning means for a documentation that is at once naturalistic, systematic, quantitative, and a basis for research leading to the comparative analyses of different families.

Plan of the Report

There exists no ready format for a book of this type. Being an admixture of clinical diagnostic problem, anthropological method, behavioral categorization and coding procedures, intensive case study, and sociologic-psychodynamic formulation, it does not lend itself to established precedents. Tried and accepted models for ordering the various aspects are lacking. As a consequence, it was decided that it might be best to permit the materials to unfold as naturally ordered. They are offered to the reader in much the same sequence in which they were encountered by the writer.

Thus, we begin by confronting a common clinical dilemma. At the behest of the public schools a boy is brought to a New England child guidance center for psychological evaluation and help. His parents accompany him, but deny the problems itemized in the school's listing of concerns. Under duress the family agrees to a treatment plan. They then fail to properly cooperate. After some months of frustration on all sides, an impasse is reached. Family and guidance center continue to disagree over basics. They cannot reach accord on whether or not a problem exists; they dispute what the data really are, and how they are to be best interpreted. In this first part of the study, then, Roscoe A. and his parents are introduced, and their background is traced much in the manner it became known to workers in the Yankee Child Guidance Center. The first year of treatment is also described.

Chapter 2 considers one attempt to come to grips with some aspects of the clinical dilemma. It details the nature of the writer's initial involvement with the A.'s and highlights a new variety of dilemma induced by the attempted solution to the old. Also described are observational methods, the home visit, and procedures for recording and coding data gleaned from home visits.

The succeeding chapters move first to a summary presentation of data in tabular form, and, second, to a review of data in narrative form. In the latter, vignettes are extracted from home visits in order to document clinical inferences and judgments made about the nature and meanings of the family's interactive patterns. Motivations of persons within the family are similarly analyzed. In these presentations there are deliberate attempts to take advantage of a number of theoretical outlooks and observational methodologies opened to clinicians by sociologists and anthropologists for the study of the family. It is hoped that the data are presented in sufficiently objective form, with enough quantification, and with enough direct, un-cluttered description of real events to allow them to speak for themselves. In other words, the data should stand on their own merits, permitting the reader to draw his own conclusions.

The family situation described is rather grim, having been purposively selected because it exemplifies the constraints and conflicts a culture can create for its members through its value orientations and social taboos. And, despite the efforts to maintain an attitude of objectivity, to invoke a measure of rigor, and to emphasize the descriptive, an interpretative, value-laden point of view makes itself felt. One cannot help but have an attitude toward the society in which one lives. At some point in time, somewhere in the course of things, there has to occur interpretation based on the individual's observations, given all its inadequacies, prejudices, and emotionality.

The next section of the book deals with aftermath. In it there is an attempt to detail events that occur to the A. family, not only in the immediate wake of the crisis central to this report, but in the years that followed as well.

The last sections of the book are more speculative. Conjectures and suggestions made there are less tightly bound to data derived from the home visits themselves. Rather, the observational data are used as springboards for some hypotheses and assertions about the nature of middle-American culture, social bias in behavioral research, the sequelae of cultural taboo, and the costs involved in many of our beliefs and mental health practices and assumptions. In addition, there is, as already noted, an attempt to utilize the observations and data on the A.'s as a nexus for examining the literature having to do with clinical interest in families, in death, and in related conceptions of "psychopathology." In these parts of the book, it is quite possible that the reader may choose to disagree completely with the conclusions and interpretations offered. There are tolerance limits in generalizing from "N of 1" research, though the setting of those limits is, for the most part, a matter of personal taste. In any event, it is hoped that the speculations offered will give the reader pause for some considered thought.

I

Clinical Problem
and Research Method

Chapter 1

Roscoe A. and His Parents

Contact with the A. family came about in the following manner: Roscoe, the fourth child, and the younger of two boys in a sibship of five, was referred by the Revere public schools to the Yankee Child Guidance Center for evaluation. He was seven years and eight months old at the time and in the second grade. The reasons for referral are embodied in the school's report of Roscoe's history from kindergarten through second grade.

Kindergarten

In kindergarten Roscoe was viewed as a highly creative child, one capable of losing himself in subjects of particular interest to him. Primary among his interests was nature study. His knowledge in this area was well advanced, and he spent much time producing elaborate and "beautiful" pictures of animals and birds. However, the teacher noted that Roscoe found it difficult, if not impossible, to shift to new activities unrelated to these interests. When the need to do so arose he became negative, unruly, and generally refused to cooperate. In addition, he manifested uncontrolled aggression toward other children, had no friends, and seemed incapable of playing well with peers. Often he provoked the teacher into excluding him through attacks on other children, or through his negativism. If he was not excluded by the teacher, his behavior would reach a frenzied pitch, and he would ultimately regress to infantile modes such as thumb-sucking, biting, crawling, and rolling about on the floor. At all times he appeared very tired in class, and during rest periods would invariably fall asleep. Despite such problems, it was felt he was bright, and that he learned easily and retained what he learned. The teacher's concerns, however, led her to refer Roscoe for evaluation by the school diagnostician.

During diagnostic testing Roscoe was extremely hyperactive, aggressive, and destructive. He found it difficult to stay seated, and began running about the office flapping his arms in imitation of a duck. His projective protocols were replete with references to birds and flying objects, and he openly expressed the wish to be a butterfly, so "I could go up in the air." In addition he told the examiner that he would "like to be the devil so I could make poison, and dump it on people and make them sick." He drew a picture of a "foreign lady" who lived in his house, and whose "husband is across the ocean." He stated that his little sister, Pamela, aged one year, was "invisible," and that all the rest of the family was invisible "when I want them to be." The diagnostician felt Roscoe to be sufficiently disturbed to warrant more extensive evaluation at the Yankee Child Guidance Center.

The school social worker then met with Mrs. A., Roscoe's mother, on a number of occasions. She tried to persuade Mrs. A. to seek help. Mrs. A. stated that professional help was not needed as far as she could see. She related that Roscoe was sometimes hard to understand at home, but that he was certainly no behavior problem at all, and that she did not see at home any of the behaviors or concerns related by the school.

First Grade

In first grade Roscoe's academic progress continued to be good, and his interest in animals and nature continued to intensify. However, he needed constant controls. His hyperactivity and aggressive meanness to other children were ever present. He refused to discuss his problems with the teacher or the school social worker. Periods of daydreaming in class were noted. He also began to bring money to school without parental permission. Both the teacher and the school social worker had frequent contacts with the mother throughout the year. The mother continued to insist that Roscoe presented no such behavior at home, and that, in fact, he was seldom in difficulty because he devoted so much time to his nature collection and pets. Mrs. A. again refused professional help.

Second Grade

In second grade Roscoe "fell apart." Self-control deserted him. His unprovoked aggression against other children mounted, and he was eventually suspended from school. Following this the mother agreed to call the Yankee Child Guidance Center for help.

Yankee Child Guidance Center Evaluation

In the guidance center's evaluation, Roscoe was described as a boy of somewhat feminine appearance who despite anxiety and almost hyperactive fidgeting was cooperative and willing to respond. His verbal abilities were good. He talked readily about his collection of bird models, his pet bird, and his hobby of studying and drawing birds. He announced, once again, that he would like more than anything else to be a bird so he could fly, and discussed his dreams of being a bird. He stated, however, that he knew he could never really be one. He related his sadness when a pet bird died. At one point he stated quite suddenly that "people think I'm ugly," and this seemed backed by the sincere belief that he considered himself ugly too. He denied problems in school other than daydreaming about birds and butterflies. His situation at home he described as unremarkable. He complained only briefly about his father's intense interest in motorcycles and his not being permitted access to this interest. Generally, he discussed home with minimal emotion. He added, however, that his best friend at home was his dog Flip.

The guidance center evaluation summary noted the absence of any special environmental stresses, the fact that his home seemed adequate, that his school adjustment was poor, that sadistic, destructive tendencies were moderate, that masochistic behavior was not present, that separation anxiety was absent, that frustration tolerance was weak, that delusional material and paranoid symptoms were mild to moderate. Hyperactivity was seen as predominant in the clinical picture.

Interview with Mother

Mr. A. did not appear at the outset of the evaluation because of work. Mrs. A. was seen alone. She was described as a rather unemotional, unsympathetic woman of average intelligence, who throughout the course of the interview "manifested no understanding of Roscoe's problems."

She saw Roscoe as no problem at home, and viewed the locus of his difficulties as the school setting. At home he was neither hyperactive nor aggressive. She was amazed to hear the school reports. She found it impossible to believe that Roscoe could strike out at other children in school with pencils and scissors. She had always been inclined to believe his version of events. She was now convinced that he must have been lying to her all along, but added that she would have had no awareness of Roscoe's difficulties except for the school reports; she intimated, in fact, that since she did not see problems at home, it might be, after all, the school's problem and not Roscoe's.

She related that Roscoe was the fourth of the five children. A sister Deedee was four years older than Roscoe, another sister, Sheila, two years older, and a brother, Ricky, eleven months Roscoe's senior. Pamela, four years junior to Roscoe, was the youngest. Roscoe's developmental milestones were normal. At two years he was fully toilet trained.

Mrs. A. stated that she had worked throughout most of her marriage, but not from the time of Roscoe's birth until his entry into school. Since Ricky and Roscoe were so close in age —less than a year apart—she had found it convenient to raise them as twins. She had not only dressed them identically, but had had similar expectations for them regarding achievement from the time Roscoe could walk. She expressed amazement that she could raise two boys so similarly and have them turn out so differently. Roscoe liked butterflies, flowers, and birds. He was not interested in playing ball, but preferred gardening. Roscoe was an amateur ornithologist and a nature lover. She described the many pets he had and elaborated on his maintenance of a "graveyard" for dead pets and animals in the backyard of the A. home. Ricky had no such interests or preoccupations. He, like the father, enjoyed working on motorcycles, playing ball, and hunting birds and animals. Mrs. A. described no problems with any of the children. She did say, however, that her husband was immature, rigid, and compulsive, a man who was an extremely hard worker. His primary interests were motorcycles and outdoor sports such as snowmobiling, ball playing, fishing, and hunting. They had married when young —Mr. A. was nineteen and Mrs. A. barely eighteen. Both had finished high school. Mr. A. now worked as a tool and die maker in a New England factory producing parts for the space industry. He earned nine thousand dollars a year. Mrs. A. worked as a seamstress in a dress manufacturing firm and earned about four thousand dollars. Mrs. A. said that her husband had frequently worked two jobs, and still did on occasion. She discussed his immaturity in relation to his habit of pouring money into motorcycles and motorcycle racing when the family could better use the money.

She finally mentioned that ever since the birth of Pamela, the youngest child, some three years previously, she and Mr. A. had had sexual difficulties. Prior to this time their sexual relationship had been highly compatible and satisfactory. In the past two to three years, however, she had been repulsed by the thought of sexual activity with her husband, and had had to force herself to undergo sexual relations. This, she said, had upset him, but she could not help herself.

Questioning Mrs. A. about traumatic incidents in Roscoe's life revealed only that Roscoe had been severely scratched when attacked by a Great Dane at age five. It was possible, however, to piece together that the following events all occurred at about the same time—during Roscoe's first year in school, in kindergarten: *a)* His mother had returned to work on a full-time basis; *b)* his sister Pamela had been born the year prior, and his mother had spent some time in the hospital; and, *c)* Mr. and Mrs. A. had begun to have sexual difficulties.

Psychological Testing at the Time of the Child Guidance Center Evaluation

Psychological testing again revealed a negativistic, hyperactive, and regressed youngster. Roscoe was highly provocative in the office, at times running from the examiner and hiding, picking up the phone, shutting off the lights, leaving the office.

At the same time, he pleaded with the examiner not to leave him, held the examiner's hand while walking down the hall, and ate all the candy in the office. He imitated birds, and got down on his haunches and waddled about the room like a duck, flapping his arms. Despite the fact that he knew he was pretending, the examiner expressed concern over whether Roscoe at times "might not get carried away." His intelligence was deemed adequate, as was his reality testing. His ability to sublimate in terms of hobbies was remarked upon. Yet, it was felt that "reality testing broke down too easily and too often," that "impulse controls were weak," and that "hobbies were often in the service of pathology." Interpersonal relations were felt to be undifferentiated. Defenses cited were denial, denial in fantasy, regression, and projection. Superego development was deemed poor. There were few indications in the protocols that Roscoe ever experienced guilt or that he had internalized moral standards. It was noted that Roscoe seemed highly ambivalent with respect to his mother, and that he had only the vaguest perception of his father. Diagnosis was "borderline psychosis," with inpatient status in a residential psychiatric setting and psychotherapy recommended. Roscoe was referred to the inpatient screening committee of a nearby residential psychiatric facility for children; there he was screened, accepted, and placed on the inpatient waiting list.

During the course of the child guidance center evaluation Roscoe had been permitted to attend school once again. Shortly after the child guidance center evaluation was completed Roscoe was excluded from public school for the second time in three months because of his aggressive outbursts. The principal visited the A. home to discuss the matter, and reported that his father expressed no concern. It further became apparent that during the time Roscoe was excluded from school, he had no supervision at home since both parents were away at work. The parents, upon learning that Roscoe had been seen wandering about downtown during the afternoons, sent him to stay with his maternal grandparents, who lived in a New England town some distance away. Roscoe's response to all this was, "I better go back to the child guidance center, so they can talk some good sense to me."

Interview with the Parents

Both parents were now seen by a social worker, and individual histories obtained from each.

Mrs. A.—Mrs. A. was born and raised in a coastal New England town. She grew up less than fifty miles from where the A. family currently lives. She had two siblings, a sister three years older than herself and a brother some five years her junior. Her mother did not work until her brother was entered in kindergarten at age five. Mrs. A., then age ten, almost immediately assumed the major responsibility for raising her brother. Because her mother worked, Mrs. A. awakened and dressed her brother each morning, cooked his breakfast, got him ready for school, brought him to school, brought him home for lunch, returned him to school for the afternoon, escorted him home from school, washed the dishes, vacuumed the house daily, dusted, supervised her brother's play, and prepared the evening meal for the entire family. She insisted that she always loved her brother, felt protective of him, and was committed to his welfare.

She herself was a shy child, quiet and withdrawn, "a girl who never stood out," and was not at all popular. She was never asked out on dates, and through her first three years of high school remained isolated from most peers—boys and girls alike. She participated in no extracurricular activities, attended no athletic functions. Instead, during adolescence, she spent increasing amounts of time with her father. She went directly from her high school classes to assist her father at a nearby marina, where he worked as a boat engine mechanic. Her interest in boats grew accordingly. She was navigating and operating fair-sized yachts at age sixteen. She was, she said, also close to obtaining her mechanic's certificate.

At sixteen, she met Mr. A. He was one of a number of teen-age boys who "hung out" at the marina. He was the only boy she ever dated. She recalled her surprise at his interest in her. He was terribly skinny, almost emaciated: six feet tall, he weighed only 120 lbs. This, she explained, was due to his childhood bouts with rheumatic fever.

Mr. A., who was also intensely interested in boat engines

and mechanics, insisted that she quit boating and stop working for her mechanic's certification. She stated with some regret that she would have been one of the only women in this field had she gone on. However, she complied with Mr. A.'s wish. They were married shortly after her graduation from high school. Initially, they lived in a small apartment not far from her parents' seaside home. Subsequently, they moved to Colorado for three years. Ricky and Roscoe were born there. Though she worked fairly consistently until Roscoe's birth—excepting periods of pregnancy and maternity leave—she did not return to work until Roscoe entered kindergarten.

Mrs. A. reiterated that the marriage had been sound, particularly in the sexual sphere, until shortly after Pamela's—the youngest child's—birth. Since then, the thought of intercourse with her husband filled her with an inexplicable repulsion. She could not control the feeling. Pamela was a "wanted" child. Mrs. A. recognized the pain her attitude had caused her husband in the past two to three years.

In the past three years she had felt extremely nervous, and reported that headaches were very frequent. She consulted doctors about her headaches and her repulsion regarding intercourse. They had informed her that there was no physical basis for either, that she was "overworked," and that her headaches were "tension headaches." These headaches persisted and often forced Mrs. A. right to bed upon her arrival home after work. At times she found it impossible to keep food down.

Mr. A.—Mr. A., seen now for the first time at the child guidance center, reported that he came from a broken home. His mother died of cancer when he was two. Three older siblings were sent to live with relatives. He and an older sister stayed with their father, who, within a year or two, married a woman with two daughters and a son by a previous marriage. The father was a dealer in farm equipment, and Mr. A. was essentially raised in the rural atmosphere of northeastern New England. He recalled his father as a stern man and a strict disciplinarian. Throughout childhood Mr. A. was responsible for many household and caretaking chores; but, nursing the hope that he might free himself from his father's yoke at an early age, he sought and obtained work on nearby farms as well. His hope of independence, however, was not to be realized. His father, seriously hurt in an automobile accident when Mr. A. was still fairly young, suffered the loss of both legs, and could not return to work. Additional responsibilities fell to Mr. A.

Mr. A. reported that his health was fine until he reached high school. It was then discovered that he had rheumatic fever. He could endure little activity, and lost considerable weight. He missed much school, and, when he could attend, he was not permitted to travel from classroom to classroom. The rheumatic fever attacks were most pronounced in the springs and summers of his high school years. They were so severe that he spent virtually four consecutive summers confined to bed. While he was in high school and in the midst of one of his rheumatic fever bouts, his father died. He was sixteen at the time. His step-mother remarried quickly, only to be divorced within a year.

After leaving high school Mr. A. went to work in a textile factory. It was while working there that he met and married Mrs. A. Two years later he moved the family to Colorado, where he apprenticed as a tool and die maker and worked in an auto-parts factory. The reasons for the move were not clear. Nor, for that matter, were the reasons for the return. The family stayed in Colorado three years before returning.

The worker who interviewed Mr. A. commented on his guardedness and his defensive need to see himself, his background, and his current family situation as unremarkable, "normal," and "average." She noted, however, "Mr. A.'s fright over his rheumatic fever might play a part in his mild manner, and also in the unconscious satisfaction he gets from Roscoe's rampant acting out."

Following these interviews, and while Roscoe was still awaiting admission to the residential facility, he was again excluded from public school. His mother wrote the child guidance center, complaining bitterly of the school's anger toward her son. She concluded her letter with, "Sometimes it seems to me the teachers can be a little more reasonable at times. I

wish I didn't even have to send Roscoe to school at all.
Frankly, I can't see that they [the school] are helping him.
. . . The sooner the better that he is admitted up there [to the
residential unit for emotionally disturbed children]."

Once more, Roscoe was reinstated at school but his stay
was short. His aggressive outbursts and attacks on other children persisted, and the school finally excluded him for good.
Faced with the public school's irreversible decision to expel
the boy, and with the fact that no residential facility bed was
immediately available, it was decided mutually, by the A.'s
and the Yankee Child Guidance Center, to have Roscoe admitted to the Day Treatment Service of the Center.[1] He would attend school at the center five days a week from 9:00 A.M. to
3:00 P.M., receive psychotherapy, but reside at home. The parents were to be involved in casework treatment.

Roscoe entered the Day Treatment Service in the middle
of the school year. The entire guidance center was immediately aware of his presence. He reacted much as he had in
public school. He had frequent aggressive outbursts, ran away
often, raged at the staff. He would fly up and down the corri-
dors of the center, burst unannounced into professional meetings and offices, tear up bulletin boards, scatter papers, sweep
desks off indiscriminately. Control and containment were constant issues the Day Treatment staff in particular, and the center staff in general, had to face with Roscoe. His public school
record, in fact, looked mild when compared to what was now
seen first hand, and there was wonder expressed at the tolerance of his public school teachers and principal—especially on
those occasions when Roscoe would suddenly, without warning, grab another child by the throat and choke him until staff
would have to forcibly remove him from the blue-faced victim.

1. The Day Treatment unit of Yankee Child Guidance Center was—at
that time—a rather newly created multidisciplinary service for "emotionally
disturbed" children, who, for reasons of severe, but functional, academic retar-
dation, or behavioral incorrigibility, could not be tolerated in the public
schools. The service typically maintained a census of twenty-four children,
aged six to twelve. School, occupational therapy, recreational therapy, and
psychotherapy on a one-to-one basis, comprised daily activities for Day Treatment children. The treatment unit itself was housed in a wing of the child
guidance center which had been added to the main building especially for
that purpose.

The Course of Psychotherapy: Roscoe's First Year

What follows is a synopsis of Roscoe's first year in psychotherapy, in a series of telegraphic quotes taken from his psychotherapist's process notes. The material, which is cited for its representativeness of typical attitudes, behaviors, and exchanges, makes abundantly clear that Roscoe acted in his therapeutic sessions much as he acted in the Day Treatment school. It also makes clear that his acting out slackened little, if at all, over the course of the year. Roscoe was virtually never given to verbalization of his difficulties, he introspected rarely, and, in fact, could seldom be slowed down sufficiently to "listen" during treatment hours. The challenge was persistently one of inhibiting his motion and his aggressive, abusive outbursts.

> April: Roscoe found it difficult to control his aggressiveness . . . Roscoe was perpetually hyperactive . . . a veritable whirling dervish. . . .

> May: . . . quite destructive . . . throwing things around the office . . . breaking toys . . . can't listen or attend . . . runs away every hour . . . often necessary to terminate sessions early. . . .

> June: . . . runs away . . . extremely upset . . . throws toys . . . refuses to talk . . . angry and furious . . . loses control easily . . . swears . . . mingled with baby talk and curling up on floor . . . has to be restrained physically. . . .

> July: . . . difficulty controlling self . . . quite destructive in office . . . self-destructive by head banging. . . .

> August: . . . running away . . . swearing . . . omnipotent . . . bossy . . . defiant, belligerent. . . .

> September: . . . finally got some interpretative connection between behavior and wish to hurt others, especially father . . . he fears wishes might be realized . . . leads to hyperactive excitement . . . becomes very destructive . . . agitated . . . throws things at me . . . destructive. . . .

> October: . . . again very destructive and very hyperactive . . . not producing . . . no shift in relationship . . . hard to keep him in office. . . .

November: . . . acting out worse than ever . . . can't stay in office . . . doesn't discuss home, parents, or Day Treatment milieu . . . but expresses feelings for first time in a while that he is naughty and crazy. . . .

December: Therapist away on vacation.

January: . . . violent acting out continues . . . Roscoe feeling rejected . . . he invites failure and punishment . . . throws things and attacks. . . .

February: . . . more of same . . . precipitates punishment . . . again try interpretations along the lines of his feeling rejected and pushed away. . . .

March: . . . finds a broken pencil in office . . . Roscoe didn't break it, but he insists he did . . . interpret his need to be blamed for something he didn't do . . . claims he is crazy . . . all efforts to convince him otherwise are to no avail . . . his reaction is explosive rage. . . .

The Course of Casework: The Parents' First Months

In order to provide a more complete groundwork for reviewing the home visits made to the A. home, and in an attempt to convey the contrasts, paradoxes, and perplexities of the center's efforts to engage and work with the A. family, a sequential account of the social casework hours with Mr. and Mrs. A. follows. The A.'s began their casework sessions at the same time Roscoe began psychotherapy, and the events of their hours may be placed side by side with the excerpts from the monthly summaries of Roscoe's therapy.

April: Time was spent discussing the family and various family routines and roles . . . father and Ricky like to hunt together . . . Ricky is mature . . . Ricky protects Roscoe . . . anger or jealousy between the two boys was denied . . . Roscoe is viewed as the clumsier, less athletic of the two . . . but Roscoe often seemed smarter than Ricky . . . there was some talk of the history of the boys and speculation on what it meant to raise two boys, eleven months apart in age, as if they were twins . . . Mrs. A. acknowledged having done this since the time Roscoe could walk . . . Mr. A. allowed that he worked many evenings, repairing motorcycles for friends . . . Roscoe was described as very well behaved at home, and both showed surprise at the stories of his behavior at the center . . . Mr. A. seemed upset that Roscoe had brought some pheasant feathers to the Day Treatment Service . . . it turned out they were from a pheasant Mr. A. had killed on a recent hunting jaunt . . . Mr. A. concluded, "Roscoe has been given all the opportunities the other kids have, but he just hasn't taken any advantage of them . . . that's all." . . . Their denial of his problems was noted to them several times. . . .

May: The A.'s came in only once this month, having cancelled the first two and last two of the weekly sessions . . . on the one occasion they were in Mrs. A. seemed highly anxious, but Mr. A. showed absolutely no anxiety . . . Mrs. A. complained of tension headaches, and how the children, especially Roscoe, got on her nerves . . . she also felt highly anxious on her job . . . Mr. A. announced that he could handle the kids, and that he has no problems or anxieties on the job . . . Mrs. A. agreed that "he never seems to worry about anything . . . at least not so it shows. . . ."

June: The parents missed the first, third, and fourth of their five scheduled appointments in June. On all three occasions they said they "forgot" . . . their avoidance and denial are extreme . . . Mrs. A. did not come in at all in June . . . Mr. A. came in on the second and fifth occasion . . . He was bland and anxiety-less . . . his affect was flat . . . he kept denying the import of Roscoe's problems . . . he denied ever seeing him act up at home . . . "the kids have always been quiet and good at home," he insisted . . . he expressed surprise again at hearing of Roscoe's behavior at Day Treatment school, since he is never that way at home . . . he reported that Mrs. A. is reluctant to ask her supervisor at work for time and permission to come to her casework hours . . . once again Mr. A. expressed the feeling that Roscoe was brighter than Ricky, but "Roscoe just hasn't used the opportunities he has been given . . . Ricky wants to get ahead . . . he is a plugger. . . ."

July: Five appointments were scheduled for the A.'s in July . . . Mr. A. called to cancel the first, and a second special make-up appointment was arranged . . . Mrs. A. appeared alone; Mr. A. was "tied up" at work . . . Mrs. A. related some worries about her husband, feeling he worked too hard and too long, day and night, and that he was "running

himself down" . . . everyone at home, including Roscoe, is
unhappy because of the tension created by his demanding
schedule . . . The A.'s neither called to cancel or reschedule
their next appointment; they simply failed to show . . . both
showed for the fourth session of the month, but they just sat
and looked out the window . . . both were content to say
nothing . . . it seems that little goes on at home . . . the parents only talk to the kids in order to discipline them . . . Mr.
and Mrs. A. seemed tired, bored, unmoved . . . their life
seems exceedingly routine and dull according to them . . . an
emergency kept me (the caseworker) from keeping my last
appointment with the A.'s in July. . . .

August: Caseworker away on vacation.

September: The A.'s kept three of their four appointments
this month . . . but to little avail . . . their denial and resistance continue despite efforts to cut through . . . in the first
session both parents were guarded and quiet, as well as fifteen minutes late . . . Pamela was ill, and Mrs. A. had been
up all night for two nights running in addition to her working
during the day . . . when Mrs. A. said she usually was in bed
by 8:30 P.M. and that she was exhausted if awake 'til 9:00
P.M., it provided some opportunity to tentatively approach the
A.'s sexual relationship . . . Mr. A. quickly made it clear that
this was off-limits and no one's business but his own and his
wife's . . . he too complained of a cold, not feeling well, and
being tired, but stated he was still working long hours . . . "a
little cold isn't going to get me down" . . . Mrs. A. complained about Mr. A.'s lack of self-care and precaution . . .
we talked about how Mrs. A. seems to worry and likes to baby
and care for Mr. A. . . . The A.'s cancelled their next hour,
but came the following one . . . both were quiet . . . they
again denied vehemently that Roscoe was a problem at home
. . . they described him as quiet, but said that the whole family is quiet . . . "it is a family characteristic," said Mr. A. . . .
The last hour of the month was also spent discussing Roscoe
. . . the parents' denial was impenetrable . . . the parents are
themselves so vacuous they can't see Roscoe's problems because they are too threatening. . . .

October: The A.'s failed to appear for their last three sessions of the month . . . they did not bother to call or cancel

. . . during the first hour, for which they appeared, they persisted in reporting that Roscoe was doing fine at home, and that he had always done well at home . . . Mr. A. reiterated that if it had not been for the school they would never have known Roscoe had difficulties . . . both parents wondered if the problem did not lie with the school and not Roscoe . . . Mr. A. said if the teachers in the public school and in Day Treatment were less afraid of the children and more authoritative Roscoe would behave as he behaved at home . . . Mr. A. directly attacked the permissiveness of the center program . . . he raised question about the need for himself and Mrs. A. to come to appointments . . . they still deny any knowledge of Roscoe's hyperaggressive-antisocial behavior . . . they missed their next three appointments, and when called were evasive, but not even apologetic . . . they resisted make-up hours, claiming lack of time and too much work. . . .

At this juncture, after some seven months of mutual frustration, Roscoe's case was brought up for reconsideration. Materials were reviewed with an eye toward altering treatment strategies—primarily in the direction of removing Roscoe from his home and hospitalizing him in a residential setting, either a state hospital or a child psychiatric installation.

Roscoe was viewed as an attention-seeking, uncontrolled, guiltless, impulse-ridden boy, with confused sexual identity, poor and undifferentiated object relations, and weakly internalized moral stantards. Diagnostically, he was deemed "a highly disturbed, borderline psychotic child who gave evidences of deep-rooted conflicts in the oral and anal stages of development," and, as a child "incapable of distinguishing people from one another," or one situation from another situation. It seemed not to matter whom he was with—child or adult, male or female—or what setting he was in—school, occupational therapy, recreational therapy, recess, schoolyard, lunch, or therapy—he would rage, attack, and destroy without provocation and indiscriminately, like a wild man "possessed of a demon." The one-sidedness of this picture was but modestly tempered by the recognition that at other times Roscoe would be regressed, clinging, and dependent. In even rarer moments it was acknowledged that he could be "sadly warm" and "softly engaging," but such moments were highly infrequent during his first seven months in the Day Treatment program; they were sufficient, though, to win the affection and devotion of a number of staff who had worked with him.

Mr. and Mrs. A. were viewed as virtually unworkable. In seven months of casework they had missed better than 50 percent of their appointments, and on those occasions when they had come they had engaged in the most blatant forms of "resistance," "denial," and "projection." They refused to "see" any disturbance in Roscoe, much less make an effort at alleviating problems; they blocked all efforts aimed at an exploration of their marital relationship, generally acted as if they were outside the problem, and seemed, for the most part, bored and unconcerned. On those occasions when they were not bored they remained outside the problem by blaming the schools and the center for failing to deal adequately with Roscoe, who, after all, "was never a problem at home."

After some extended discussion and closer deliberation, however, it was decided to defer, at least for a time, further consideration of inpatient status for Roscoe. In part it was felt that Mr. and Mrs. A. would "resist" this alternative as they had all else; in part, a number of the Day Treatment staff saw enough positive glimmers amidst Roscoe's perpetual, angry acting out that *they* resisted an alternative which they felt tantamount to admitting failure and throwing in the towel. Finally, once again, the practicalities of timing, and the unavailability of inpatient bed space in the residential facility, dictated a substantial delay, if not indefinite postponement, of the move toward hospitalization. Given these sentiments and circumstances, it was decided to maintain Roscoe in Day Treatment and to continue offering casework to the parents. Simultaneously, it was realized that to do this and nothing more would be to perpetuate the status quo, which seemed to be of no therapeutic value to anyone. It was resolved that new data, added sources of information, and fresh vantage points needed to be introduced, especially regarding the family and its investment.

Chapter 2

The Home Visit

Background

The Method

It was at this point that I was first contacted about the A's. Along with a number of colleagues, I had been engaged in the study of families for some time. Most particularly, we had been studying families in which at least one male child manifested a severe reading disability of functional origin. As a research group, we were most attentive to the role of the child's symptom in the maintaining of the equilibrium of psychological forces within the family system (Miller and Westman, 1964; 1966). In the course of our work we had evolved a variety of techniques for assessing family patterns and interaction (Bermann, 1967; Lebby, 1971; Schmidt, 1971). Many involved the use of paper and pencil forms, questionnaires, interviews, or experimental tasks. One which did not, however, was the "home visit." We had adopted this technique from Robert Blood (1958), who, in turn, had drawn on the work of Charlotte Buhler (1939) done some twenty-five years earlier. It is a naturalistic method of observation that Anthony (1970) has since termed "unroofing." The method entails the use of nonparticipant observers in the homes of families who have agreed to the visit. Usually there is an attempt to observe at a time when all family members are together, such as at dinner. The aim is to observe unobtrusively and to record subsequently the "solitary and interactional activities of the family members minutely and intimately" (Anthony, 1970, p. 145). Each visit is approximately an hour and a half in duration. A number of visits at weekly or biweekly intervals are made over a period of time—sometimes over the course of a few months.

At the time the social worker and the psychiatrist working with the A.'s first approached me, the home-visit technique was still being developed, and we were experimenting with ways to deal with a number of problems.

As is probably obvious, the technique is a highly delicate one, fraught with intensified sensitivities about the invasion of familial privacy. Concomitantly, there are issues of how the data may or may not be used clinically, of whether note taking ought be done by the observer while in the home, of assessing to what extent the presence of an observer alters the everyday behaviors of the family, of gauging the rate of habituation in family behavior that occurs with time, of evolving ways and means for responding to the family's defensive maneuvers and to its efforts to incorporate or expunge the observer. We will have occasion to discuss all of these matters in the later sections of this book. One major problem deserves special mention at this time, though it too will receive fuller treatment further on. This problem has to do with the observer's defined role, his commitment to that role, and the counter forces that tug him in the direction of nonneutrality and intervention in family affairs. There are cruelnesses in family life that challenge the resolve of any observer committed to noninterference. As it turned out, the A.'s had more than a fair share of cruelness. There were times when the situation seemed to cry out for active participation and abandonment of the passive, onlooker stance. Just what arrangements were made to handle situations of this kind, and what implications such contingencies had for the writer will be detailed in subsequent sections. Suffice it to say that this problem constituted the largest single pressure point for the author in the observations to be reported. The visits substituted the dilemma of knowing for the dilemma of not knowing.

There were also, at the time, other matters relevant to home visits that we as researchers had simply not considered. Among them was the need for a scheme for coding the recorded observations and a means for analyzing quantitatively generated data. These we evolved subsequently. At the time, we were primarily preoccupied with the technical and mechanical difficulties of carrying out the observations themselves. And we were eager for any opportunity to expand our knowledge and use of the method. Until approached about the A.'s, I had visited only the homes of families having a son with reading disabilities. No one in our research group had observed the interaction of other classes of families. While we were beginning to formulate hunches about the qualities characteristic of reading-problem children and their families, we had not selected a comparison group. The opportunity to do observations on the A.'s was, therefore, much welcomed. We willingly, and all too naïvely, accepted the clinical challenges it offered. Our needs seemed to dovetail with the desire of the A.'s treatment team—we were both seeking new information and fresh vantage points.

To these ends it was agreed that Mr. and Mrs. A. ought to be approached about the feasibility of home visits. This was done. The request was presented, quite genuinely, in the light of the apparent discrepancy between the parents' reports of Roscoe's behavior at home and the center's report of Roscoe's behavior in the Day Treatment school. The suggestion, as might be imagined, was not without its complications.

Ground Rules

Laying ground rules was a matter of utmost importance. During a joint meeting with the A.'s caseworker, Roscoe's therapist and Mr. and Mrs. A., I outlined the proposal and the procedures entailed. It was emphasized that the visits would be strictly observational. The observer would not intervene in family activities, nor would he expect to participate in family routine. He would visit once every two weeks, or every week when possible, would remain in the background as much as possible, and would stay for about an hour and a half each time—arriving before dinner and leaving sometime after the completion of the meal. He would not, however, be wooden or unresponding. It was also made clear that the observations would be communicated to the staff persons working with Roscoe and the A.'s, and that the family would be expected to continue in treatment with the social worker and the child psychiatrist. Whether and how the clinicians or the A.'s decided to use the home observation data was a matter for each to decide. Judgment would clearly be involved. I raised some potential difficulties for the group to discuss. What, for example, if the caseworker drew on the home visits in his efforts to underscore a point and the parents disagreed with the basic observations? All agreed that there ought to be open and free discussion of data and feelings in such a case. In this way the observations could become a point of departure for meaningful therapeutic work. Other feelings were also anticipated. The A.'s sense of being invaded, their probable discomfort in the early stages, the awkwardnesses of explaining the observer's presence to their friends, the possibility that the whole venture might resolve nothing and culminate in disappointment all around, were all reviewed. We spent time trying to work through these feelings of concern and apprehension, gave the A.'s a week to turn matters over in their minds, and awaited their response.

The following week the parents met with their caseworker. Their initial response was most predictable. They reacted to the proposal as if a spy were going to be placed in their home to check the veracity of parental reports. Yet, Mr. A. was also able to articulate that he had already felt accused and discredited by the center. It was with some anger—the first he had displayed—that he surprised the caseworker by accepting the home visits. They were for him a vehicle for vindication. The fact that the visits would be made by an "outsider" —one who, at that point, had not been involved or even acquainted with Roscoe or the family—and the knowledge that the visitor would be a person who had routinely made visits to many other homes for research purposes were reassuring to the A.'s. Equally appealing was the understanding that the visits were to be strictly observational, and not therapeutic. The very conception of visits to the home served to balance the ledger regarding felt responsibilities—i.e., the clinic was now going to approach the A.'s, meet them on their turf, so to speak, rather than leaving them to feel the burden of all the psychological press to make and keep appointments at the child guidance center. In sum, Mr. and Mrs. A. concurred readily with the suggestion for home visits, granted that they did so with some visible apprehension, some anxiety; this was counterbalanced by a sense of relief and a degree of renewed challenge and hope.

The Format

Over the course of the next year, twenty visits were made to the A. home. All visits were made by me, and all took place during the evening hours—virtually always around the dinner hour. The dinner hour seemed a logical time since all family members would likely be present and family interaction would be maximized. Typically, I would arrive a half hour before dinner, and stay a half hour past the completion of the meal. I tried to be as unobtrusive as possible in order to reduce the chance of biased involvement and contamination of data. I therefore refrained from asking questions of the family. I initiated as little conversation as possible; but, on the other hand, I was not awkwardly unnatural in a social sense and did not maintain monastic silence. Instead, I sought to bring conversation directed to me to a close as quickly, but as politely, as possible. I never dined with the family, asserting, usually truthfully, that I had already eaten. I endeavored to seat myself away from the family, and rather quickly came to rely on a single vantage point that permitted me a vista on all or most of what transpired, but, at the same time, left me peripheral to, and outside of the mainstream of family events. I selected a chair situated some fifteen to twenty feet across the family room from the dining table, to the right of the television set. This spot also allowed observation of the kitchen and the activities therein. And, since the A. family ate their meals in the family room and usually moved across the room after finishing dinner, relocating themselves on chairs and couches before the television set, the same chair served as a good location for postdinner interaction. (See Fig. 1.) Occasionally, of course, this one vantage point proved impossible, particularly on special anniversaries or holidays—Christmas, Easter, Valentine's Day—when the family gathered in the front living room for group activities. On such occasions, I followed the family to the front room. Warm and pleasant weather also posed some problems for observation; members of the family would be dispersed outdoors before or after dinner while others were in-

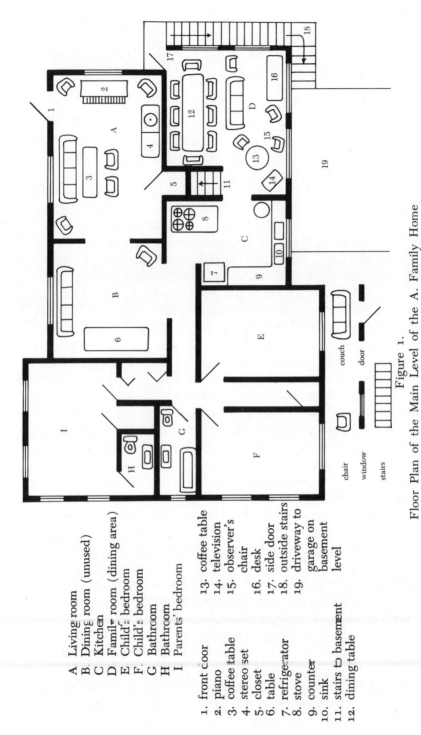

A Living room
B Dining room (unused)
C Kitchen
D Family room (dining area)
E Child's bedroom
F Child's bedroom
G Bathroom
H Bathroom
I Parents' bedroom

1. front door
2. piano
3. coffee table
4. stereo set
5. closet
6. table
7. refrigerator
8. stove
9. counter
10. sink
11. stairs to basement
12. dining table

13. coffee table
14. television
15. observer's chair
16. desk
17. side door
18. outside stairs
19. driveway to garage on basement level

chair
window
stairs
couch
door

Figure 1.

Floor Plan of the Main Level of the A. Family Home

side. The rule of thumb was always to search out interaction between family members where they gathered in greatest number, or where they were involved in situations which had not been previously observed—playing catch, fixing a motorcycle, or gardening.

During the first visits it proved somewhat difficult to maintain a strictly nonparticipatory, inconspicuous presence. Obviously, merely being in the A. home was enough to call attention to me. Moreover, during the second and third visits, the parents attempted to convert me from neutral observer to therapist. On one occasion, for example, they cleared the room of children and pulled up chairs before me, seated themselves, and began first relating family history and then inquiring what they might do about Roscoe. Reiteration and clarification of the observer's role in their home, as well as urging the A.'s to discuss family material and concerns about Roscoe with their caseworker persuaded them to reaccept the visits as regular and routine periods of observation—i.e., as times when the family's life should proceed as always. By the fourth or fifth visit, I felt fairly sure that I was seeing the A. family in natural interaction.[1]

No note-taking took place during the visits. Visits to other families had already lead us to the conclusion that note-taking was a source of distraction for both family and observer. Instead, upon leaving the A. home I proceeded directly to a dictaphone and dictated my report much as one might process notes from a psychotherapy hour—with the same attempt to describe as faithfully, and in as much detail as possible, the sequence of interaction observed. Transcription followed. A visit

---

1. The neutrality of the observer, fairly well attained and accepted by the A. family by the fourth or fifth visit, did not mean that the observer was wooden, or impolite, or unfriendly. I was responsive when approached, but within limits. By the same token, neutrality does not imply that I was totally without meaning to the various family members. The very fact of my observing often forced the family members to look at their own behaviors and wonder what an outsider made of them, and in periods of family stress, it was frequently apparent that I was a ready object for the transfer of intrafamilial feelings and attitudes precisely because I was neutral and something of a "blank screen"; thus, despite the early conviction that the visits had no therapeutic intent, one may wonder in retrospect if they were entirely free of therapeutic effect. This whole intriguing area will be treated in greater detail in the concluding chapters.

of one and a half hours yielded an average of five to six pages of single-spaced typed notes.

In all, a total of twenty visits were made to the A. home. The visits extended over the ensuing year—a year in which Roscoe remained in the Day Treatment program and individual psychotherapy, and a year in which his parents continued in casework, although their participation was, as before, marginal and highly sporadic. With the exception of vacation periods, visits were generally made at two-week intervals. Observations on two visits were lost because the dictaphone failed to record audibly. As a consequence, the report that follows is based upon data from eighteen home visits to the A. family.

The Observations

Their Presentation

The problem of presenting home observation data adequately is a vexing one. At first, one seeks to summarize it all—everything—in a set of master strokes; to render a "still picture" which both arrests and represents in complete form the usual patterns of family interaction. But, such a rendering threatens to stultify and categorize the workings of a vital group and, at the same time, eliminate the flow of time. Yet, it remains, perhaps, the most useful way of providing an introductory overview of the A. family.

On the other hand, one hopes to preserve the observer's own experience of discovering the A. family through time—as an organic, psycho-social, dynamic whole moving in time and through events with an inevitability that cannot be slowed or stopped. In this regard, one wishes, more than anything else, to let the data speak for themselves. It would be important, for example, for the reader to discover contextually, as the observer did, in a moment of thunderous silence at the close of the fifth visit, that Mr. A. would "not be home" for the next scheduled visit, as Mrs. A. so quietly put it, because "Mr. A. needs open heart surgery," and that "without it he is not expected to live until the fall." Of course, it turned out, all the A.'s had known this for some time, and then some. For the observer it was tantamount to being ripped from ignorance. Suddenly, so much fell into place. But, some very real limits—of available space and of novelistic skill—attach to this approach to the presentation of observational data. Even if the visits could be presented verbatim and as dictated, they would not come close to communicating the palpable nature of the events themselves.

On the assumption that neither means of presenting the data on the A. family could be consummately achieved, a compromise has been struck. Both approaches are attempted in circumscribed and delimited fashion. The first, which endeavors to summarize the interactional configurations of the A. family, rests upon the outcome matrices obtained from a systematic coding of the eighteen transcribed home visits. Where possible they are supported by examples drawn from the visits themselves. The limitations of this approach are those of the category scheme employed, and the fact that the matrices are for one-step, dyadic contingencies. Two- or several-step contingencies, and three-cornered or larger interaction patterns remain well beyond the scope of this effort. That extended contingencies are a very real aspect of family functioning must be borne in mind, despite their lack of treatment here.

The second approach, which seeks to retain the "clinical richness" of the material and which presumes to "let the observational data speak for itself," is also circumscribed—in this instance, by organization around those "family themes" that, either in their striking presence or absence, seem to most characterize the A. family and its concerns. This approach, more ideopathic than the first—the first, in its way, might be stylized as nomethetic—permits one to unfold the salient themes in the A. family. Through citing vignettes, these themes can be introduced as they emerged or were experienced over time by the family and/or by the observer. The very selection of prominent themes or nonthemes dictates the omission of much data, and, therefore, runs the risk of weakening the contextual feel for the significant events described. In a word, there is some unavoidable loss. That which one seeks to preserve is, to some degree, always undermined by the very need to select.

The Code for Interaction

Before turning to a discussion of the summary tables of inter-action in the A. family, the coding system employed for cate-gorizing the behaviors between family members should be de-scribed.[2]

The code is an elaboration of one aspect of a system first devised by Charlotte Buhler (1939) in a study of Viennese chil-dren and their families in the 1930's. It was chosen as the basis for the current code because the content categories seemed particularly suited to family observation data obtained from home visits—that is, to descriptive data, recorded retrospec-tively in the form of process dictation, where resultant interac-tional units are of molar rather than molecular size.

As mentioned earlier, Buhler's study was nearly the first anywhere to utilize home observations as a source of data. Her methods of data collection and transcription were similar to those reported here. Her code, however, was presented in what is virtually outline form—categories are labeled rather than defined and exemplified. Hence it was necessary to gen-erate a coding scheme having rounded definitions, criteria, and guiding examples. In part, these are provided in the ap-pendix.

2. This code is but a part of a more general coding scheme now being created and processed for the analysis of family interaction. Considerable test-ing and refinement of the code in all its aspects as yet remains to be done. The ultimate goal is to apply it to the transcriptions of the many home visits accumulated on families of various types, ethnicity, and social class, that have already been collected over a period of time. Clearly, it is beyond the scope or intent of this work to review all methodological details relevant to the use of the code. For that matter, space does not permit full description of the code itself—i.e., the presentation of the complete coding manual. The full code seeks to cover a broad range of psychological phenomena, including in-tentions, behaviors, and response sets. As a method, the coding system is in various stages of development—intercoder reliabilities, much less interobserver reliabilities, have not been formally attempted in all aspects. Its application to the A. family is in the service of illustration and convenience of summary, and involves but a piece of the larger coding manual. That part of the code rele-vant to the material presented on the A. family is contained in the appendix. Intercoder reliabilities for the segmenting of interactional units, for designa-tion of initiator and target persons, and for agreement on category have been obtained for much of this subsection of the code. The reliabilities are, in all cases, quite respectable—on the order of 0.70 or better. However, their mean-ings and intricate interrelations make their discussion here infeasible, and re-quire that their consideration be deferred to another time and place.

It also should be noted that the present code is organized for one-step interaction contingencies—that is, for discrete sequences of approach or initiating acts which are followed by reactive behaviors. The approach is similar to stimulus-response models: an interactional unit consists of Person *A*'s initiation(s) and Person *B*'s reaction(s).

Finally, it is important to mention that coding was conscientiously directed at paralleling reality as nearly as possible— for remaining as close to the raw data as one reasonably could. Therefore, behaviors were *not* coded in a mutually exclusive fashion, since a given act can, and usually does, carry a multiplicity of meanings. Telling a child to "sit down at the dinner table" is undoubtedly a "directive" or "influencing" initiation (see appendix), but it may also be said angrily—with "antagonism"—or supportively—with "affection"—and should, as a consequence, be coded as something beyond simply an "influencing" act. In this respect, the present coding system departs substantially from the usual means employed by other investigators in the analysis of interaction sequences. Typically, and for reasons of statistical clarity and convenience, the rule of mutual exclusivity in coding is adopted almost as a matter of course. However, what the rule is likely to gain in terms of methodological respectability and statistical manipulability, it is just as likely to lose in terms of truncations and distortions. In short, the rule is certain to introduce artificialities into representations of how actual communicative processes take place between people.

Synopsis of Coding Categories

To familiarize the reader with the coding categories, and in the interest of easy reference, a brief overview of the coding scheme is provided below:

A. Initiating actions toward another
   1. *Cooperative-affectional:* expressions of friendliness, warmth, cooperation, charity, nurturance, or helpfulness
   2. *Conversational:* personal statements, story telling, expressions of opinion or subjective attitudes

3. *Objective:* questions, explanations, informing communications, which are neutral in tone and devoid of personal valence

4. *Mild influencing:* directing, convincing, proposing, urging, controlling the other

5. *Strong influencing:* insisting, demanding, threatening, forcing the other

6. *Disapproving* (emotional-evaluative): being critical, negative, devaluating of the other short of blame, anger, or contempt

7. *Blaming-accusing* (emotional-evaluative): holding the other responsible for objectionable, disapproved behavior

8. *Joyful* (emotional-evaluative): expressions of pleasure, enthusiasm, glee, strong approval, laughter

9. *Antagonistic:* displays of contempt, disaffection, hate, ill will, disgust toward the other

B. Reactions by the other toward the initiator

1. *Positive-direct:* responses which are made directly, straightforwardly with no evasion or negativism

2. *Passive-objective:* responses that are indirect, but complying; passive-submission; the responder reacts to the situation or object, but not to the initiator directly

3. *Cooperative-affectional:* friendliness, warmth, assisting, giving, mutual cooperation

4. *Negative:* refusal, negation, obstinacy, opposition, all in direct form

5. *Avoidant:* diversion, evasion, hesitation, delay, defensiveness; negativism in an indirect sense

6. *Ignoring:* extreme avoidance; refusal to respond in any visible fashion

7. *Embarrassed-withdrawal:* anxious responses; shyness, awkward laughter, leaving the field

8. *Antagonistic:* responses of contempt, hate, ill will; hitting, hurting.

With this overview in hand, we now turn to some tabular summaries of interaction patterns in the A. family.

II

Configurations

Chapter 3

Interaction Frequencies in Behavior Exchange

Overview

Contacts Made and Received

Table 1 summarizes the frequencies of interactions between the A. family members totaled over the eighteen coded home visits. The table contains no reference to the nature of the behavioral exchanges, but provides information about who initiated

Table 1

Matrix Summarizing Interaction Frequencies between Members of the A. Family

		TARGETS								
		Mr. A.	*Mrs. A.*	*Deedee*	*Sheila*	*Ricky*	*Roscoe*	*Pamela*	*All*	*Total*
INITIATORS	Mr. A.		47	26	11	34	28	42	26	214
	Mrs. A.	54		54	28	33	38	36	18	261
	Deedee	20	47		12	3	2	5	9	98
	Sheila	4	19	13		12	11	32	0	91
	Ricky	16	38	0	6		69	9	12	150
	Roscoe	12	23	1	4	17		3	2	62
	Pamela	22	16	1	6	3	9		4	61
	Total	128	190	95	67	102	157	127	71	937

interaction with whom. Nine hundred thirty-seven coded interactions were initiated during the eighteen observations, for an average of fifty-two per visit. The table shows that Mrs. A. initiated the most interactions, followed by Mr. A. and Ricky. Fewest interactions were begun by the two youngest children, Roscoe and Pamela. Mrs. A. not only initiated more interactions than anyone else in the family, but she was also the recipient of more behaviors than anyone else. Roscoe ranked second among family members as a target of initiated interactions.

A number of general observations about Table 1 seem warranted. First, it is apparent that most of the behaviors in the A. family emanate from the parents—Mr. and Mrs. A. account for some 50 percent of the initiated acts. Coordinately, since family members are listed in descending order of age, it seems apparent that there is considerable positive correlation between chronological age and the initiation of interactions— the single exception to this is Ricky. Equally noteworthy is the fact that the same ordering does not apply to targeting. There is no readily observable relation between chronological age and being the object of others' initiations. These relations suggest the possibility that in the A. family at least, the frequency with which one begins interactions is a function of status and/or power, while being the target for others' behaviors is not.

It might be noted in passing that this suggestion is at some variance with the findings of other investigations. Received and transmitted verbal units have been used as measures of influence by Bales and Slater (1955), Mills (1960), and Murrell and Stachowiak (1967), and all have reported that talking *and* receiving are associated with leadership in small groups—including families—and that high frequencies of receiving rather than talking tended to be somewhat more closely correlated with status. Findings with respect to receiving in the A. family run counter to these results, while those for initiation do not.

It must be emphasized, of course, that Bales and Slater, Mills, and Murrell and Stachowiak obtained their results from experimental studies conducted in laboratory settings, while the data on the A. family came from observation in natural settings. Whether this is the crucial difference is not clear. But early returns from the coding and analysis of a small number of research families who were observed in situ in the home indicate that initiation and status are consistently more highly correlated than are receiving and status. However, the most promising, because in our current, limited experience the most

powerful, index of influence or status in the family is the ratio
of initiations to receptions. The greater the frequency of one's
initiations relative to one's frequency as object of other's initiations, the greater one's attributed or attained authority in the
family social system.

Viewed in this light, Table 1 reveals Roscoe to be by far
the weakest member of the family. The four oldest persons in
the group initiate interactions more often than they receive
them; Roscoe and Pamela are both more often targets than initiators, but Roscoe has an unfavorable ratio of 2 : 5 compared to
Pamela's less drastic 1 : 2. When one remembers that Pamela is
some four years Roscoe's junior and yet enjoys commensurate
if not greater status in the A. family, it can readily be discerned that Roscoe has some special meaning—a particular,
low-status-linked significance in the family constellation. Table
1 does not provide data for conjecture as to what the meaning
might be, but two immediately prominent hypotheses based
on the writings of others suggest that his low standing may be
a function of (a) his "emotional disturbance," his "patient status" at the guidance center or (b) his occupancy of the "scapegoat" role in the family's dynamics. Subsequent data will shed
further light on these possible interpretations.

Dyadic Interchanges: Frequencies

Moving, for the moment, from the marginals of Table 1 to the
internal cells, more specific statements about the dyadic interchanges in the A. family can be made. Mr. A.'s heavy involvement with his wife and with his youngest daughter, Pamela, is
clear. He approaches them more than he does other persons in
the family, and they, in turn, initiate more behaviors toward
him than they do toward others. By the same token, Mr. A. interacts almost not at all with Sheila, the middle daughter; he
directs little toward her and she virtually nothing toward him.
By contrast, Mrs. A.'s exchanges with family members tend to
be more evenly distributed—both in terms of initiation and
reception—than is the case with any other family member. In
part, no doubt, her seeming lack of selectivity or bias must be
attributed to her heightened centrality during the dinner hour.
Since nearly all visits occurred at this time, Mrs. A. was unsurprisingly often the hub of much organizational activity and in-

teraction; that she looms in Table 1 as the most interpersonally active individual in the family requires some cautious interpretation because of this fact. Indeed, it is the distinct impression of the observer that her highly instrumental, task-oriented behavior—preparing dinner, getting the table set, serving dinner, having the table cleared and the dishes washed and dried—brought her into significantly greater interaction with everyone than might have been the case otherwise. Interestingly, her postdinner-time behavior formed a sharp contrast with the welter of action just ascribed to her; as many mothers do, she often withdrew into herself after dinner, becoming subdued and self-contained as she sought to recoup some of her expended energy. To have sampled her behavior during this time alone would have made her appear the least engaging or engaged of the A. family. This period, of course, seldom lasted more than ten or fifteen minutes during a visit.

Yet, despite these possible limitations, some features of Mrs. A.'s relationships seem of more than passing consequence. She is, for example, generally sought out by all persons in the family, and she may, in fact, be the most popular of the group. As fulcrum for family interaction—451 of the 937 exchanges, or 48 percent of interactions involve her—Mrs. A. may be seen as instrumental in holding the various members and subunits of the A. family together. She may be *the* unifying force.

Certainly, she is the only member of the family to substantially engage or be engaged by Deedee. Deedee, it will be observed, virtually never approaches her three younger siblings and has only modest contact with Sheila and father. Reciprocally, others seldom approach her, and the three youngest children avoid her assiduously. Hence, her relation to and participation with the family is primarily mediated by or through mother. Better than 50 percent of Deedee's interpersonal exchanges involve Mrs. A. It would not be an overstatement to assert that without Mrs. A., Deedee's place in the family would be more peripheral than it already is. And, as will be clear later on, most of what Mrs. A. does *is* directed at maintaining persons within the family circle—her efforts with Deedee are simply the most extreme (see Fig. 2).

On first glance, and indeed in reality, other members of

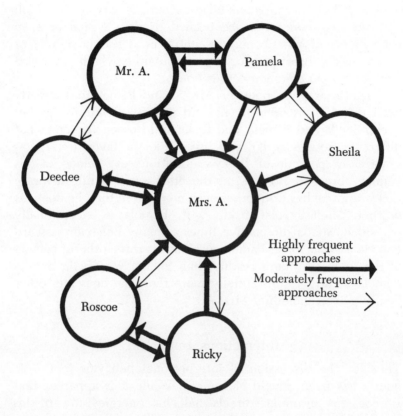

Figure 2.
Depiction of the Major Interpersonal Alignments
Based on Relative Frequency of Approach
in the A. Family

the A. family appear to be less isolated than Deedee, and therefore less dependent on their interactions with Mrs. A. for maintaining them in the family. A number of interactional alignments [1] are prominent—Mr. A. with Pamela, Sheila with Pamela, Roscoe with Ricky. All these are markedly dyadic in their distribution unless one takes account of Mrs. A., in which case the alignments may be termed triadic. As can be seen from Figure 2, Mrs. A. plays a central or at least a significant role as nexus for disparate subunits, subunits which otherwise would have no common connection.

The interaction between Mr. A. and Pamela has already been noted. It is both strong and mutual. Relationships between Sheila and Pamela, and Ricky and Roscoe are somewhat different. Roscoe is far and away Ricky's favorite target— exactly 46 percent of Ricky's initiations are aimed at his younger brother. Roscoe, on the other hand, while favoring Ricky, approaches his mother even more often than he does his brother. Sheila's relationship with Pamela is exceptionally one-sided. Sheila directs five times as many behaviors toward Pamela as vice versa. Pamela approaches three other members of the A. family more readily than Sheila; yet Sheila prefers Pamela as target substantially more than she does any other family person including Mrs. A.

Interactions Initiated

Thus far the discussion of interpersonal behavior in the A. family has been devoid of content. While it is apparent that Roscoe, for example, directs half his energies toward his brother, Table 1 does not make it possible to describe the nature of those approaches. Table 2 presents the content categories for initiated acts (as noted before, categories are defined and exemplified in the appendix).

Table 2 is perhaps best understood as a statement of prob abilities. Given the fact that the coding categories employed

---

1. The term "alignment" is not used here to connote necessarily harmonious or mutually supportive alliance. Rather it refers to high frequency of mutual interaction—the quality of which may be predominantly positive, negative, neutral, or mixed.

for analyzing the A. family's interactions were intentionally *not* mutually exclusive, Table 2 reports the likelihood that any act initiated by a member of the family will communicate joy, antagonism, or affection. Thus the table makes possible a global description of each A.'s characteristic mode of engaging other members of the family.

Table 2

INTERACTIONS INITIATED OF EACH FAMILY
MEMBER'S TOTAL INITIATIONS
(IN PERCENTAGES)

Initiated Interactions	Mr. A.	Mrs. A.	Dee-dee	Sheila	Ricky	Ros-coe	Pa-mela
Cooperative-Affectional	11.2	9.2	21.4	52.9	5.4	17.7	29.5
Conversational	31.8	21.5	35.7	1.0	22.7	29.0	16.4
Objective	25.2	16.1	21.4	8.8	44.0	41.9	27.9
Influencing							
Mild	23.8	36.8	16.3	30.8	10.0	25.8	4.9
Strong	7.0	14.6	7.1	7.7	10.0	3.2	13.1
Emotional-Evaluative							
Disapproving	17.3	18.4	4.1	4.4	14.7	0.0	9.8
Blaming-Accusing	2.3	5.8	0.0	1.0	13.4	0.0	0.0
Joyful	3.7	1.1	3.1	0.0	.7	12.9	4.9
Antagonistic	14.0	11.1	6.1	11.0	32.7	0.0	18.0

Mr. A.

The table shows that Mr. A. is likely to initiate a "coopera-tive-affectional" interaction only once for every nine interac-tions he begins—i.e., 11.2 percent. He is far more inclined to engage others via conversation—about one in every three initiations—or, via objective statements of fact—one in every four initiations. He is far less likely to approach in "pleasura-ble-joyful" ways—one in every twenty-five—or, "blaming-ac-cusing" ways—one in every fifty.

Mrs. A.

As with Table 1, some caution must be taken. Mrs. A. seems to emerge as a woman who, in her actions, is predominantly con-cerned with "influencing" others. More than half the inter-actions she begins appear aimed at exerting control or at getting others to comply. The view must be tempered by an allowance for her need to direct the pace and flow of dinner-time activities. Her low percentage of "cooperative-affectional" approaches, as well as her relatively high inclination to disapprove, may be attributable to similar causes—her intense task orientation, and the attendant premium on timing.

Deedee

Deedee's profile is remarkable for its minimized emotional expressiveness—13.3 percent; only Roscoe manifests a lower relative proportion. On the other hand, while Deedee may not, by frequency count, volunteer as much as either of her parents, she is more likely than anyone else in the family to make conversation when she does initiate interaction. Telling stories and relating extrafamilial events are her major ways of making contact with her family. This makes sense in view of the limited nature of her intrafamilial exchanges—something already observed in Table 1. In her own way, she is the A.'s major link to the outside world.

Sheila

Sheila's profile is phenomenal for its preponderance of "cooperative-affectional" approaches, as well as for its total absence of joy-like initiations. It is also clear that Sheila is a girl invested in influencing and controlling. Since we already know from Table 1 that Sheila spends one-third of her efforts engaging Pamela, it seems reasonable to surmise, even at this juncture, that her approaches to Pamela are basically serious and of a maternal nature—sober, affectionate, and influencing.

Ricky

Ricky is most outstanding for his antagonism. One in every three of his initiations contains an element of dislike and malice. This is virtually twice the relative percentage manifested by any of the other A.'s; and insofar as Table 1 tells us that fully 46 percent of his behaviors are directed at Roscoe, it seems safe to assume that Roscoe receives a good share of Ricky's ill will. Concomitantly, Ricky indulges in the lowest relative percentage of "cooperative-affectional" approaches, but the greatest percentage of objective statement. Hence, it may be surmised that he communicates factual information and purportively neutral data; however, he does so to essentially hostile, rather than friendly, ends. Roscoe is his likely target in this process.

Roscoe

Roscoe, who in Table 1 is seen to initiate rather little, emerges in Table 2 as a boy who, when he does engage other A.'s, is prone to do so in a moderately cooperative, highly objective, and frequently enough joyful rather than pejorative or hostile fashion. Relatively speaking, he manifests almost three times the pleasure displayed by any other member of the A. family. He shows *no* acrimony, *no* hostility, *no* disapproval. He is totally unnegative—perhaps, alarmingly so.

One must conjecture about this boy, for years the scourge of classmates and teachers, who in his own home appears terrified of initiating any display of anger. One must also conjecture about the efficacy of theoretical models and conceptual vantage points adhered to by mental health professionals—orientations which frequently dispose the professional to indict his clientele as dishonest, mendacious, unconcerned, rejecting, or unmotivated; these are orientations that leave precious little conceptual elbow room for testing out, in any significant fashion, the self-same, long standing, "technically justified" assumptions about "resistance."

Table 2 makes clear that Mr. and Mrs. A. were not simply engaging in "denial" when they disclaimed any first-hand knowledge of Roscoe's hyperaggressiveness. That they reasoned the school mishandled him is, in the light of Table 2, something other than "projection"; it is, in fact, a not increditable supposition. In a year of visits to the A. home, Roscoe was never once observed to initiate an act in anger. During that same year, in the Day Treatment school he did so with regularity.[2] On the other hand, one must certainly wonder about

2. Naturally, it might be argued that the parents were "denying" and that Roscoe was on his best behavior during the twenty home visits. But this is not likely. His behavior during the visits was worn naturally by him, which is hardly to suggest it was tension free or relaxed. Roscoe certainly looked

the dynamics of a family system that would encourage or demand a Jekyll–Hyde existence in one of its members. This, of
course, is a major focus of this work, one to be developed in
detail throughout what follows.

Stimulus Values

Table 3 describes, in percentage figures, the stimulus values
that each of the A.'s has for all the other family members. It
informs about what kinds of initiations are likely to be elicited
or received by each individual.

Mr. A., for example, is primarily the object of conversation—39 percent of the time—and objective statements—36 percent of the time—when approached by others
in his family. He is almost never on the receiving end of a
"strong influencing" act. Mrs. A.'s profile is rather similar to
her husband's. They are engaged by others mostly as targets
for objective comments and conversation.

Deedee seems to draw proportionately more acts of
"strong influence" than anyone else in the A. family, while
Sheila is reacted to cooperatively or affectionately better than
four times in every ten approaches to her. Yet people seldom
make conversation with her. Hence, Sheila's movement toward
other persons (see Table 2) mirrors their orientation to her
(Table 3)—she converses and shares information minimally,
but mediates great amounts of affection and cooperation.

Ricky seldom finds himself a target for others' antagonisms. He is somewhat more often a target for cooperative and
affectionate approaches. When people interact with Ricky it is
often to influence him in mild fashion—one in every three
approaches—or to make objective (neutral) remarks to him. He
is, however, seldom approached with joy.

---

awkward and embarrassed much of the time, but his own, as well as others',
reactions made it apparent his behavior was usual, even expected. No one, not
even Pamela, who, at age four, might have been counted on to do so, betrayed any hint that Roscoe ever acted differently. However, Roscoe on occasion encountered the observer at the child guidance center in the Day Treatment service, where despite his awareness of the observer's presence, he
would continue to engage in outbursts of unchecked aggression. And, as it
turned out, a not insignificant moment in his treatment occurred when the observer confronted Roscoe with the dramatic disparity between his school and
home behavior.

Roscoe's profile in Table 3 is significant on four counts. Proportionately, he is the object of more antagonism, more disapproval, and more accusing initiations than any other family member. No one ever approaches him with joy. It is noteworthy that every family member except Roscoe is approached with a favorable "cooperative-affectional" to "antagonism" ratio; for all but Roscoe positive approaches balance or outweigh antagonistic approaches. For Mr. A. it is 9 : 8, for Mrs. A. 2.5 : 1, for Deedee 3 : 2, for Sheila 4.5 : 1, for Ricky 11 : 8, for Pamela 2.5 : 1. For Roscoe, however, antagonistic

Table 3

STIMULUS VALUE OF EACH A. FAMILY
MEMBER FOR ALL OTHERS
(IN PERCENTAGES)

Behavior directed toward	Mr. A.	Mrs. A.	Dee-dee	Sheila	Ricky	Ros-coe	Pa-mela
Cooperative-Affectional	9	16	21	42	11	5	37
Conversational	39	26	20	4	18	17	3
Objective	36	43	17	10	24	18	8
Influencing							
Mild	19	13	20	31	31	23	43
Strong	1	6	20	4	13	17	13
Emotional-Evaluative							
Disapproving	9	3	17	7	8	30	11
Blaming-Accusing	0	0	9	2	1	15	3
Joyful	8	13	1	0	11	0	2
Antagonistic	8	6	14	9	8	43	14

approaches outweigh "cooperative-affectional" approaches in a ratio of better than 8 : 1. He receives untempered hostility.

Piecing together Roscoe's profiles in Tables 2 and 3, we obtain the following: Roscoe is inclined to make contact with others via objective means. His approaches are devoid of hostility, and are, in fact, occasionally touched by joyful pleasure. Yet, he is the object of disapproval, anger, and blame, while receiving no affection, cooperation, or pleasant affect from others. Clearly, there is little, if anything in the objective data to indicate that he does anything to earn his unfavored position. Quite the contrary. He seems to avoid assiduously any behavior which might justify his negative valence. It must be concluded, therefore, at least on the basis of the home observations, that Roscoe is being scapegoated by his family.

Reactions to Initiations

Table 4 offers a summary of reactions to the initiations of others, given in percentages and by category. It reveals that "direct-positive" reactions are adult prerogatives in the A. family, while "passive-compliant" responses are inversely related to age. Inspection of individual profiles shows Mr. A. to be proportionately the least cooperative responder in the family. This

Table 4

REACTIONS TO INITIATIONS BY OTHERS OF EACH
A. FAMILY MEMBER'S TOTAL REACTIONS
(IN PERCENTAGES)

Reactions	Mr. A.	Mrs. A.	Dee-dee	Sheila	Ricky	Ros-coe	Pa-mela
Positive-Direct	36.7	35.3	20.0	14.9	19.6	11.5	18.9
Passive-Objective	16.4	11.6	26.2	35.8	31.4	42.7	56.7
Cooperative	7.8	12.6	23.2	44.8	10.8	14.0	22.0
Negative	17.9	24.7	16.7	1.5	23.5	7.0	22.0
Avoidant	19.5	26.8	17.9	7.4	19.6	18.5	18.1
Ignoring	19.5	22.6	10.5	10.4	15.7	15.9	15.8
Embarrassed-Withdrawal	3.9	0.6	0.0	1.5	5.9	23.6	5.8
Antagonistic	2.4	4.7	9.5	0.0	16.7	3.8	8.7

is not really surprising since Tables 2 and 3 indicate that he offers little affection and cooperation to others and receives little from others.

Ricky, who similarly initiates proportionately few "affectionate-cooperative" acts, is also low, relatively speaking, as a cooperative reactor. Ricky's rank as the most antagonistic responder of all the A.'s is consonant with his initiating behavior, despite the fact that relatively few antagonistic behaviors were received by him (see Table 3). In other words, Ricky's disagreeableness, both as initiator and responder, cannot be accounted for on the basis of others attacking him. Just as Roscoe seems not to earn the animosity directed at him, so Ricky seems to have minimal cause for his angry, belligerent attacks on others.

Sheila's behavior as initiator and as reactor is consistent. When approached by others she is prone to respond with cooperation and compliance, but never negativism or belligerence. Similarly, according to Table 3, Sheila elicits a predominance of "cooperative-affectionate" behaviors from others. She is seldom attacked or blamed. Possibly more than any other member of the A. family, Sheila's profiles in Tables 2, 3 and 4 reflect an isomorphism, a congruity, indicative of the fact that she is treated by others as she treats them. Her salutatory offerings and responses are repaid in kind.

Roscoe and Pamela are the two members of the family most likely to react with "passive-submission"—more than half of Pamela's responses are of this kind. This reiterates the earlier assertion that Roscoe and Pamela enjoy the lowest status in the family. But beyond this, Roscoe and Pamela's profiles differ markedly. Pamela is moderately negative, moderately hostile in her responses. One in every five of her reactions is negative. But she is as cooperative as she is negative. Roscoe, on the other hand, is seldom negative or hostile. What truly sets Roscoe apart from Pamela, and, indeed, from the rest of the A. family, is his tendency toward embarrassed withdrawal. He responds to others' approaches with embarrassment and/or by leaving the field almost one in every four times he is engaged. Once again, the picture of Roscoe at home stands in sharp relief to the vision of his malevolence in the public and Day Treatment schools. Rather than "a raging animal," he seems a browbeaten, thoroughly whipped puppy.

Chapter 4

Pairs

Mrs. A. and Some Noteworthy Dyads

Perhaps the most interesting way to approach the coded interactional data is to consider various of the dyadic relationships
within the A. family constellation. Obviously, not all can or
really need be reviewed. The nature of the splits and alignments, as illustrated in Figure 2 (p. 51), suggests a basis for selection. Certain pairings may allow further and more finely
grained comprehension of the A. family's dynamics. Other
pairings assume significance because they defy intense analysis
—they are significant by virtue of their absence. For instance,
one cannot analyze the nature of Ricky's relationship with
Deedee from this data since they interacted just three times in
the eighteen coded visits. The fact that they mutually avoid
contact is likely of some import—just what, however, we cannot say. The dyads chosen for closer inspection are those represented in Figure 2: Mrs. A. and Deedee, Mrs. A. and Mr. A.,
Mr. A. and Pamela, Sheila and Pamela, and Ricky and Roscoe.

Mrs. A.

It will be recalled from Figure 2 that Mrs. A. was the hub of
family activity, the nexus of family networks. The degree to
which she is central can be surmised from the following: with
seven members in the family there are twenty-one possible
dyads available for study. The dyads may be ranked according
to their frequency of interaction. This frequency is obtained by
adding Partner X's initiations toward Partner Y to Partner Y's
initiation toward Partner X. Mrs. A. is involved as a partner in
five of the seven highest ranked dyads; and all six of the pairings in which she is involved rank among the top nine of the
twenty-one pairings. It seems necessary, therefore, to begin

any discussion of dyads with a discussion of her as an individual playing a vital family role.

We have recognized earlier Mrs. A.'s indispensible, cohesive role as coordinator, mediator, organizer, and impeller of the continued functioning of the A. family. Now we may characterize it in its particulars. Tables 5, 6, and 7 summarize Mrs. A.'s behaviors toward specific persons in her family—initiated acts in Table 5, reactions in Table 6, and reactions toward specific kinds of initiating actions by others in Table 7.

Table 5

MATRIX SUMMARIZING INITIATIONS BY MRS. A.
TO MEMBERS OF THE A. FAMILY

	Mr. A.	Dee-dee	Sheila	Ricky	Ros-coe	Pa-mela	All	Total
Cooperative-Affectional	1	7	9	2	2	3	0	24
Conversational	30	10	1	3	4	3	5	56
Objective	15	10	4	6	3	1	3	42
Influencing (mild)	16	8	12	15	19	21	5	96
Influencing (strong)	0	17	1	6	8	6	0	38
Disapproving	10	9	2	3	8	7	9	48
Blaming-Accusing	0	8	0	0	3	3	1	15
Joyful	0	1	0	0	0	0	2	3
Antagonistic	1	12	1	0	7	6	2	29

Mrs. A. is a woman intent on running her family—especially at dinner time. While forty-two of her initiations are objective, and fifty-six conversational, she is not, comparatively speaking, a woman given to sharing information, idle chit-chat, gossiping, or story-telling. She does not recite the events of her day. She contributes 17 percent of all objective statements made in the A. family—roughly one-sixth among seven people—and 25 percent of all A. family conversation. Similarly, she offers but 17 percent of the "cooperative-affectional" approaches made in the family. While these figures are not outstandingly low, and may even be construed as somewhat above chance expectation (14 percent for one person in seven), they are considerably overshadowed by her task-oriented, "foreman" like qualities.

Her ninety-six "mild-influencing" efforts constitute 43 percent of all attempts at "mild-influencing" made in the family. So too, she accounts for 41 percent of all "strong-influencing," 40 percent of all "disapproval" and 36 percent of all "blaming-accusing." Clearly, she asks that people perform certain behaviors, makes demands, and tries to coerce them when they don't comply. Her approach is not especially antagonistic, nor is it cheered by a joyful orientation. Rather, it is intent on involving everybody in the business of family functioning and task performance. Thus, Pamela, for a four-year-old, seems to get very little from her mother, in part, perhaps, because Pamela lacks instrumentality and is not capable of contributing heavily to task implementation—her mother's goal.

Table 6

MATRIX SUMMARIZING REACTIONS BY MRS. A. TO
INITIATIONS BY A. FAMILY MEMBERS

	Mr. A.	Dee-dee	Sheila	Ricky	Ros-coe	Pa-mela	All	Total
Positive-Direct	25	17	3	12	6	2	2	67
Passive-Objective	4	5	2	1	3	5	2	22
Cooperative	2	8	8	2	2	2	0	24
Negative	11	9	5	9	11	2	0	47
Avoidant	14	13	3	14	4	3	0	51
Ignoring	12	1	1	15	9	5	0	43
Embarrassed-Withdrawal	0	0	0	0	0	1	0	1
Antagonistic	0	3	0	6	0	0	0	9

Mrs. A. frequently responds positively and directly to her family—in fact, she alone accounts for one-third of all "direct-positive" reactions in the A. family. But she also accounts for a similar percentage of the A.'s' total "negative" reactions, total "avoidant" responses, and total "ignoring" reactions. It appears she is willing to listen to and respond directly to others when their initiations are task-relevant; otherwise she is discouraging or unresponsive. She does not tend to react to others with antagonism and/or withdrawal, nor is she especially inclined to submit passively to the demands of others or to cooperate with them because they request it. She dispenses less in the way of compliance and cooperation than is asked of her. This is quite apparent from Table 7, where the content categories in the far left column represent the approaches to Mrs. A. by the family, and the numbers in parentheses the frequency of the particular initiating action. Here we see others trying to influence Mrs. A. on thirty-seven occasions—twenty-five "mild" and twelve "strong." She never cooperates with the demand, is seldom directly positive in her response, and is only occasionally to moderately compliant. On the other hand, she is frequently negative, frequently avoidant, and sometimes ignoring. It can readily be seen that the "negative," "avoidant," and "ignoring" columns of Table 7 contain cells gener-

Table 7

REACTIONS BY MRS. A. TO VARIOUS INITIATIONS
BY A. FAMILY MEMBERS
(IN PERCENTAGES)

	Positive-Direct	Passive-Objective	Cooperative	Negative	Avoidant	Ignoring	Embarrassed-Withdrawal	Antagonistic
Cooperative-Affectional (29)	7	7	52	0	4	7	4	0
Conversational (50)	46	6	10	20	26	34	0	0
Objective (82)	47	5	3	20	29	35	0	7
Influencing (mild) (25)	16	44	0	72	60	24	0	8
Influencing (strong) (12)	0	8	0	17	25	0	0	8
Disapproving (6)	66	0	0	66	66	50	0	33
Blaming-Accusing (1)	0	0	0	0	0	0	0	0
Joyful (12)	8	8	0	58	33	66	0	0
Antagonistic (10)	30	0	0	40	50	60	0	20

ally having higher percentages than the columns for "positive," "passive," and "cooperative" responses. Finally, while twelve joyful behaviors—some 46 percent of all "joyful" initiations among the A.'s—are directed at Mrs. A., she manages to negate, avoid, or ignore most of them. Indeed, her style would appear to be all business.

To a considerable degree her business-like approach works. She gets things accomplished via group interaction and effort—but at considerable cost. People do not cooperate extensively with her, but then she rarely asks for or depends upon cooperation. Rather, she makes demands, and seeks to influence, compel, and cajole others into getting family functions fulfilled and family tasks accomplished. She relies on others complying and ultimately obtains their compliance in about the proportion she requests. But it is a struggle. And in doing so, she overrides the personal needs and desires of others, and, one suspects, personal wants and hopes of her own as well. She is without fun and relatively low on nonessential exchanges—such as conversation or idle talk. When others seek to gain her attentions for their own needs, she puts them off, ignores them, or tells them outright no—unless it happens to appear that recognition or fulfillment of the other's need is somehow consistent with family task performance. Unfortunately, consistency of this kind is not frequent. Examples of her general behavior, drawn from the transcriptions of home visits, follow:

Home Visit 4, December 5

There was a phone call for Mrs. A. which she answered. She spoke on the phone for a number of minutes. After hanging up the phone Mrs. A. emerged from the kitchen. She sat down on the couch, and Mr. A. asked her who had called. She replied that it had been a friend—Marge. Mr. A. asked what Marge had wanted. Mrs. A. replied that Marge had invited them to come over later that evening, but that Mrs. A. had replied that they could not since they had to go shopping this evening. At this point Ricky, who had been reading a volume of the World Book while seated on the living room floor, began to ask his mother questions. He showed her a picture of a Japanese emperor and asked Mrs. A. if she knew who it was. Mrs. A. tried to evade the question by simply not responding, whereupon Ricky persisted in asking it two or three more times. Finally, with some tiredness, Mrs. A. said Hirohito.

At this point Sheila appeared with some Christmas cards that she had begun making in school. Mrs. A. began constructing some too, working side by side with Sheila. Ricky kept asking all sorts of questions. He asked his mother what would happen in case of a world war—would Germany fight on our side. Mrs. A. said she didn't know. Ricky wanted to know if China would fight on our side. He specifically said Red China. Mrs. A. again shrugged her shoulders and said she didn't know, brushing off the question. Then Ricky asked about numerous other countries, including Russia. To all of these questions, despite the fact that Ricky knew and Mrs. A. knew they had obvious answers, Mrs. A. replied automatically, "I don't know." When Ricky asked if Russia would fight on our side in a war, Mrs. A., almost as if she hadn't heard him, said simply, "I don't know. . . ."

Home Visit 5, December 12

As I went through the kitchen I noted that Mrs. A. was on the phone. It seemed she was talking to a friend. Sheila was doing the dishes. Ricky and Roscoe were in the living room playing with planes on the floor. Both were wearing G.I. caps. Mrs. A. finished her phone conversation and then proceeded to call someone else—a business office of some kind. Pamela was in the living room with a small toy rake trying to sweep up the carpet. She apparently jabbed herself in the stomach with the rake and began crying loudly. Mrs. A. was still on the phone. Pamela went immediately to her mother. She clung to her mother trying to explain to her what had happened, but crying all the while. Mrs. A. at first did not acknowledge her. Then she half pushed, half waved her away. Ricky appeared from the living room and seemed quite concerned about Pamela's having hurt herself. Mrs. A. paid no attention to Pamela, and Pamela eventually returned to the living room and began playing again while continuing to sob.

Mrs. A., finished on the phone, now came into the living room and sat down. Pamela began crying in earnest again. She held a handkerchief to her stomach and indicated that she was very badly hurt. She wanted her mother to fix it. Again, Mrs. A. hardly acknowledged Pamela, much less the fact that she seemed to be in pain. My own impression was that Pamela was not in real pain; she had played for a number of minutes with soft crying while her mother was still on the phone. I had the feeling she was now putting on an act to pull some solicitous and nurturant response from her mother, who did not so much as inquire what had happened. Mrs. A. seated herself anew on the couch. Pamela disappeared into her bedroom for a moment and then reappeared with her security blanket. While she was gone, Sheila finished the dishes and sat herself down in a chair in the living room. Pamela climbed on Sheila's lap, security blanket in hand and thumb in mouth.

The tendency to subvert the socio-emotional sphere of concern, to pretend that it doesn't exist, or to delegate it to others by default, earns Mrs. A. considerable animosity and resistance. She may be the task master in the home—at least around dinner time—but she is not necessarily a popular leader who inspires willing and enduring commitment from her family. She receives 35 percent of all the "negative" reactions given in the A. family, 28 percent of the "avoidance" responses, 25 percent of the "ignoring" responses, and fully 31 percent of all the "antagonistic" reactions. Her struggle to keep the family intact and operative is a decided hassle. One does not wonder at her complaints of exhaustion, her need to retire to bed at 8:30 P.M., her extreme nervousness, her tension headaches, her inability to keep food down, all mentioned to her caseworker at the center. One wonders, instead, why the task falls so very heavily on her, what alternatives she sees for herself, and why she doesn't beg for, or at least welcome, outside support and assistance.

Mrs. A. and Deedee

Just how taxing the struggle of holding the A. family intact can be for Mrs. A. is illustrated by her relationship with Deedee, the oldest daughter, aged thirteen.

But for her contacts with Mrs. A., Deedee would be, for all intents and purposes, thoroughly outside the family. She was certainly the most invisible of the A.'s during the home visits and frequently disappeared from the home after dinner was over. In many ways, she typifies the young adolescent beginning to find her way out of the home and into peer activities and relationships. Yet her autonomy and growing separateness has a starkly driven, one-sided, even premature quality. She relates not at all to her siblings. While she exchanges cooperative behaviors with Sheila, they are the automatic, hard-programmed exchanges of long standing reciprocal role-functioning around the dinner chores. Otherwise, she does not speak to Sheila. There remains only her relationship with her parents. Here Mr. A. is almost incidental. They speak to each other, but usually because both are engaged with Mrs. A. or because Mrs. A. sometimes tries to encourage their contact, suggesting that Deedee ought to ask permission from her father, that Mr. A. ought to counsel or advise Deedee. Deedee's only real connection with the family is through Mrs. A.

Their relationship is a highly charged, heavily ambivalent one for both of them. It is overtly characterized by tension, anger, and struggles for control and freedom. Deedee seems unaware of the subtleties of the relationship. Whether Mrs. A. fully appreciates its dynamics is also questionable. In a variety of very significant ways, Deedee would seem to be Mrs. A.'s long envied but despised alter-ego—a wished-for but unattainable and undesirable would-be self. It will be recalled that Mrs. A. described herself as a shy child, quiet, withdrawn, not popular, isolated from peers, never dating, highly responsible and committed to family, especially her younger brother. Deedee is none of these things.

Thirteen and in junior high school, Deedee is well developed, has a trim figure, and by eighth-grade standards is surely one of the more sexually attractive girls in her class. Her face is not strikingly pretty, but she is very much aware of her looks, obviously spends much time attending to herself, and by way of makeup and hairstyling makes the most of her appearance. In sharp contrast to Sheila and Mrs. A., Deedee wears clothes that accentuate her figure—tight sweaters, slacks, mini-skirts, shorts. When she and her mother engage in conversation it is about school dances, local skating parties, and Deedee's clothes.

Deedee is clearly popular and very much a part of peer group activity. She regales her parents, and especially Mrs. A., with news of her world. Mrs. A. is often dubious, sometimes critical of what she hears, but she always listens. Table 6 indicates that Mrs. A. only once ignores an approach by Deedee, though she frequently (forty-three times) ignores others and accounts for 31 percent of all the "ignoring" reactions in the A. family.

The relationship between Mrs. A. and Deedee is, along with that between Mrs. A. and Mr. A., the most active of all the dyads. Next to that between Ricky and Roscoe, it is also the most conflictive. Table 5 indicates, for example, that Mrs. A. is highly intent on strongly controlling Deedee, on directing

her, and that she is more admonishing, blaming, and antagonistic toward Deedee than she is toward anyone else in the
family. By the same token, Table 8 informs us that Deedee,
while making many cooperative, objective, and friendly ap-

Table 8

MATRIX SUMMARIZING INITIATIONS BY DEEDEE
TO MEMBERS OF THE A. FAMILY

	Mr. A.	Mrs. A.	Sheila	Ricky	Ros- coe	Pa- mela	All	Total
Cooperative-Affectional	1	8	12	0	0	0	0	21
Conversational	7	19	0	0	0	0	9	35
Objective	11	9	0	1	0	0	0	21
Influencing (mild)	5	9	0	0	0	2	0	16
Influencing (strong)	0	2	0	1	1	3	0	7
Disapproving	0	2	0	0	2	0	0	4
Blaming-Accusing	0	0	0	0	0	0	0	0
Joyful	1	1	0	0	0	0	1	3
Antagonistic	0	3	0	0	2	0	0	5

proaches to her mother, also seeks to influence Mrs. A. more
than any other member of the A. family dares to do. The battle for control ends in a mutual standoff. Mrs. A. gives in, responds positively, and cooperates as much as she negates and
avoids. For her part, Deedee does the same, except that on occasion she ignores Mrs. A. and/or expresses antagonism toward

Table 9

MATRIX SUMMARIZING REACTIONS BY DEEDEE
TO INITIATIONS BY A. FAMILY MEMBERS

	Mr. A.	Mrs. A.	Sheila	Ricky	Ros- coe	Pa- mela	All	Total
Positive-Direct	8	11	0	0	0	0	0	19
Passive-Objective	10	14	0	0	0	1	0	25
Cooperative	2	8	12	0	0	0	0	22
Negative	1	13	0	0	1	1	0	16
Avoidant	5	11	0	0	0	1	0	17
Ignoring	1	8	1	0	0	0	0	10
Embarrassed-Withdrawal	0	0	0	0	0	0	0	0
Antagonistic	0	7	0	0	1	1	0	9

her mother. Eighty percent of Deedee's "negative" responses, 52 percent of her "avoidant" reactions, 80 percent of her "ignoring," and 78 percent of her "antagonistic" responses are re-

Table 10

REACTIONS BY DEEDEE TO VARIOUS INITIATIONS
BY A. FAMILY MEMBERS
(IN PERCENTAGES)

	Positive-Direct	Passive-Objective	Cooperative	Negative	Avoidant	Ignoring	Embarrassed-Withdrawal	Antagonistic
Cooperative-Affectional (20)	50	5	80	0	0	0	0	0
Conversational (19)	5	16	0	5	5	5	0	5
Objective (16)	44	19	0	13	7	13	0	19
Influencing (mild) (19)	0	58	0	21	37	5	0	0
Influencing (strong) (19)	0	32	0	52	27	37	0	16
Disapproving (16)	0	50	0	32	63	19	7	25
Blaming-Accusing (9)	33	11	0	0	22	11	0	44
Joyful (1)	100	0	0	0	0	0	0	0
Antagonistic (13)	23	23	0	31	31	8	0	38

served for Mrs. A.'s initiations. The following excerpt is typical of the interaction between Mrs. A. and Deedee:

Home Visit 14, March 27

Mr. A. finished eating ahead of the others. He got up from the table and disappeared from the family room without a word of explanation. Apparently everyone in the family understood where he was going. The sound of an electric shaver came from the bathroom. Mr. A. was shaving. The meal ended for the rest of the family. Deedee disappeared almost immediately into the front living room. Roscoe and Ricky also disappeared. Pamela sat down in front of the TV set sucking her thumb and began watching TV. Mrs. A. also sat down. Mr. A. came out into the family room and with a wave said he was leaving for the scout meeting. Mrs. A. and Pamela continued to watch TV very intently. At this point Sheila had apparently finished clearing, scraping, and stacking the dishes in the kitchen and came out to the family room. She sat down and asked her mother what the plot of the TV program had been thus far. Mrs. A. filled her in briefly, and in so doing apparently caught Roscoe's attention. He had been passing through, but now sat down to watch. Pamela got up and disappeared shortly thereafter.

When the program ended some minutes later, Mrs. A. became aware that Pamela was no longer around. She asked Sheila where Pamela had gone. Sheila said she did not know. Mrs. A. went to the living room. Pamela was not there, but Deedee was. She was sitting next to the stereo set listening to rock music at high volume. As she listened she polished her fingernails. Mrs. A. asked Deedee where Pamela was. Deedee said Pamela had gone outside. At this point Mrs. A. lost her temper. She almost totally lost control. Full of anger, she started yelling at Deedee about her negligence. How could Deedee just sit there listening to that horrible music and polishing her fingernails, and let Pamela go outdoors without anything on except a pair of trousers and a shirt. Deedee said she had been busy listening and polishing her fingernails. This only irritated Mrs. A. more. In fury she told Deedee that the dishes had been stacked and ready for washing for some twenty minutes already, and asked why she hadn't washed them already. Deedee denied awareness that they were ready. Mrs. A. retorted it was her business to be aware of her responsibilities. Deedee defended herself by saying she couldn't do them now until her fingernails had dried. Mrs. A. in a rage reiterated that Pamela was not supposed to go outside by herself, dressed or not dressed. With a final blast at Deedee she went out the front door to find Pamela. Pamela emerged from the family room just as Mrs. A. returned. She gave Pamela a smack on the backside and a bawling out. Pamela didn't react. As I departed through the front door some minutes later, Deedee was still sitting, polishing her fingernails and listening to music. She didn't look up from her task to say good-bye.

The next excerpt exemplifies a more sanguine aspect of the relationship between Mrs. A. and Deedee.

Home Visit 1, November 14

Conversation at the dinner table was initially slow. Eventually, Deedee began talking about some activity at school. She asked her parents if she could go to a dance at the junior high school. The dance was a week away and was to be a dance for eighth-grade boys and girls. Deedee asked her parents if they would chaperon. Mr. A. seemed not to know what Deedee was talking about, though Mrs. A. did. Mrs. A. tried to remind Mr. A. of the dance. She had told him about it before, but he seemed to have forgotten. Deedee seemed quite anxious to go to the dance and she reminded her parents of the seventh-grade dance the prior year. This jogged Mr. A.'s memory. He recalled that he and Mrs. A. had chaperoned last year's dance—there had been movies about motorcycles at the dance. Deedee said she couldn't promise movies this time, but would her parents please come as adults to chaperon? Mrs. A. agreed to do so. She agreed for herself and Mr. A. Deedee was jubilant.

Deedee now talked about the dance in terms of how wonderful it would be. She rambled on about the couples who would go—who was currently going steady with whom. Mrs. A. expressed surprise at some of the pairings. She and Deedee were the only two at the table who appeared to know the personalities involved. Deedee commented that one of the teachers, a Mr. C., who was extremely funny, and who taught dramatics, would be the disc jockey for the dance. She assured Mrs. A. that Mrs. A. would "love" him, and probably "die laughing" at his antics. Deedee talked about all the advertisements that were posted around the school for the dance.

The conversation then turned to what Deedee would wear. Mrs. A. asserted it would have to be something new—a new dress. She told Deedee that she had "lent" some of Deedee's clothes to a daughter of a neighbor who also wanted to go to the dance, but who had nothing to wear.

The conversation for some minutes had been exclusively between Deedee and her mother. It continued as such around the topic of clothes and dresses—especially the ones that had been "lent" out. There was some discussion of how well these things really fit Deedee. Deedee, quite conscious of her body, said that the neighbor girl could have the dresses since they no longer fit her (Deedee) around the bust; she then fumbled momentarily for a word and added "or around my bottom either." Mrs. A. smiled, both in pride and embarrassment. She turned toward Mr. A. to point out that even though the neighbor girl was some months older than Deedee, Deedee was way ahead "developmentally." Mr. A. did not respond. He poured himself a second cup of coffee and began to talk about events at his work.

Similarly revealing of the vicarious, identificatory relation of Mrs. A. to Deedee and Deedee's willing complementariness is the following:

Home Visit 5, December 12

Deedee came up from downstairs in a tight fitting pair of slacks, and a bulky-knit sweater. She announced she was ready to go skating at the school. She then requested if she could use her mother's snow boots. Mrs. A. said it was okay for her to use them. Deedee did. Deedee then disappeared from the family room only to reappear a few minutes later. In full view of the family she brushed her hair and put on her lipstick. A few moments later she shouted good-bye to her mother as she went out the front door. She did not mention anyone else. Her mother shouted good-bye back, and told her to have a good time.

This relationship is essentially bellicose. Its calm, private moments of mutuality are, of course, real enough, and they point up the interplay of Deedee's unabashed narcissism, her blatant sexuality, and Mrs. A.'s projective and vicarious identifications. They are short lived. Mrs. A. finds in Deedee all that is forbidden and repressed in herself. She indulges the forbidden for brief periods, then she rages at her lapses. Or, more precisely, she projects her lapses and consequent guilt to Deedee, and rages at them in Deedee. For her part, Deedee is given to flaunting her possession of what mother never had. She teases Mrs. A. with glimpses of a world Mrs. A. never experienced. In this way, Deedee becomes a foil and a scapegoat for Mrs. A.'s jealousies and displaced self-loathings.

Their entire relationship may be viewed a quid pro quo that is currently tenuously balanced, but is, for developmental and social-psychological reasons, of problematic duration. There is no doubt that at age thirteen Deedee needs her mother as much as her mother needs her. She needs a "chaperon," and there are certain pleasures she derives from provoking her mother's vicariousness. But, Deedee's trajectory is away from the family. Already, one-third of her "family hours" —around dinner time—are spent outside the home. When she is home she relates essentially only to her mother. While it may never fully come to pass—in a psychological sense—it seems only a matter of time before extrafamilial contacts replace or reduce Mrs. A.'s value for Deedee as a major source of gratification. Deedee's narcissism and sexuality promise to enhance the process. Early departure and/or early marriage are not unlikely prospects for her.

One may guess, however, that Mrs. A.'s need for Deedee will not reduce. Judging from her struggle to control Deedee and her condemnation of Deedee's extrafamilial activities, she seems unmistakably begrudging of Deedee's autonomy, of Deedee's ability to leave the cares of the family behind. The fleeting recognition of that wish in herself threatens to bring Mrs. A.'s wrath down on Deedee. One begins to surmise that Mrs. A. would indeed like to follow Deedee out of the family but instead dictates to her, seeks to dominate her and to keep her tied to the family—out of need and jealousy. Some questions remain. Why is Deedee *so* impelled to leave her family at age thirteen? And, aside from factors of age and felt responsibility, why is Mrs. A. *so* invested in keeping Deedee within the family? What accounts for the intensity of these wishes?

Mrs. A. and Mr. A.

As mentioned earlier, Mrs. A. and Mr. A.'s relationship ranks as the most active dyad in the family. And, as with the relationship between Mrs. A. and Deedee, this is ostensibly a somewhat surprising finding, insofar as Mr. A. is absent from the home for substantial portions of many of the visits; during some visits he is not present at all.

It may be that interaction between family members simply increases in frequency as the age or status of the participants increases, overriding even issues of absenteeism. Or, it may be that there is an effort to compensate for interactional short changing when a frequently absent member is around. Or possibly, Mrs. A. is trying to keep Mr. A. in the family group—just as she endeavors to maintain Deedee's ties. There is no definitive way of deciding the relative contributions of these factors. All three likely contribute to the high frequency of interactions in the mother–father dyad. There is, however, less reason to feel that the third factor (inclusion) contributes as greatly, or at least in the same fashion, as it does in the mother–daughter relation. Deedee relates to no one but her mother. Mr. A. relates to everyone, and mostly to Mrs. A. Yet, as will be seen, Mrs. A. has good reason to be concerned about Mr. A.'s leaving the family. But the fear is differently based and is dealt with differently. The patterning of interaction profiles between Mr. and Mrs. A. is, in major respects, unlike that between Mrs. A. and Deedee. At a minimum, it reflects the differences in role relations.

Mrs. A. is properly respectful of her husband. She approaches him with conversation and information, tries to influence him moderately, but only mildly. She responds to him directly more than does any other A., and more than she does to any of her children. She is almost never antagonistic, blaming, or strongly insistent toward him. She is all of these things to other family members. While she does disapprove of Mr. A.'s behavior—or of him—and does ignore and avoid him fairly frequently, this characterizes her behaviors toward other members of the family as well and cannot be described as unique to her relationship with her husband. Yet her interaction with Mr. A. is remarkably low in "cooperative-affectional" exchanges. Of the 101 interactions coded between Mr. and Mrs. A., only five involve the cooperative-affectional category. This despite the fact that Mrs. A. accounts for 17 percent of all "cooperative-affectional" initiations in the family, 13 percent of all the family's responses in that category. For Mr. A. the comparable percentages are 17 and 8 percent respectively (see Tables 11, 12, and 13).

It must be concluded that Mr. and Mrs. A. are less disposed, at least during the observation periods, to offer each other warmth or colleagual exchange than they are to their children. In view of Mrs. A.'s statements to the social worker at the child guidance center about the sexual repulsion she has felt toward her husband for more than three years, the impres-

Table 11

MATRIX SUMMARIZING INITIATIONS BY MR. A.
TO MEMBERS OF THE A. FAMILY

	Mrs. A.	Dee-dee	Sheila	Ricky	Ros-coe	Pa-mela	All	Total
Cooperative-Affectional	1	1	1	0	0	21	0	24
Conversational	19	8	2	9	6	1	22	67
Objective	27	5	1	13	1	3	4	54
Influencing (mild)	2	11	4	8	8	15	3	51
Influencing (strong)	2	1	0	3	4	5	0	15
Disapproving	2	7	3	4	10	7	4	37
Blaming-Accusing	0	1	1	1	1	1	0	5
Joyful	4	0	0	0	0	3	1	8
Antagonistic	5	1	2	4	11	7	0	30

sions gained from the home visits seem to be an accurate reflection of the general relation between Mrs. A. and her husband.

For the most part, Mr. A. is a man given to neutral or distanced interactions with his family. His favored modes of encounter are objective statements and conversation. This is especially true of his initiations toward his wife. In the emotional realm, his behavior toward Mrs. A. is weak to moderately low. He does not seek to control her, blame her, or express anger toward her. His reactions tend to be negative,

Table 12

MATRIX SUMMARIZING REACTIONS BY MR. A.
TO INITIATIONS BY A. FAMILY MEMBERS

	Mrs. A.	Dee-dee	Sheila	Ricky	Ros-coe	Pa-mela	All	Total
Positive-Direct	17	6	2	10	2	10	0	47
Passive-Objective	12	4	0	1	1	3	0	21
Cooperative	1	1	2	1	0	5	0	10
Negative	10	2	0	1	10	0	0	23
Avoidant	14	4	0	3	2	2	0	25
Ignoring	9	4	0	3	6	3	0	25
Embarrassed-Withdrawal	0	0	0	0	0	5	0	5
Antagonistic	0	1	0	0	2	0	0	3

avoidant, and ignoring, and he maintains an affective remoteness. She generally mirrors these proclivities, except, perhaps, for her inclination to disapprove.

The basis for this mutual relation is, of course, not clear from the tables. It is apparent, however, that this unemotional, low evaluative, uncooperative, disaffectionate dyadic relationship is more characteristic of Mr. and Mrs. A. than of any

Table 13

REACTIONS BY MR. A. TO VARIOUS INITIATIONS
BY A. FAMILY MEMBERS
(IN PERCENTAGES)

	Positive-Direct	Passive-Objective	Cooperative	Negative	Avoidant	Ignoring	Embarrassed-Withdrawal	Antagonistic
Cooperative-Affectional (11)	13	0	73	0	9	9	0	0
Conversational (50)	40	8	4	6	22	28	0	0
Objective (46)	39	20	7	26	17	22	4	2
Influencing (mild) (24)	17	29	0	38	25	17	0	4
Influencing (strong) (1)	100	0	0	0	0	0	0	0
Disapproving (12)	0	17	0	33	58	8	0	0
Blaming-Accusing (0)	0	0	0	0	0	0	0	0
Joyful (3)	33	0	0	0	0	100	67	0
Antagonistic (10)	0	20	10	10	20	60	50	0

other family pair that interacts to any degree whatsoever. The parents give the impression of mutual toleration and minimal cooperation. They treat each other with kid gloves.

Mr. A. and Pamela

All that is present in the relation between Mr. A. and his wife is absent from Mr. A.'s relation to Pamela. Conversely, what is missing between Mr. A. and Mrs. A. is manifest between Mr. A. and his youngest daughter. Where Mr. A. relates objectively and conversationally to Mrs. A.—as perhaps befits public interaction between adults—he is neither objective nor conversational toward Pamela. Where he is uncooperative, unaffectionate, undemanding, and unemotional toward Mrs. A., he is singularly affectionate, cooperative, influencing, disapproving,

---

antagonistic, and embarrassed with his daughter. He avoids, is negative, and ignoring toward his spouse. He is virtually none of these to Pamela. He is highly direct and passively compliant to his wife; he is less so to Pamela. He expresses some joyful pleasure to both his wife and this daughter, but 83 percent of his "affectionate" initiations belong to Pamela.

Pamela initiates in kind (see Table 14). She is both affectionate and antagonistic in her approaches to her father. Her reactions are compliant, negative, antagonistic, embarrassed, ignoring, avoidant, and cooperative in moderate to large degrees. Better than 50 percent of her "negativism," 73 percent

Table 14

MATRIX SUMMARIZING INITIATIONS BY PAMELA
TO MEMBERS OF THE A. FAMILY

	Mr. A.	Mrs. A.	Dee-dee	Sheila	Ricky	Ros-coe	All	Total
Cooperative-Affectional	8	6	0	4	0	0	0	18
Conversational	1	1	0	0	0	4	4	10
Objective	5	6	0	1	2	3	0	17
Influencing (mild)	0	2	0	1	0	0	0	3
Influencing (strong)	0	3	0	1	1	3	0	8
Disapproving	2	0	0	0	0	4	0	6
Blaming-Accusing	0	0	0	0	0	0	0	0
Joyful	2	0	0	0	0	0	1	3
Antagonistic	8	0	0	0	0	3	0	11

Table 15

MATRIX SUMMARIZING REACTIONS BY PAMELA
TO INITIATIONS BY A. FAMILY MEMBERS

	Mr. A.	Mrs. A.	Dee-dee	Sheila	Ricky	Ros-coe	All	Total
Positive-Direct	5	4	0	15	0	0	0	24
Passive-Objective	19	15	2	25	8	3	0	72
Cooperative	6	4	0	17	1	0	0	28
Negative	15	6	3	3	0	1	0	28
Avoidant	7	6	0	10	0	0	0	23
Ignoring	5	6	0	0	1	0	0	12
Embarrassed-Withdrawal	6	0	0	1	0	0	0	7
Antagonistic	8	1	0	0	1	1	0	11

Table 16

REACTIONS BY PAMELA TO VARIOUS INITIATIONS
BY A. FAMILY MEMBERS
(IN PERCENTAGES)

	Positive-Direct	Passive-Objective	Cooperative	Negative	Avoidant	Ignoring	Embarrassed-Withdrawal	Antagonistic
Cooperative-Affectional (47)	34	62	49	19	9	11	13	17
Conversational (4)	25	25	0	0	25	50	0	0
Objective (10)	20	60	10	10	10	10	0	10
Influencing (mild) (55)	7	58	0	22	29	11	0	7
Influencing (strong) (17)	0	47	0	41	11	18	0	0
Disapproving (14)	0	50	0	29	0	50	0	14
Blaming-Accusing (4)	0	25	0	0	50	25	0	0
Joyful (3)	33	0	100	0	0	0	0	0
Antagonistic (18)	0	67	0	0	22	22	33	0

of her "antagonism," and 86 percent of her "embarrassed-with-drawal" occur in response to her father. Their relationship is almost exclusively based on emotional-evaluative interchanges, devoid of neutralized or articulated communication, and often fraught with sudden shifts from one affective extreme to the other. For example:

Home Visit 3, November 28

Sheila and Pamela were involved in watching television. Pamela sucked her thumb continuously. A few minutes into the Yogi Bear show Mr. A. returned to the family room. He took off his jacket and sat down in the seat that Pamela was in. He picked her up and sat her down on his lap. Pamela reacted to this by laughing and giggling in a very happy and almost silly way. She then jumped off her father's lap and said she did not want to sit on his lap. This was in contrast to the affect she expressed at the time.

And again, later in the same visit:

Pamela asked for her father's hand and he reached over and gave it to her. She then began pounding at it with her fists. Mr. A. seemed somewhat startled at this and Mrs. A. intervened, stating that possibly Pamela was trying to wake her father up. Mr. A. withdrew his hand without saying anything.

Home Visit 10, January 30

Pamela went over to her father, jumped on his lap and began teasing him. Mr. A. responded by trying to embrace Pamela and caressed her and she said, "Stop doing that." Mr. A. reacted somewhat hurt and told Pamela to come back. She had jumped down from his lap and he grabbed after her. Pamela refused to return. As soon as Mr. A. had ceased his efforts to restrain her and his efforts to get her back, Pamela began to leap at her father and to provoke him by poking at him. Mr. A. was somewhat embarrassed by the situation and laughed weakly.

The oedipal and counter-oedipal features of this relationship are unmistakable and perhaps even unremarkable for a four-year-old girl and her father. Yet the intensity of the relationship—especially its seductive, teasing, hurting qualities —may be buttressed by the tepid relation between Mrs. A. and Pamela. It will be recalled from Tables 5 and 6 that Mrs. A. does little for Pamela except try to control her. Mrs. A. appears to have retreated from the competition for Mr. A.— except when it is too late and she intervenes reparatively in the counter-oedipal fighting and defense between father and daughter. She then makes peace. As noted earlier, she also seems to have surrendered her motherly role toward Pamela.

Again, we may conjecture why all this should be so. It is not unreasonable to assume, for example, that Mr. A. has turned to Pamela for sexual-affectional gratifications. Moreover, he has done so not simply because her oedipal phasing has triggered counter-oedipal feelings in him, but also because he can obtain from her, in substitute fashion, some of the gratifications absent from his relationship with Mrs. A. One might, in fact, speculate parenthetically that Mrs. A., feeling the same lack, has sought gratifications in her identification and vicarious experiences via Deedee. Be that as it may, Mr. A. and Pamela have a highly sexualized, provoking, and teasing relationship.

Pamela and Sheila

It is from Sheila that Pamela gets her nurturing. She does not seek it from her however. Pamela's approaches to Sheila are few. She approaches her mother two and a half times as often.

Since their relationship ranks twelfth in frequency of interaction among the twenty-one possible dyads in the A. family, Sheila must be considerably active as the instigator. A glance at Table 17 will indicate this is so. Moreover, the interactions Sheila initiates toward Pamela are characteristically of a positive maternal cast—they are almost exclusively "cooperative-affectional" and efforts at mild influence. For example, it is Sheila who sees to it that Pamela eats. Their relationship is somewhat out of balance: Sheila pursues Pamela; Pamela pursues her parents. When Mr. A. gets overengaged with Pamela, or when Mrs. A. fails to respond to her needs, both of which

Table 17

MATRIX SUMMARIZING INITIATIONS BY SHEILA
TO MEMBERS OF THE A. FAMILY

	Mr. A.	Mrs. A.	Dee-dee	Ricky	Ros-coe	Pa-mela	All	Total
Cooperative-Affectional	1	10	12	2	2	21	0	48
Conversational	0	0	0	1	0	0	0	1
Objective	0	5	0	1	2	0	0	8
Influencing (mild)	1	3	0	3	5	16	0	28
Influencing (strong)	1	2	1	2	1	0	0	7
Disapproving	0	0	0	1	3	0	0	4
Blaming-Accusing	0	0	0	0	1	0	0	1
Joyful	0	0	0	0	0	0	0	0
Antagonistic	0	0	0	4	3	3	0	10

Table 18

MATRIX SUMMARIZING REACTIONS BY SHEILA
TO INITIATIONS BY A. FAMILY MEMBERS

	Mr. A.	Mrs. A.	Dee-dee	Ricky	Ros-coe	Pa-mela	All	Total
Positive-Direct	2	4	0	0	1	3	0	10
Passive-Objective	4	15	0	1	1	3	0	24
Cooperative	1	9	11	2	1	6	0	30
Negative	1	0	0	0	0	0	0	1
Avoidant	0	5	0	0	0	0	0	5
Ignoring	3	1	0	0	3	0	0	7
Embarrassed-Withdrawal	1	0	0	0	0	0	0	1
Antagonistic	0	0	0	0	0	0	0	0

Table 19
REACTIONS BY SHEILA TO VARIOUS INITIATIONS
BY A. FAMILY MEMBERS
(IN PERCENTAGES)

	Positive-Direct	Passive-Objective	Cooperative	Negative	Avoidant	Ignoring	Embarrassed-Withdrawal	Antagonistic
Cooperative-Affectional (28)	7	11	75	0	0	0	0	0
Conversational (3)	0	0	0	0	0	67	33	0
Objective (7)	71	43	29	0	0	0	0	0
Influencing (mild) (21)	14	95	14	5	24	14	0	0
Influencing (strong) (3)	0	33	0	0	0	0	0	0
Disapproving (5)	0	80	0	20	0	20	0	0
Blaming-Accusing (1)	0	0	0	0	0	0	0	0
Joyful (0)	0	0	0	0	0	0	0	0
Antagonistic (6)	0	17	0	0	0	17	17	50

happen often, Sheila is there to pick up the pieces. She approaches Pamela, engages her, comforts her, and Pamela is glad to have her.

Home Visit 3, November 28

Mr. A. picked Pamela up and sat her down on his lap. Pamela reacted to this by laughing and giggling in a very happy and almost silly way. She then jumped off her father's lap and said she did not want to sit on his lap. This was in contrast to the affect she expressed at the time. She then looked around her. She was hesitant about where to sit. In the moment of hesitant searching Sheila patted the couch next to her. It was near where the dog was. Pamela scrambled up on the couch and sat next to Sheila. Sheila proceeded to wrap her sister in a blanket and cuddle her. She kissed her a number of times and all of it seemed quite spontaneous and very natural. Pamela did not object and seemed to enjoy the attention she was getting from Sheila.

Still, Pamela will seek out her mother before she will Sheila.

Home Visit 14, March 27

Pamela was crying and whiney. She had all the fingers of her right hand in her mouth except her thumb. She dragged her blanket about as she followed her mother. Mrs. A. commented that Pamela had not felt well all day. She took the opportunity to add that she herself was "beat." She slumped on the couch with a sigh. Pamela situated herself beside her mother. Mrs. A. complained that "it was warm." She motioned Pamela away. Sheila, watching from the doorway, asked if Pamela would like to watch TV. Pamela said yes. Sheila crossed the room and turned on the set. The two girls lay down on the floor to watch.

Then too, Mrs. A. will sometimes ask Sheila to take over her maternal responsibilities.

Home Visit 16, May 1

Dinner ended, and Sheila got up and went into the kitchen to begin clearing and stacking dishes. Deedee remained seated and watched TV. Ricky bolted from the table and ran downstairs to the basement. He came back up with a catcher's mitt and a ball. Pamela ran over to Mrs. A. and said she wanted to go out too. Mrs. A. shrugged with a tired gesture and shook her head. She glanced at Deedee watching TV, momentarily closed her eyes, and said flatly that Pamela should go into the kitchen and ask Sheila to dress her in a coat for outdoors. Pamela left, soon to return in a heavy winter-like coat. Mrs. A. looked at her but said nothing. Pamela went outside.

Sheila is Pamela's surrogate mother and in many ways she is like Mrs. A. She has her mother's efficiency and her mother's hausfrau drabness. She is thin, undeveloped, unpretty, with sharp facial features and stringy hair. Her clothes always seem to fit her badly, and she wears only full skirts. Her appearance stands in sharp relief to Deedee's well-coiffed, beauty-minded glamour. Like Mrs. A., Sheila is industrious and fatigued by turns. Compare:

Home Visit 7, January 9

Mrs. A. was busy making pancakes throughout the meal. She did not sit down. She seemed particularly haggard and worn: she did not look at all well. As she was bringing the pancakes in to the family she tended to move more slowly—almost as if in pain—there were lines in her face and her cheeks were more hollowed than they had seemed before. She tended to be forgetful of things—sugar, syrup, butter knives—and had to be reminded by members of the family. After the meal she sat down at the table, and Sheila got up and made pancakes for her mother. She said nothing and ate limply, taking long times between bites and staring vacantly off into space. She did not eat very much, and on a couple of occasions she pressed her fingers against her temples, the sides of her head, as if she had a headache. She did not say anything about having a headache however.

Home Visit 5, December 12

Now, everyone except Sheila had left the dinner table. Sheila was still seated, and it was not clear what she was doing. She had an empty milk carton in front of her and was either peering down into the carton, or holding her head while looking down at the table behind the milk carton. She sat motionless in this way, her elbows on the table and her hands holding her head up, for some five or six minutes. No movement at all. It almost appeared as if she weren't feeling well or as if she were fighting a headache. Eventually, Mrs. A. turned around and noted that the table was still piled with dishes and Sheila hadn't moved. She suggested that Roscoe and Ricky clear the table.

Sheila is identified with the ego-syntonic side of her mother, just as Deedee is with the dystonic side. Mrs. A. is able to say quite candidly that Sheila reminds her of herself as she was a child—not to mention as she is today as an adult. It hardly seems accidental that Mrs. A. has delegated to Sheila the same child-caring role she fulfilled with her younger brother throughout middle childhood and adolescence. The intergenerational repetition allows Mrs. A. some welcome escape, and frequently seems to foist a mother surrogate on Pamela. There seems little question regarding choice of escape mechanism.

The question at this point is why the need to escape? Escape from what? Is it, as Mrs. A. was told by doctors, a matter of "overwork"? She is tired, to be sure. But, as contended elsewhere in this study, there seem to be more forces at play than simple fatigue and overwork.

Ricky and Roscoe

The last dyadic relationship to be reviewed here is that between Ricky and Roscoe. In many ways it is the most telling. If nothing else, it highlights what some critics of modern psychoanalysis have already pointed out (Finch and Cain, 1968) —that relationships between siblings have a life and meaning all their own; that in them more than concern about displacement and ordinal positioning is at stake.

The relationship between Ricky and Roscoe ranks third in frequency of interaction among the twenty-one dyads possible in the A. family, and it is the only relationship among the top eleven which does not include a parent as one member of the pair. It has been suggested that Roscoe is of low, if not lowest, status in the A. family; that he is the favorite scapegoat for family members; and that he is most often abused by Ricky. The data in Tables 20, 21, and 22 make these suggestions explicit assertions.

Ricky appears as the bain of Roscoe's existence. True, he approaches Roscoe with conversation and neutralized statements, but far more often he dictates to Roscoe, disapproves of him, blames him, and attacks him. In terms of initiations, Ricky is antagonistic to Roscoe ten times more often than he is cooperative toward him. Ricky's reactive behaviors look somewhat more benign—he is no less cooperative than antagonistic, negative, or ignoring of his brother. But, these ratios are mis-

Table 20

MATRIX SUMMARIZING INITIATIONS BY RICKY
TO MEMBERS OF THE A. FAMILY

	Mr. A.	Mrs. A.	Dee-dee	Sheila	Ros-coe	Pa-mela	All	Total
Cooperative-Affectional	0	2	0	1	4	1	0	8
Conversational	5	6	0	0	12	0	11	34
Objective	11	26	0	1	20	6	0	66
Influencing (mild)	1	4	0	0	4	1	5	15
Influencing (strong)	0	2	0	1	10	2	0	15
Disapproving	0	2	0	0	20	0	0	22
Blaming-Accusing	0	1	0	0	19	0	0	20
Joyful	0	0	0	0	0	0	1	1
Antagonistic	1	2	0	3	41	2	0	49

Table 21

MATRIX SUMMARIZING REACTIONS BY RICKY TO
INITIATIONS BY A. FAMILY MEMBERS

	Mr. A.	Mrs. A.	Dee-dee	Sheila	Ros-coe	Pa-mela	All	Total
Positive-Direct	9	3	1	1	5	1	0	20
Passive-Objective	10	12	1	6	2	1	0	32
Cooperative	0	2	1	3	4	1	0	11
Negative	3	17	0	1	3	0	0	24
Avoidant	7	10	1	1	1	0	0	20
Ignoring	8	3	0	1	3	1	0	16
Embarrassed-Withdrawal	6	0	0	0	0	0	0	6
Antagonistic	1	9	0	3	4	0	0	17

Table 22

REACTIONS BY RICKY TO VARIOUS INITIATIONS
BY A. FAMILY MEMBERS
(IN PERCENTAGES)

	Positive-Direct	Passive-Objective	Cooperative	Negative	Avoidant	Ignoring	Embarrassed-Withdrawal	Antagonistic
Cooperative-Affectional (11)	9	27	9	9	9	0	0	9
Conversational (18)	22	17	0	6	0	44	28	0
Objective (24)	50	21	5	21	25	5	0	25
Influencing (mild) (32)	6	50	6	38	16	16	0	16
Influencing (strong) (13)	8	62	8	46	46	0	0	8
Disapproving (8)	0	39	0	39	0	50	13	25
Blaming-Accusing (1)	0	0	0	0	0	0	0	0
Joyful (1)	0	0	0	0	0	0	0	0
Antagonistic (8)	0	0	0	0	0	39	13	25

leading. In terms of Roscoe's approaches to Ricky (Table 23), Ricky has little basis for anything but positive, cooperative responses. Indeed, Roscoe's responses (Table 24) to Ricky's belligerent approaches do not appear to warrant Ricky's further wrath. Yet, this is precisely what they seem to elicit. Roscoe, however, is far more likely to comply, cooperate, avoid, and withdraw than to assert himself or strike back. Even Ricky's positive behaviors toward Roscoe are to be re-

Table 23

MATRIX SUMMARIZING INITIATIONS BY ROSCOE
TO MEMBERS OF THE A. FAMILY

	Mr. A.	Mrs. A.	Dee-dee	Sheila	Ricky	Pa-mela	All	Total
Cooperative-Affectional	0	2	0	1	7	1	0	11
Conversational	7	5	1	0	5	0	0	18
Objective	4	9	1	0	1	0	0	15
Influencing (mild)	1	5	0	4	6	0	0	16
Influencing (strong)	0	1	0	0	0	1	0	2
Disapproving	0	0	0	0	0	0	0	0
Blaming-Accusing	0	0	0	0	0	0	0	0
Joyful	0	7	0	0	1	0	0	8
Antagonistic	0	0	0	0	0	0	0	0

Table 24

MATRIX SUMMARIZING REACTIONS BY ROSCOE TO
INITIATIONS BY A. FAMILY MEMBERS

	Mr. A.	Mrs. A.	Dee-dee	Sheila	Ricky	Pa-mela	All	Total
Positive-Direct	0	2	0	2	13	1	0	18
Passive-Objective	10	25	1	4	25	2	0	67
Cooperative	0	2	0	3	16	1	0	22
Negative	0	6	1	0	4	0	0	11
Avoidant	1	1	0	3	22	2	2	29
Ignoring	7	7	0	1	6	4	0	25
Embarrassed-Withdrawal	16	5	0	0	16	0	0	37
Antagonistic	0	0	1	0	4	1	0	6

garded as tainted as they are prelude to, and ultimately serve the interest of, ridicule or abuse. The following excerpt exemplifies a skillful, though not unusual setup:

Home Visit 15, April 10

During dessert Mr. A. asked if Ricky had gone to the Day Treatment school with Roscoe that morning. Ricky and Mrs. A. replied simultaneously that he had. Mr. A. did not pursue the matter further. Roscoe picked it up, however, and asked Ricky how he had liked the center school. Ricky said he liked it very much. Roscoe brightened visibly. He said that Ricky had been included in the Easter party they had had

Table 25

REACTIONS BY ROSCOE TO VARIOUS INITIATIONS
BY A. FAMILY MEMBERS
(IN PERCENTAGES)

	Positive-Direct	Passive-Objective	Cooperative	Negative	Avoidant	Ignoring	Embarrassed-Withdrawal	Antagonistic
Cooperative-Affectional (8)	0	13	88	0	0	0	0	0
Conversational (26)	23	8	0	0	8	12	65	0
Objective (29)	38	55	41	7	10	0	10	7
Influencing (mild) (36)	0	64	4	11	5	28	14	0
Influencing (strong) (27)	4	44	4	4	4	11	22	7
Disapproving (47)	2	28	0	4	19	6	55	4
Blaming-Accusing (24)	0	0	0	4	33	8	66	4
Joyful (0)	0	0	0	0	0	0	0	0
Antagonistic (61)	6	36	12	4	21	11	48	6

in school and that everyone had had a good time. Ricky agreed. He asked Roscoe about Jim, wondering why Jim was in the center school. Roscoe said he wasn't sure, but that Jim wasn't too good at reading. Ricky said he had liked Jim. Obviously encouraged, Roscoe asked if Ricky had liked his teachers, especially Mr. N. Ricky said they were fine.

Roscoe now began a vivid description of the day at school. Before he had gotten too far, however, Ricky interrupted by saying he knew it wasn't the usual day at the center school since it was a half day before a holiday and was a party day. He added that he did not think he would like to go to that school. On other days he was sure it wouldn't be good. He said the kids didn't know how to be friendly or behave. Roscoe, suddenly stunned, began to protest that he liked his classmates. Ricky said flatly, "Then how come they don't like you?" Roscoe fell silent. Ricky added, "It was a school for mentals."

As devastating as an interaction like the one above can be to Roscoe's self-esteem, they do not equal the devastation resulting from what fails to take place—any parental intervention. Mr. and Mrs. A., in virtually every circumstance in which Roscoe is demeaned, do not make their presence felt as buffers

or protectors, despite the fact that they are often privy to the
assault. Their failure to do so is an implicit sanction for Ricky's
derogating approaches to his brother. They make Ricky their
all too willing agent of action. At other times, they model ways
and means of deflating Roscoe.

Home Visit 11, February 13

Dinner was ended. Mr. A. carried his cup of coffee from the
table to the chair in front of the television set. He began sip-
ping his coffee. He asked me about the Day Treatment program. How many children, he wanted to know, were in the
program. I indicated about twenty-four. Roscoe chimed in
and confirmed the estimate. Usually, he said, the lunchroom
has that many people. Roscoe began describing what he
knew. There were so many children at a table—six per table
—and there were four tables. He talked about his table and
who the other children at his table were—Jim, Harry, etc. He
described how the tables were arranged according to the ages
of children. He talked about which adults sat at which tables.
He was quite animated and very involved. Mr. A., however,
said nothing. He had become disinterested as soon as Roscoe
began talking. He barely listened to the answer to his question before he withdrew completely into the TV set. When he
next spoke he asked his wife about the weather.

Home Visit 12, February 27

The family sat in almost total silence while watching TV.
There were now some cartoons on. Roscoe got up and got an
Indian feather and headband from his room. He returned to
the family room wearing it. Mrs. A. told him to put it away.
Roscoe said he liked wearing it. Mrs. A. went back to watching TV. Roscoe returned to his seat and began telling his
mother that he had been swimming that day and had done 174
lengths of the pool. That was the equivalent of a mile, and he
related his experience with excitement. Mrs. A. did not react
to the content of Roscoe's statements. Hearing him talking to
her, she merely turned to him, and, in the midst of his explanation of how the mile was tabulated, she interrupted with,
"Turn around and sit up straight in your chair." There was no
acknowledgement of what Roscoe was saying or trying to

convey. Roscoe straightened up, and Mrs. A. returned to watching TV. Roscoe discontinued talking about swimming.

Home Visit 16, May 1

The other kids came in from the street and began to toss the ball around on the lawn. Pamela came back down the side steps. Mr. A. greeted her with, "How ya doing, Tiger?" He laughed as he said it. Ricky was squatting in a catching position and trying to catch Roscoe's pitches. Roscoe was trying to effect major league form. He would wind up, kick and throw. His movements were somewhat awkward. His body would move after he moved his arms and he certainly was not the most graceful of athletic figures. Mr. A. laughed quite openly and loudly whenever Roscoe threw a pitch. On a couple of occasions Roscoe simply blanched and did not say anything, though he was quite obviously hurt by his father's laughter. Finally, he turned to Mr. A. and asked what was so funny. Mr. A. continued laughing and said, "That is sure a new kind of pitch, Roscoe. Where did you pick it up?" Roscoe sort of shrugged and swallowed hard. It was almost as if he pretended not to have understood his father.

In many ways, then, the relationship between Ricky and Roscoe is a function of parental default and sanction. Ricky is not required to pull his punches. Table 22, for example, makes

Table 26

MATRIX SUMMARIZING "BLAMING-ACCUSING" INTERACTIONS BETWEEN MEMBERS OF THE A. FAMILY

		TARGETS							
	Mr. A.	Mrs. A.	Dee-dee	Sheila	Ricky	Ros-coe	Pa-mela	All	Total
Mr. A.		0	1	1	1	1	1	0	5
Mrs. A.	0		8	0	0	3	3	1	15
Deedee	0	0		0	0	0	0	0	0
Sheila	0	0	0		0	1	0	0	1
Ricky	0	1	0	0		19	0	0	20
Roscoe	0	0	0	0	0		0	0	0
Pamela	0	0	0	0	0	0		0	0
Total	0	1	9	1	1	24	4	1	41

INITIATORS

Table 27

MATRIX SUMMARIZING "DISAPPROVING" INTERACTIONS BETWEEN
MEMBERS OF THE A. FAMILY

		Mr. A.	Mrs. A.	Dee-dee	Sheila	Ricky	Ros-coe	Pa-mela	All	Total
					TARGETS					
INITIATORS	Mr. A.		2	7	3	4	10	7	4	37
	Mrs. A.	10		9	2	3	8	7	9	48
	Deedee	0	2		0	0	2	0	0	4
	Sheila	0	0	0		1	3	0	0	4
	Ricky	0	2	0	0		20	0	0	22
	Roscoe	0	0	0	0	0		0	0	0
	Pamela	2	0	0	0	0	4		0	6
	Total	12	6	16	5	8	47	14	13	121

it abundantly clear that despite his angry demeanor, Ricky receives very little disapproval, blame, or antagonism from his family. One would expect him to receive 14 percent of the family's initiations in these categories. Instead, he receives 7 percent of all "disapproval," only 5 percent of the "blame," and 6 percent of the "antagonism." Only Sheila receives better treatment, but Sheila does not persistently assault the esteem of her brothers or sisters. One has to conclude that all the A.'s permit Ricky to abuse Roscoe because they don't care, deem it

Table 28

MATRIX SUMMARIZING "ANTAGONISTIC" INTERACTIONS BETWEEN
MEMBERS OF THE A. FAMILY

		Mr. A.	Mrs. A.	Dee-dee	Sheila	Ricky	Ros-coe	Pa-mela	All	Total
					TARGETS					
INITIATORS	Mr. A.		5	1	2	4	11	7	0	30
	Mrs. A.	1		12	1	0	7	6	2	29
	Deedee	0	3		0	0	2	0	0	5
	Sheila	0	0	0		4	3	3	0	10
	Ricky	1	2	0	3		41	2	0	49
	Roscoe	0	0	0	0	0		0	0	0
	Pamela	8	0	0	0	0	3		0	11
	Total	10	10	13	6	8	67	18	2	134

deserved, or fear Ricky will turn his guns on them if they attempt intervention or challenge. All three explanations may deserve credence. The last certainly deserves attention. Ricky has little to fear in the A. family. The proper measure of this is that he is not even afraid or dissuaded from attacking his mother. No one, not even Mr. A. or Deedee, responds to Mrs. A.'s initiations with more antagonism than does Ricky. His license exceeds that of all the others.

The same conclusions may be reached via other routes. One could, for example, simply compare Mr. and Mrs. A.'s relationships with Ricky and Roscoe respectively. Mrs. A. (Table 5) accords Roscoe more disapproval, blame, and scorn than she does Ricky. Mr. A.'s differential contacts with the boys are even more pronounced (Table 11). He converses with Ricky, but not Roscoe; he relates objectively to Ricky, and not Roscoe; he disapproves and is antagonistic to Roscoe, and is decidedly less so toward Ricky; reactively, he is direct and positive with Ricky, but negative and ignoring of Roscoe. What is more, the other members of the A. family—the three girls—follow suit. In similar, if less exaggerated fashion, they are hostile toward Roscoe and neutral or tolerant of Ricky. Tables 26, 27, and 28 tell the story in a way that needs no elaboration whatsoever.

III

Death-Terror

Chapter 5

Fear as an Organizing Theme

Threat and Secret

Questions

In the foregoing pages we have summarized salient interaction patterns in the A. family. Despite some quasi-systematic coding of interpersonal exchanges in the family the summary has been less than fully descriptive. Configurations of the interactions between members of the A. family resulted in certain conjectures about typical power structure, role assignments, and group alignments, exemplified, where possible, by excerpts from the recorded home visits. Nonetheless, these conjectures, often in themselves inferential and teased from data derived from coding in categories, raised numerous questions. Why these splits and these alignments? Matters of cause, source, origin, and speculations about dynamic content or substance were left relatively untouched. They were deferred to the present section.

Why is the A. family seemingly threatened with disintegration? What are the sources of stress? Why does the responsibility for maintaining family integrity, membership, and status quo fall so heavily to Mrs. A.? Why is Deedee embarked so early on a course of separation from home? What forces impell her to leave and Mrs. A. to cling so desperately to her? Why the "kid gloves" treatment of Mr. A. by all family members except Pamela? Why the intensity of Mr. A.'s relationship to his youngest daughter? What causes Mrs. A. to default her maternal role so readily to Sheila, and why does Sheila so assiduously avoid her father? Why does Roscoe, in spite of all his efforts to earn affection and tolerance, obtain scorn and rejection? Why is he such a prominent scapegoat? What accounts for Ricky's

95

sanction as agent of family abuse and his concomitant "good standing" and high level of esteem?

Some possible answers are here offered as relatively parsimonious explanations for these interactional patterns. Admittedly, they cannot account for all the variance. Indeed, a cause and effect model applied to a changing, complex, semi-open social system—such as a family—runs the risk of oversimplification. Parsimony is not always a virtue nor an end in itself. It is argued, nonetheless, that certain themes permeating the A. family are so deeply and palpably felt by all its members that their immediate impact and far-reaching effects cannot be denied attention.

Death-Terror and the A. Family: Tacit Agreement to Silence

Terror is frequently made obvious to us by the absence of manifest concern where concern is supremely in order. To recognize it, however, all too often requires some special knowledge—the knowledge that a given concern *is* very much in order. Without this knowledge, idiosyncracies in behavior and irregularities in attitude and orientation, while discernible, are not easy to fathom. They have the nagging quality of hints and, indeed, they are derivative bits of information meant to conceal or disguise the source of terror. This is especially so when the source of the terror is socially taboo.

Sources of terror in family life are manifest in "family secrets" and conspiracies of silence. Everyone in the family knows the source and behaves in ways consistent with that knowledge. Yet, they pretend otherwise. To maintain silence is to pretend that there are no reasons for concern or fear. It is as if word and deed are construed as synonomous by the entire family. An outsider talking to members of the family or observing the family is easily bothered (something seems wrong or missing) but all too often fooled especially when he also shares the accepted outlook with respect to a social taboo.

The A. family terror is a terror of death. The family "secret" is that father—Mr. A.—may die at any moment. This is no fantasy. The possibility is very real. All the A.'s live and behave in accord with this knowledge at the same time they endeavor to demonstrate they are uninfluenced by it. After nine months of casework with the parents, and nine months of individual psychotherapy with Roscoe, the secret is divulged. It is revealed in neither treatment situation, but almost as an aside at the close of the fifth home visit. Even then, it is not mentioned in the course of interaction between family members. *This never occurs.* Instead it is offered off-handedly to the home visitor in the following affectless way—the terror seemingly well insulated from the substance of the secret itself:

Home Visit 5, December 12

Mr. A. returned to the family room, where Mrs. A. and Pamela were still sitting watching TV. Things were silent for some minutes, with only the noise of the television in the room. I began to get up to leave, on the assumption that no more interaction would take place. The television program had only just gotten under way and had some twenty-five minutes to run. Besides, I had already run over my scheduled time. As I rose, Mr. A. inquired if I would still want to visit in two weeks. He then announced that he would not be home at that time. I was puzzled. Without looking at her husband, in fact without looking away from the TV set, Mrs. A. said flatly, "Mr. A. will be in the hospital then . . . he needs open heart surgery . . . they want him in for a week to do some tests . . . he has a leaky valve which allows the blood to flow backwards . . . the operation will come later . . . without it he is not expected to live until the fall." I said I was surprised to hear this, that I had had no idea; I commented that no one had ever said anything about it. Had they talked to Mr. L., their caseworker, about it? "No," said Mrs. A. Had they known about the heart problem long? "Yes," Mrs. A. replied, "for years," though the need for surgery was a more recent development. Silence, except for the sound of the TV set, enveloped the room. Mrs. A. suggested I not visit since she and the kids would likely be up in Boston at the hospital visiting Mr. A. Visiting hours were 6:30—8:30 P.M. Maybe I should visit earlier. I told her I would call during the week to check arrangements. I wished Mr. A. well and indicated I would stop by to see him in the hospital if I could get away to Boston. He had not said anything for some minutes; not since he mentioned he wouldn't be home. Now he said I should make the trip to Boston and come to visit him in the hospital. There would be "lots of pretty nurses."

As it turned out, the next home visit took place one week later, before Mr. A. entered the hospital for his tests. That visit was absolutely devoid of any mention of the prospect of hospitalization, tests, or surgery. No family member so much as hinted at it in their interactions. It was mentioned again only in the context of the observer's leave taking, and then it was the observer who did the mentioning. The following visit—home visit number seven in early January—contained but a single reference to the hospitalization. It was made by Mr. A.

Home Visit 7, January 9

Mr. A. greeted me at the door and asked me how I had enjoyed the holidays. He then told me that he had just gotten out of the hospital on Sunday. This had been a relatively short stay, he said. The next stay would be more serious in nature and longer in duration.

On no occasion did a member of the A. family discuss any aspect of the matter with another member of the family. The next reference to the surgery and heart problem occurred May 1. Once more, it was directed at the observer, and not brought up as a subject for family discourse.

Home Visit 16, May 1

It was almost 7:15 P.M. and I indicated to Mr. A. that I had to be going. He said this would be the last time he would be seeing me for a while, and explained that he was entering the hospital for surgery. I told him that I hoped things certainly went well in the hospital and that I wished him the best of luck. He said that he was sure he wouldn't need it, that things would go perfectly all right. We shook hands. I told him I would visit him in the hospital and then I left.

Visit seventeen was made to the A. family home during Mr. A.'s hospitalization. There was not one spontaneous comment about Mr. A.'s condition. I found it necessary to inquire after him. He was doing fine; better than expected. By the eighteenth visit—May 29—he was back home, his recuperation being miraculously rapid. During this somewhat unusual visit

—unusual in that Mr. A. talked primarily with me—the full meaning and full history of Mr. A.'s heart condition came to light.

Home Visit 18, May 29

I arrived at the A. home a few minutes late. There was nobody in the family room and, rather than enter unannounced, I walked around to the front and knocked on the front door. I was greeted by Sheila in a rather warm and friendly manner. Sheila said that they had finished eating, that her father was down back, and that she would call him. She said her mother was washing her hair and Deedee was washing the dishes. No one else was around. Pamela, Roscoe, and Ricky were not to be seen. Sheila went to get her father.

A few minutes later Mr. A. came up. He moved in a very careful manner. He had always moved somewhat rigidly but now it was particularly pronounced, and he appeared to be consciously cautious in his movements at this point. We said hello. I had not seen him since I visited him in the hospital after his surgery, and he looked far better than he had then. I told him how much better he looked and said I was glad he was doing so well. I told him I was impressed that he was home far ahead of schedule. He thanked me and apologized for not being able to talk better in the hospital when I visited. He blamed the medication for his drowsiness and distractibility at that time. I told him I understood. Mr. A. smiled and said he had been "very lucky." Throughout the rest of the visit and my talk with him he continued to reiterate how very lucky he had been.

He moved rather carefully across the room and very gently sat himself down in the chair that I usually occupied during my visits to the family—the one to the right of the TV set facing the dining room table. The television was going as usual, despite the fact that no one had been watching it when I arrived. Mr. A. sat down and I seated myself opposite him. We were alone for the next twenty to thirty minutes.

Mr. A. sat silently for a few minutes. I said nothing; only watched him. He kept shaking his head and nodding by turns, much as if he were preoccupied with his thoughts. Physically, he appeared to be rather well off. He did not look as if he had lost a great deal of weight and, aside from his careful movements, one would not have suspected that he had undergone a very serious operation of the proportions he had. Psychologically, however, he still seemed to be in considerable shock. He appeared abstracted, vague, would talk to a point for a few minutes, then would drop it, become silent, and begin restating phrases over and over again to the effect that, "My gosh, I sure was lucky." There was, apparently, no external stimulus to these statements. Another phrase he kept reiterating was, "That's the way it goes." He must have made these statements a dozen to two dozen times in the next twenty minutes. They were not said to me particularly. I had the feeling he would have said them even if I hadn't been there. At least he would have thought them. My presence was enough to prompt his saying his thoughts aloud.

Most of his discussion, interspersed among his ruminative wonderings and silences, revolved around the operation and his recovery. He also reviewed the history of his heart disease. He said he had indeed been very lucky in that he had done so well. The doctors had never expected him to do so well. He had bounced right back and had surprised himself with his recovery. He said he had been taken into surgery earlier than expected. And, he was out of the hospital earlier than anticipated. He commented that he had fully expected to die in surgery, on the table. He had done it once before, he said. I did not interrupt him at this point to inquire after what he meant. He ambled on. He felt he would be going back to work much sooner than anyone expected—maybe by late June.

Throughout his talking he kept turning his head, almost as if he were trying to adjust some obstruction in his neck or throat, and occasionally he would cough or clear his throat. He explained that the surgery had simply been that of cutting down the middle of his chest from about the neck area all the way down to the lower part of the rib area, and that they had simply opened up the ribs in order to get at his heart and put in the valve. He said he had very little pain except when he moved suddenly or got up or down.

He became more involved in discussing the operation. He explained there had been a number of people in the Boston area who had been awaiting this particular heart surgery. He said the heart valve used was a new one—one that had just recently been developed, he thought, at the University of Texas at Houston, and nine people in the nearby area alone had been waiting its shipment for several months. All nine people had undergone surgery at the hospital within a few days of each other. Mr. A. recounted how five of the nine had died, some in surgery, some shortly afterwards. Three of the remaining four were still in critical condition and not expected to live. He was the only one who had had a successful recovery. He stated that he was the third in the group of nine to undergo the surgery.

He was quite visibly shaken by the experience and had a good deal of trouble now in talking about it clearly, continually clearing his throat, swallowing, jerking his head aside, and ruminating about it all with statements of "I sure was lucky" and "That's the way things go." He stated that one of the men who had died as a result of the surgery had been a very good friend of his. He recounted how, one Thursday night, he had gone up to see his friend and the friend had been in good spirits and how two days later his close friend was gone. He shook his head. He reiterated that he had been sure that, like his friend, he was going to die on the operating table. It was a fear, he said, that he had never divulged to anyone.

Mr. A. then went on to say that about four years earlier he had gone into the hospital for some minor surgery—"a hernia operation as a matter of fact." While in surgery he had suffered heart failure. It was totally unexpected. His planned stay of a few days in the hospital had been converted to a stay of nearly three months, and an additional two months at home recuperating. It was an event that had "really shook things up"; he was out of work for almost half a year; Pamela had just been born, but Mrs. A. was forced to return to work well ahead of her plans; Mr. A. had stayed home and cared for the children for a few weeks. He remembered it as a frightening time. His life seemed so tenuous. It was the first aftermath of his rheumatic fever; and ever since his heart stoppage he has had to be "careful" with his activity "regulated" and his regimen dictated by his doctor.

He stammered through this history, often pausing for extended periods of time, staring straight ahead as he related things. He closed by once more shaking his head. "I sure was lucky," he said.

At this point Mrs. A. came in. Her hair was still very wet and she sat down on the couch. I commented that her husband was looking quite well and seemed to be doing excellently. She said, "Well, nobody could ever keep him down. He always had to do things his own way. This is just another example."

Mr. A.'s surgery and his history of heart trouble were not mentioned again during the home visits. Yet their thematic omnipresence, both before and after the fact of surgery, seemed to dictate virtually every facet of A. family life. Just how this was so will be discussed in the sections that follow.

Death-Terror and the Clinician: The Clinician's
Tacit Digression from Death Material

First, however, it may be instructive to consider briefly why Mr. A.'s surgery or the history of his heart condition never found its way into casework with the parents or Roscoe's psychotherapy spontaneously. One reason, of course, was the A.'s terror. They could not discuss the subject directly among themselves, and there is little reason to expect that they would readily raise the matter with outsiders. Yet this does not mean they did not want to, or did not try. In fact, they did test the receptivity of outsiders in a number of circuitous or symbolic ways. Mrs. A. asked for help, but the doctor she consulted told her that her headaches, vomiting, and sexual aversions were due to tensions resulting from "overwork"; certainly a less loaded, more benign explanation than one related to Mr. A.'s bilateral hernia surgery, cardiac arrest, and very precarious health. Mr. A.'s regimen required "no excitement" or "strenuous activity." One need not subject Mrs. A. to a reconstructive psychoanalysis of her early years to recognize the probable source of her repulsion from Mr. A. At a minimum, she likely dreaded the prospect of her husband dying during intercourse. Her sexual aversion dated from his cardiac arrest. The explanation of "overwork," while possibly having some validity, is at the same time an easy—and unhelpful—bit of professional denial.

Mrs. A. was not the only one to give off signals and cues.

Roscoe did as well. He too was discouraged from open expression of concern. Roscoe's ritualistic behavior around, and preoccupation with, the burying of dead animals in a backyard gravesite was looked upon as "morbid" by professionals and teachers. They recommended aversive training as a remedy. The behavior was not seen as a piece of anticipatory mourning, nor understood as an effort at active mastery. Its healthful and adaptive functions were overridden by cultural squeamishness and clinical adherence to notions of psychopathology. Hence, a second major reason that Mr. A.'s surgery and cardiac problems did not emerge spontaneously in the A.'s treatment was the willingness of professional helpers to avert their eyes and/or to try to stamp out the "eyesore." That the A. family was not alone in their dread of death can be seen in examples drawn from their therapists' process notes. The first excerpt illustrates evasion via complementarity by the caseworker. He skillfully assists the parents in the move away from the theme of death.

Casework Hour with Mr. and Mrs. A., December 14

Both parents were looking worried and fatigued today. I knew from talking with Mr. B (the home visitor) after his last visit to the A. home that Mr. A. will need to go into the hospital right after the holidays for tests and a heart catheterization with prospect of open heart surgery imminent thereafter. I raised this with Mr. and Mrs. A. today. Mr. A. explained that without the surgery he could not expect to live more than six to eight months. Father did not display any noticeable anxiety as he discussed this. He tended to deny the significance of the diagnostic procedures to be done in the next two weeks. Mother was exceedingly anxious and looked as if she were about to blow apart. I asked Mrs. A. what was troubling her. She indicated that she had had a "terrible time" with the children this week. She found their behavior almost intolerable in the house. They had gotten into everything and had provoked each other at every turn. They would be the death of her yet. I teasingly commented to Mrs. A. that she ought to take a page from her husband's book. He was calm and cool in the face of his illness, while she fretted about household matters and the kids. Mrs. A. said he never worried about anything, "at least not so it shows."

A long silence followed. Finally, I asked Mrs. A. how she had reacted to the children. She said she responded with extreme anxiety and a tension headache which sent her to bed late Saturday afternoon. I attempted to explore with her the specifics of her handling of the children, but she became very, very vague about what she had actually done. Mr. A. gave her very little support, and only said he never had that kind of trouble with the kids. I commented that Mr. A.'s success must make her angry. She agreed.

Mrs. A. then brought up her trouble in getting off work to make her casework appointments. She said her supervisor and co-workers are quite critical of her. They don't understand her situation. They won't listen to her side of things. She is extremely anxious at work and troubled by tension headaches—she "hates" her job. I indicated I would be happy to call or write her supervisor if she wanted me to. Mrs. A. said we could try, but she didn't think it would help. . . .

The same caseworker again betrays his cultural aversion and the wish to evade when he describes the first session following Mr. A.'s surgery:

. . . devoted to father's depicting in excruciating fashion the lurid and gory details of his surgical procedure. . . . He talked about the many stitches in his body and about the fact that he can now hear his heart at night when he is in bed because a small metal ball inside a cage has replaced the damaged valve in his heart and it makes a whirling and thumping noise as it works. . . . He seemed to take particular delight in unnerving his audience, and trying to steer him to a consideration of the pressing issue of helping his wife get to these appointments proved exceedingly difficult. The whole hour was somehow very Edgar Allan Poe-like. . . .

Roscoe's experience in psychotherapy is not dissimilar. His therapist seems to somehow miss Roscoe's attempts to convey his dread of death, and generally manages to pursue instead less salient themes of orality and dependency. The excerpt below is drawn from the therapist's process notes at the time Roscoe's father has entered the hospital for catheterization of the heart. Roscoe's metaphor is effectively ignored by his therapist.

Roscoe was more spontaneous today. He saw some candy on the desk and I invited him to take a piece. He took five minutes deliberating. He had to ask me questions and tried to get me to give him instructions as to which one he should pick. He took none. He looked toward the toys and he chose the guns, looked at them briefly, then put them down and looked at and picked up an airplane. He said the plane was on a trip, flying to Mexico with a bunch of passengers, but that it would crash before it got there because one of its motors had gone dead. He then put the plane down and eyed the candy again. I commented how hard it seemed for him to make up his mind, that he seemed afraid of taking good things to eat, and that he would like it if I would choose for him, because then he wouldn't have to worry or feel guilty about wanting good things or too many things. It would be up to me. . . .

The next sample comes from a treatment hour a week or so before Mr. A. was to undergo surgery, and illustrates how Roscoe's attempted communication about his wish for past security as opposed to current danger is misconstrued as regressive dependency.

. . . Roscoe then went to the play table and told me that he was going to finish the house he had started the same way that houses looked when they lived in Colorado, how bright and sunny it was, and how everyday seemed good and alive. Roscoe said a number of times he wished he could go back there now—back to those good times. I told him it was nice to dream of the past, especially of times when we were younger and taken care of. That then he was young and didn't have to worry since Mom did lots of things for him that today he was expected to do for himself. Roscoe agreed and said he didn't think they would return to Colorado. I said one never could go back in time, and that his wanting to but knowing that he couldn't or shouldn't was like his battle over whether or not to take lots of candy for himself in the office. He wanted to eat lots, but also felt it was babyish to do so. All of a sudden he became very destructive. He threw the house he had been building on the floor and shouted that it had blown up like a volcano. I tried to connect his explosion with his studying volcanoes in school. But, he continued to be upset and started throwing toys. Before the hour was over he left the office and ran away from me. . . .

Naturally, it can be argued that it is unfair to second guess the caseworker and the therapist in the A. case. Retrospective insights are all too easily come by. Lacking the vantage point of hindsight, it is frequently difficult to comprehend all that transpires in treatment. The relationships of contemporaneous events to each other are elusive, and the therapist has trouble finding bearings since he himself is in the midst of all that transpires. He must, in most instances, rely on his theory to orient him, to help him take readings. The contention here is not that these therapists deserve to be faulted for lack of knowledge or insight. Quite the opposite. It is contended that they are quite representative of mental health practitioners who, even when well intentioned, are ill prepared culturally, professionally, theoretically, and attitudinally to deal with death materials.

Death-Terror as a Psychological Construct

We have asserted that terror of death is the prepotent organizing theme—the eminent "psychological construct"—in the A. home. Members of the family do not discuss it. It exists in the family atmosphere and awareness. It must be inferred. Yet all interaction seems to hinge on it, and family reactivity is best explained as a function of it. We now seek to demonstrate how this is so—how the dread of death permeates all aspects of family functioning; how it provides the basis for selective attention and inattention; how it colors perception, affects cognition, and directs activity; how it has altered role assignments; and the ways in which it has, in the service of adaptation, seriously distorted interpersonal relationships. Finally, perhaps most importantly, we seek to demonstrate the ways in which a family that operates according to the rules of a death-denying society is forced to deviate from some major value-orientations of that society by virtue of its very effort to observe the societal norms. Because the salient values are internalized, the result is cultural strain, abundant paralysis, and "psychopathology." In short, we shall attempt to convey the ways in which the family is both abandoned and victimized by the surrounding social order and its own internal creed.

IV

Some Defenses against "Knowing" and "Feeling"

Chapter 6

Thanatophobic Countermeasures

The Drive to Master, The Press to Deny

The Culture

To seem impervious or unmindful of death is fast becoming an American trademark, albeit a defensive and costly one. This attitude toward death and dying is of a piece with, if indeed not the ultimate outgrowth of, our guiding cultural policy.

This policy was phrased some years ago by Florence Kluckhohn (1956) as a "first-order emphasis on mastery over nature." The designation of middle-American values was derived from Kluckhohn's (1950, 1954, 1956) theory of variation in cultural value-orientations, and, more specifically, from the classification of such orientations for purposes of describing the similarities and differences between and within cultures.[1]

1. F. Kluckhohn's scheme is an especially useful device for analyzing intra- and interpersonal conflict and strain. "More formally, a value-orientation may be defined as a generalized and organized conception, influencing behavior, of nature, of man's place in it, of man's relation to man, and of the desirable and non-desirable as they relate to man-environment and interhuman relations" (C. Kluckhohn, 1951, p. 409).

Spiegel, who has productively applied F. Kluckhohn's scheme to the analysis of family dynamics (1957, 1971), outlines some major assumptions that attach: "First, there is a limited number of common human problems for which all peoples at all times must find some solution . . . second . . . while there is variability in solutions of all the problems, it is neither limitless nor random but is definitely within a range of possible solutions . . . third . . . is that all variants of all solutions are in varying degrees present in all societies at all times . . . every society has, in addition to its dominant profile of value-orientations, numerous variant or substitute profiles . . .

"Five problems have been tentatively singled out as crucial ones, universal to all human societies . . . stated in the form of questions . . . (1) What is the character of innate human nature? (human-nature orientation); (2) What is the relation of man to nature? (man-nature orientation); (3) What is the temporal focus of human life? (time orientation); (4) What is the modality of human activity? (activity orientation); (5) What is the modality of man's relation to other men? (relational orientation) . . ." (Spiegel, 1959). It will be of interest to trace the fate of the A. family's attempted answers to each of these crucial questions.

Our culture in offering solutions for the universal human problem of man's relation to nature overwhelmingly favors belief in mastery rather than the alternatives of subjugation to, or harmony with, the forces of nature. We abide in the belief that given sufficient time, effort, and money, nature can be made to submit to man's will. Nature is to be exploited, overcome, and made to serve. It follows logically that control of one's fate resides within the individual and is a function of his skill and resources. Acceptance of obstacles, surrender to failure, or tragic outlooks on life are badly tolerated, receive little understanding, and less sympathy.

Unabashed optimism and nonsentimentality—so highly consistent with American technology, organization, and professionalism—embrace matters such as chronic illness and death, though not without problems. Death, for example, tends to be regarded as an accident, a mistake, a momentary failure for mankind as if it were fully believed that given time to plan, much hard work, and the application of scientific principle, man will ultimately prevail. Medical research and its clinical application epitomize this orientation. And Mr. A. and his surgery are but one small success in this long, hard struggle.

Death remains a major problem for this belief system. It is an occurrence whose finality and inevitability cannot be accommodated by a philosophy based on the goodness of supreme effort. At present, human ingenuity merely succeeds in staving death off for a time. Its full significance must therefore be denied outright, or dealt with via substitute orientations or philosophies—outlooks that give death some proper or rightful place in the scheme of things.[2]

2. According to Kluckhohn (1956) the alternatives to a Dominance-over-Nature position are (1) the Harmony-with-Nature orientation—reflected in naïve animism or in belief systems which view man as but a part of the universe or some large eternal plan; systems where man is essentially in balance with nature, where nature is to be lived with and neither violated nor submitted to; and, (2) the Subjugated-to-Nature position—evidenced in cultures requiring men to admit their helplessness before the fates, thereby necessitating appeals to religious deities, supreme authorities, and supernatural powers.

In middle-American culture it is presumed that in times of great crisis —economic depressions, death—when the Dominance-over-Nature orientation fails, the second-order position of Subjugation-to-Nature will take precedence over the third-order Harmony-with-Nature position (Spiegel, 1959). The ordering is based on an evaluation of the relative strength of the Judeo-Christian

The Man: Mr. A. as Jack Armstrong
In his presented self, Mr. A. is the very best of Americans. He seems to observe all the rules and carry the standard. His entire life-style is geared to the attainment of mechanical and technological perfection, to the achievement of daring feats, to intense competition with other men, and to some symbolic as well as direct contests with natural forces.

Mr. A. works as a tool and die maker for a New England firm producing designs and manufacturing parts for the space industry. Before that, he was employed in an automobile factory. During the evaluation interviews his wife described him as "interested in motorcycles, outdoor sports, hunting, and fishing." In the first home visit, it came to light that Mr. A. worked evenings in the garage behind his home on the motorcycles of friends and bike dealers. Subsequently, it became evident that he spent long hours maintaining special racing motorcycles for motorcycle manufacturers. Still later, it became apparent that he raced them, and was in fact a "drag-bike" champion. He could, he said, get a twin-engine bike from zero to 160-plus miles per hour in a quarter of a mile. "That is not the world record," he stated, "but that is really flying." He felt that being a tool and die man gave him a distinct advantage in customizing motorcycles and in making and recommending changes to manufacturers. "You've got to race to know what breaks down and what can be improved," he said.

Mr. A. also has a mechanic's license for yacht engines, and it was in the course of frequenting the engine shop of a marina that he met his wife. He played right field for a local amateur baseball team, and his exploits as hunter and fisherman were loudly proclaimed by Roscoe. When not actively competing himself, he relaxed by watching athletic events or discussing sports. His particular favorites were baseball, football, hockey, and basketball.

In one early visit Mr. A. beamingly showed me his "pride and joy," a perfectly preserved and excellently functioning 1933 Indian 74 motorcycle—a motorcycle upon which he lav-

---

ethic—an embodiment of the Subjugation orientation—versus the strength of the Harmony orientation—which is little appreciated by the American middle class.

ished attention and care. It was, he said in "better shape than most new models" and "worth more than $1,000." He had no intention of "getting rid of it, since the Indian motorcycle company went out of business in the early 1950's. This machine can't be replaced; besides it's as old as I am." Mr. A. was born in 1933. On one occasion Mrs. A. laughingly commented to her caseworker that Mr. A.'s "old motorcycle is my greatest competition."

In brief, to hear about Mr. A., to listen to him, to have an accounting of his drivenness, his competitiveness, his perfectionism, his daily activities, one would not—short of extraordinary acumen or extensive clinical experience—suspect he had severe cardiac problems. On the other hand, it is almost as if a certain morbid and poetic justice attaches to the fact that he is the subject of pioneering efforts in open heart surgery and the recipient of an artificial, plastic valve. The surgery and the component part seem so admirably suited to his life-style that one hardly marvels at his speedy recovery.

The truth is, of course, that Mr. A. does have a severe heart condition, one imperiling his life, and that underneath it all, Mr. A. is quite terrified of dying. Moreover, being the threatened one, he is the person least able to contemplate his own death, for to "know" personal death is, as Freud pointed out years ago, a contradiction in terms. As a consequence, Mr. A.'s Americanism and his insistence on dominating nature succeed in pushing him unremittingly to counterphobic denial. His behavior takes on the pointed exaggeration of caricature, and more than an edge of sadism.

Home Visit 10, January 30

I arrived at the A. home at 6:00 P.M. . . . the A.'s had not started dinner though dinner was ready. Mr. A. was "out fishing" and Mrs. A. said she was waiting for him before serving dinner to the family. . . . It was obvious that Mrs. A. was quite upset and angry by her husband's lateness. . . . The older girls wanted to go ice skating and they began nagging at their mother to let them have something to eat . . . Mrs. A. put them off saying they could wait until their father got home so they "could eat as a family." Time passed, however, and the girls became increasingly insistent. Finally, in despair

Mrs. A. told them they could go ahead and make themselves some toast.

A few minutes later the girls called from the kitchen and asked if they could have some of the meat that was for dinner . . . Mrs. A. said no. They could wait for their father . . . more time passed . . . more requests . . . at 6:45 Mrs. A. told the girls they could make themselves some sandwiches. Now the younger children became insistent too . . . at 7:00 P.M. Mrs. A.'s resistance broke down . . . all the children were munching on toast.

Mrs. A. was increasingly annoyed and angry. But she did not express it overtly. . . . Most of the time she sat in front of the TV set attempting to watch it, but she would often close her eyes and set her jaws with clenched teeth. I took this as an indication of her rage.

A little after 7:10 P.M., Mr. A. arrived. . . . He had a friend who had been fishing with him come in as well, though the friend seemed reluctant and hung back some at the family room door. Ricky asked his father if they had had any success. Mr. A. said "absolutely none," not one fish. He laughed, and as he and his friend shed their winter coats, Mrs. A. served them hot coffee. Mr. A. nodded hello to me and introduced his friend. The two men sat down at the table. Mrs. A. asked Mr. A. if he were ready to eat. Mr. A. indicated that he was not, and would prefer to finish a cup or two of coffee before dinner. Mrs. A., intensely angry, retreated to the kitchen.

It was some minutes later before she emerged again. In the meantime Mr. A. and his friend discussed the ice fishing. They had had no protection from the cold and wind—no little house in which to sit, no tent. They had simply cut holes in the ice and fished, taking off on a whim directly from work in early afternoon. Mrs. A. sat on the couch when she returned. She looked tense and angry and closed her eyes frequently. Eventually she turned to Mr. A. and asked him how cold it had been out there. She suggested it must have seemed very, very cold since it had not gotten above zero in town all day. The temperature was, in fact, five below zero at the time. She accused Mr. A. of not having dressed warmly—just a jacket and no sweater. Mr. A. denied that it had been cold. He turned to his friend and asked how cold it had been. The friend looked uncomfortable and indicated weakly that he did not know. Mr. A. said it hadn't been too bad, that it seemed warmer than the last time or two. Apparently, Mr. A. has been ice fishing a number of times since he got out of the hospital in early January. Mr. A. turned to me and said that he hadn't been cold while on the ice. Mrs. A. commented that Mr. A. had been out there since before three o'clock, better than four hours in the freezing cold. Mr. A. said time had passed quickly and he hadn't even felt a chill. He talked about how thick the ice had been, how he could see the fish coming up for air, but they just did not bite.

It was now nearly a quarter of eight. Mr. A.'s friend got up to leave. Mr. A. and his friend had been talking in low tones for some minutes previous and I couldn't hear what was said, but they had been laughing aloud readily. As soon as Mr. A.'s friend left, with no goodbyes from any of the A.'s except Mr. A., a silence fell over the house and there was a great deal of perceptible tension.

Mrs. A. began to put things on the table for dinner. Mr. A. moved in front of the TV set, leaving the table to Mrs. A. and her activities. At this point Mr. A. began to talk to me. He spoke loudly enough so his wife could overhear. He acknowledged that it had been extremely cold out on the ice. He said it had really been bitter out there, that the wind had really been something and had cut right through everything, and that he had really been quite frozen. He then turned to his wife and asked her what the temperature was outside. Mrs. A. said she didn't know. Mr. A. asked her to go out and look at the indoor–outdoor thermometer. Mrs. A. did so, came back and reported without comment that it was eight degrees below zero. Mr. A. said, "Gee, it must have been at least twenty-five or thirty below on the lake with all that wind." He shook his head, lit himself a cigarette, and could not suppress a smile. He summed it up by saying that "it was really something."

Home Visit 20, October 24

Mrs. A. said they had waited with dinner tonight. Mr. A. reaffirmed this and said that he was anxious to get back to work on the motorcycles that he had out back in the garage. He was fixing up these bikes on his own time. He said that rather than begin working on a motorcycle and being interrupted for dinner, he would prefer to work right through without a break for eating. He smiled as he said this, and Mrs. A. made a comment about his working too hard anyway and that the visit was a good opportunity for him not to work so hard to-night. Mr. A. explained that he had quite a number of motor-cycles in recent weeks and that he had spent virtually every evening and night working on them. Mrs. A. said he was aver-aging fifteen- and sixteen-hour work days. . . .

Dinner ended and Mr. A. got up and said that he was going to get back to the motorcycles. He asked me to follow him but did not wait for me. He disappeared out the side door . . . I went out the side door and down into the back yard where Mr. A. was working on a motorcycle in the driveway. He explained what was the matter with it. Later, he took me over to the curb and pointed out a new Harley-Davidson Sportster and indicated that this was one of the racing bikes he customized, tuned up, and took care of for the manufac-turer. He worked on it during the week, and raced it week-ends. Roscoe had arrived on the scene, and pointed out the exhaust pipes on the sides directly beside the back wheels. He said his father raced every weekend and has never lost a race.

I was curious about this, to say the least, in view of Mr. A.'s physical condition. Roscoe said he had never seen his father race. Mr. A. was very hesitant to acknowledge that he did race motorcycles, but eventually said he races at a drag strip or a dirt oval every weekend. He said it takes a number of hours to tune up the bike for a race. This Harley-Davidson Sportster has never lost. He has had it up to 150 miles per hour in a quarter of a mile. He then discussed some of the competi-tion and the motorcycles he has beaten and said that the owner of this motorcycle has made quite a bit of money as a result of the races and the betting that goes on. . . .

Fear Tactics

Exacting Dread while Disowning Death: A Lesson in Control via Provocation

Both of the foregoing excerpts reveal Mr. A.'s counterthana-tophobic mechanisms. They of course reveal more as well. They make clear that there is an underside to Mr. A.'s death-defiant conduct, an aspect hinged on his own experience of impotence and rage. While not given overt expression, these feelings emerge at times in sadism that is but thinly veiled. The sadism—sometimes calculated, most times not—occurs when Mr. A. succeeds in placing other members of his family in the impotent position he himself dreads experiencing. The process is tantamount to an unburdening, a discharge, of his own sense of beleaguerment by transferring it wholesale to his family. In that way he does not experience fear but they do. The particular pleasure that seems to accompany the transfer gives it a sadistic tinge. Thus, Mr. A. is given to frequent taunting of his family. He seemingly holds them in check or at bay by feeding them constant reminders of his challenge to danger and death; he reminds them simultaneously that life is hazardous, that men are vulnerable and often in imperiled positions. The messages are blatantly contradictory. On the one hand, he implies that man can dominate nature; and, on the other, that man is not in control of his fate. Because of the unspoken social and familial taboo surrounding discussion of death, comment on the contradiction is proscribed. Hence, much conversation in the A. home takes on the proportions and attains the impact of the classic double bind. Absorption, embarrassment, tension, trepidation provide the only recourse. Mr. A. rather neatly succeeds in cowing his family.

Home Visit 1, November 14

The meal proceeded in silence until Mr. A. spoke again. This time he talked about a fellow employee in his shop who apparently had been injured in a fire that day. The man had been engaged in forging some metal and had been standing too close to the forging iron. His pants had caught fire, and the fire had gone up his leg. Mr. A. said the burn had been pretty bad. He wondered aloud if this incident would prevent this employee from leaving for a hunting trip he had planned for the weekend. Following his comments the meal again became silent. . . .

Mr. A. began talking about work again. Again his topic was injury to a fellow employee. He talked about another friend, one nobody at the table knew, who had been in the Korean War. Mr. A. explained that this man had suffered a skull wound and had had a steel plate put in his head. Mr. A. then went on to explain that this man had injured himself at work fixing a rotor tiller for a friend. He had cut off the tip of one of his fingers. Mr. A. said that the man had had the tip stitched back on his finger, but it had not healed well. Finally, they had had to operate on his finger and had taken it off down to the knuckle. The man was currently in the hospital. Mr. A. talked about the possibility of visiting him. He said he did not know how serious things were. Nobody said anything by way of response or comment. Silence reigned. . . .

Home Visit 4, December 5

After dinner Mr. A. began to talk to the family about some of the items he was reading in the newspaper. He read about the fog being so thick in England that a man had ridden his bike into a river and drowned. No one in the family said a word. . . .

The dilemma is over where fate control resides—inside or outside the individual. The dominant value-orientation in middle-American culture favors boundless optimism, and this attitude is most directly realized in Mr. A.'s behavior. But it is so exaggerated and insistent as to be given the lie by its very extremeness. It is given the lie as well by Mr. A.'s revealing anecdotes. These act to raise to the level of familial awareness man's inherent fallibility and vulnerability. Thus the dominance-over-nature orientation fails to outstrip, as it otherwise might, the bafflement of human control created by the reality and gravity of Mr. A.'s cardiac condition. This reality serves to greatly reduce the distance that ordinarily exists between the dominance-over-nature and subjugation-to-nature orientations in our society.

In other times, in other places, the outcome of this strain might not be so destructive of the family operation. For example, Spiegel suggests that when subjugation-to-nature is a competitive alternative to domination, "religious attitudes . . . determine, but do not quite take up the slack of, the emotional environment of failure" (Spiegel, 1971, p. 375). This is certainly not true of the A. family. Spiegel fails to take cognizance of what has been noted elsewhere (Fulton, 1965); that the influence of religion in mid-twentieth-century urban America has been greatly diminished. The A.'s are not church goers nor are they particularly religious in any observable or formal sense. A Christmas tree and Christmas cards comprise the high water mark of their religiosity and hardly exceed their celebration of St. Valentine's Day.

The A.'s have precious little to buffer or counter the heightened subjugated-to-nature position in which they find themselves. A strain between the two contrary orientations is experienced. The results are, at a group level, psychic paralysis, a sense of frustrated rage and impotence. The rage and impotence are in turn a function of the lack of fate control where fate control has always been expected. There is, additionally, some deeply felt guilt, since in middle-class America responsibility for failure must be assigned at some level. How it has been assigned in the A. family will be discussed later.

When Provocation Fails to Suffice: The Move to Cruelty

When Mr. A.'s anxiety gets especially high, the engineering of subtle fear tactics does not in itself suffice. There are times when it is simply not enough to disown one's sense of helplessness by transferring it to members of one's family. Something more extreme is needed. Mr. A. then acts out mastery and control while rendering the other family members impotent. Sadism is most prominent in these instances. The two examples that follow are drawn from visits that directly precede his hospitalizations—the first takes place a few days before his hospitalization for tests, the second just prior to his surgery.

Home Visit 6, December 19

After dinner the entire family went to the living room, except for Deedee and Sheila who cleared dishes and prepared to wash them. Mrs. A. played the piano and Ricky and Roscoe sang. Mr. A. and Pamela got involved in a game of retrieving. Pamela had apparently found an unused metal thimble and having picked this up she put it on one of her fingers. She would run to her father holding out the finger. Mr. A. would reach out and grab the finger taking the thimble off. He would then pretend to throw it across the room. He would not actually release the thimble. Pamela would turn around believing that her father had thrown it across the room and would go and try to find it. She would get down on all fours and crawl around the furniture at the opposite end of the room searching for the thimble. After some time, when Pamela's back was turned to him, Mr. A. would throw the thimble in her direction. Pamela would then find it never knowing her father had withheld it for some minutes. She would laugh gleefully, put the thimble back on her finger, and approach Mr. A. again. He would once more grab the thimble and pretend to throw it. This game went on for some fifteen or twenty minutes.

Mr. A. did much teasing, often to the point of upsetting Pamela—she was often quite frustrated and helpless. She shed tears. But every time she found the thimble, she would recover nicely and laugh happily. Gradually a good deal of aggression crept into Mr. A.'s play. While Pamela's back was turned, he would throw the thimble quite hard in her direction. On two or three occasions, when Pamela was totally unaware, he hit her on the side of the head or face with very healthy throws. The thimble obviously stung as it struck her. Her crying would be delayed by her total surprise. She looked bewildered and disbelieving, then would cry. But I do not believe she ever fully comprehended what had occurred or what her father had done. At least she did not blame him. Mr. A. for his part would laugh awkwardly and glance in my direction.

Still another aspect of the game developed. Now, Mr. A. would pretend he had the thimble in his hand, when, in fact, he did not. Instead, he had put it in a trouser cuff or under a pillow of the couch. Yet he would pretend that he had the thimble in one of his hands, close both fists, and have Pamela try to guess which hand it was in. Since it was in neither, Pamela was always unsuccessful. Though she guessed again and again, Mr. A. always opened an empty hand. She became frustrated and did cry. At this point Mr. A. would ask her to look for something across the room. Her back turned, he'd retrieve the thimble, have her guess again. Then he'd hide it again and repeat the game. . . .

Home Visit 16, May 1

Mr. A. was playing catch with Ricky and Roscoe outside. On a couple of occasions he threw over Roscoe's head, and the ball rolled down the hill some hundred yards or more. Roscoe would run to retrieve it. He'd carry the ball back up the hill until he was within throwing distance of his father. He'd throw it to Mr. A. Mr. A. would wind up and throw it over Roscoe's head again—deliberately. Roscoe would have to go the distance to the end of the block again. He'd make the hike up the hill, return the ball to his father only to see the return throw sail over his head once more. This sequence was repeated a number of times. . . .

Man as Machine

Displacement and Metaphor, Dehumanization and Death-Fear

Some fifty years ago, Victor Tausk (1933) wrote a paper on the psychoanalytic theory of the psychoses entitled "On the Origin of the 'Influencing Machine' in Schizophrenia." Its central premise was that in reality, as well as in fantasy, machines represent man's projection of his body image into the external world. Tausk, much under the influence of early Freudians, of course meant most specifically that the machine symbolized the patient's genitals. We need not narrow the conception so. No matter what its specific form, there is scarcely a society where people have not managed to associate a prized resource or innovation—whether food or manufactured material goods —with the self-image. In Western culture—as Leger and Grosz made obvious in their art of thirty years ago—and especially in technologically driven, industrially preoccupied America today, the machine is a most apt symbol of the human body. Indeed, the subtlety of the symbolism is increasingly reduced as synonymity is approached. Robots and computers simulate human operations; respirators and hemodyalysis units replace human processes; artificial valves supplant human tissue. The machine–body equation has become mundane.

For a man like Mr. A., who so epitomizes American devotion to the machine-God, the choice of machine as metaphor for bodily concerns is nearly inevitable. The displacement of the animate by the moving, functioning inanimate is readily discerned by his vigilant family. Nevertheless, its meaning is just a shade more concealed than Mr. A.'s anecdotes of environmental danger and human jeopardy making it a prime device for embodying preoccupations, a communicative device in which all the A.'s can share and participate. At times it seems as if their interactions invoke little else.

Home Visit 1, November 14

I arrived at the A. home at 6:00 P.M. Their house was well lit as if they were expecting me . . . I rang the door bell and got no immediate response. I peered in through the pane and saw the A. family. Mrs. A. came to the door and opened it for me. She let me in saying that the front door bell did not work. It had been broken for some time, and her husband kept meaning to repair it, but had not got around to it yet. It made it necessary for her to "keep a watchful eye out," she added . . .

Mr. A. left the table and went to talk on the phone. In the background I could hear him talking to someone who was apparently a friend. The conversation was about motorcycles. When he returned to the table he commented that it had been Max on the phone. Max had called to find out what he should do about his motorcycle, and said he had been having trouble with control and handling. Cornering was especially bad. Mr. A. said he had asked Max when he had last had the motorcycle in for a check up or had its front fork oiled. Max had said he didn't know, but he thought maybe sometime last summer. Mr. A. had suggested to Max that he have the suspension checked and front fork oiled and the handling trouble might clear up. He then said it was extremely silly of his friend Max not to know better than that. It was really foolish to own a motorcycle and not take care of it, to even abuse it as Max did, and never to check it regularly. Mr. A. seemed to be forcing conversation at this point. His voice had taken on a moralizing, lecturing tone, and Mrs. A. did not respond. In fact none of the family responded. There was silence. The silences continued throughout the rest of the meal. Periodically Mr. A. would comment in an effort to break the silence—"Isn't it silly that people do not know enough to adjust the front suspension of a bike, to attend to possessions of value . . ."

Roscoe appeared with a small battery-run radio. He showed it to me. He said the radio had been made at school. He attempted to play it. It did not work. He said the batteries were run down and no good any more. We continued to talk about the radio, and then Roscoe went to get a model ship—a schooner—which he had earlier docked on the floor between the pedals of the piano. He brought it over and let me look at it. He said it was given to him by a friend for fifty cents. He liked it very much. He explained that some of the parts of the ship were broken, that some of the masts were crooked because the wiring had broken on them. He disappeared down the hall only to reappear with a plane. It was a biplane and he said it belonged to Ricky. Roscoe showed me the plane and indicated that it too was broken in a number of places. He said he liked the plane anyway. . . .

Home Visit 2, November 21

Mr. A. said he had had a very rough day . . . people were preparing for the Thanksgiving bike rally weekend and lots of people wanted lots of things done for their motorcycles. He had been working long evenings—doing little tune-ups and things for people so they could make the trip. It always helped to take extra precautions, he said. "No need for risks . . ."

Home Visit 4, December 5

People started dishing up their plates at dinner. Mrs. A. commented that it was chilly in the family room. Mr. A. said that he had to get a new space heater for the family room since the present one was not working effectively. "There is something the matter with it. It needs some new parts." They would cost the price of a new one, he explained to his wife.

Mr. A. looked up from the newspaper. He explained that he was now fixing his old Indian 74 motorcycle again. He said by not taking it to a garage he was saving lots of money. What it needed now, and what he was doing, was a "valve job." He talked about other technical aspects and mechanical problems of the motorcycle, which I did not begin to understand.

Home Visit 12, February 27

I arrived at the A. house a few minutes late, pulled up in the drive, and found the house looking as if nobody were home. I went to the front door and knocked a few times. There was no response. I concluded no one was home, or that they were already out in the family room eating and so I went around to the side of the house.

The family was eating in the family room. I went in through the family room door and Mrs. A. asked how long I had been at the front door waiting. I said I had been there only a moment. She commented that the front doorbell really needed fixing very badly and wondered if it would ever get done. She said she tried to keep an eye out for people, but there were times when she just couldn't take care of everything at once. She shook her head and asked if it were still snowing. I nodded. She commented on the snowy weather and wondered if summer or spring would ever come. How long, she asked, could this bad weather persist? Would it ever end?

During the eighteen coded home visits to the A. family there were a total of forty-one independent references to injury, damage, illness, and repair, not including any of the statements made directly to, or exclusively for, the observer. This is better than two references per visit. Not included among these forty-one intrafamilial references are statements about Mr. A.'s heart condition or surgery because neither topic was openly discussed by family members among themselves. One must conclude that when people cannot talk directly about their outstanding concerns, they do so in symbol and metaphor. Moreover, the relationship between overt discussion of fears and the degree and frequency of metaphorical displacement would appear to be inverse.

Chapter 7

Time Out of Mind

Timelessness: A Royal Road to Mindlessness

Bucking the Culture to Serve It Better

The A.'s behave as if the world and their lives were timeless or, more precisely, as if they were bound by time—were, figuratively, marooned in it. This is unusual for families of their social status.

Spiegel (1959) and Kluckhohn (1956), among others, have emphasized that the dominant orientation in middle-class America is on the future. Second and third considerations are given the present and the past respectively (Spiegel, 1971). It is our style to anticipate, to plan ahead, to seek "change for the better." In so doing, we place our children on a pedestal; they come to signify the future, and we esteem their long years ahead as if they were a prize commodity.

Because of the imminence of death this does not occur in the A. family. Or rather, phrased in a more accurate way, their attempts to fulfill the cultural life plan seemed badly aborted. The A. children—with the possible exception of Ricky—appear to lose their societal significance as harbingers of a better future.

As is obvious and has already been suggested, hope, in our culture—and thereby investment—reside in the belief that a future exists and that that future can be superior to the present. The A. family's belief in this has been badly shaken. They cannot afford explicit pronouncements in word or deed to the effect that they still unqualifiedly endorse the belief. Denial of that purport would verge on group psychosis. Yet they cannot deny the belief either, as they were raised into a world which propagated the internalization of a future orientation.

124

What has been internalized is not easily disowned. Here as before, their ambivalence finds expression in avoidance and muted commitment. The children as investments in the future are not central to the family's functioning—at least not for the present and not in and of themselves. Instead, the children are simply displaced.

Even in the youth-culture of America, Mr. A.—as a man in his mid-thirties—enjoys a reasonable "future." Still potentially productive and active, his heart condition threatens his fulfillment, and this threat to all that he has not yet realized assumes prominence in the A. household. It preempts the more typical American family's child-centeredness. That his family deems Mr. A. entitled to his future, even if he must jam it into weeks and months rather than count on spending it over years, may also help explain their "tolerance" for his counterphobic acting out.

The welfare and future of the family as a whole, and of children in particular, take a back seat to his needs. For example, one would expect, given all the circumstances, that Mr. and Mrs. A. had completed their family. Five children, a modest income, a father in highly precarious health, and the lack of any religious conviction to dictate otherwise would certainly recommend they not have more children. Yet between the time of the home visits and the present writing, Mrs. A. has had two additional children. This cannot be reasonably attributed to rational planning, and must instead be ascribed to the primacy given Mr. A.'s needs, the most prominent of which is his need for a continuing sense of masculine prowess.

One may construe the "futureless" quality of the A. family, as well as the lack of family planning for children, as a short-range expediency. The future of the family and of the children are obviously contingent on Mr. A.'s continued existence. Logically, his situation and welfare should be of first priority. Besides, even to hint at a major investment in the future of the children may, in and of itself, smack of "giving up" on the future of Mr. A. This brings us to a final consideration.

If the A. family cannot unambivalently behave in accord with the future orientation of American culture, and if as a family they are not to be considered child-centered, but rather father-centered, then some very substantial alterations in the usual role assignments and their attendant identity formations must take place. These have, in fact, been outlined earlier in the review of their interaction patterns.

We earlier noted that Mrs. A. assumes the functional role of task leader and organizer. She engages not at all in socio-emotional activities. She strives to maintain the family against forces threatening to fragment it. Other than occasional asides and jokes, she tampers very little with Mr. A.'s counterphobic attempts at adjustment. Instead she labors, both literally and figuratively, to circumvent him. She does so at considerable psychic cost to herself, and does violence to her maternal role in addition. It will be recalled that she clings desperately to Deedee, her oldest girl; Deedee, for her part, seems bent on escaping the duress of the home situation as soon as possible —even if it means premature and precipitous leave-taking. Sheila, on the other hand, is given and accepts the maternal socio-emotional assignment. Mrs. A.'s psychic fatigue from her struggles on other fronts creates a vacuum in this realm into which Sheila is invited or moves willingly by default. Roscoe assumes the major role of family scapegoat, Ricky of terrorist, while Pamela acquires many of the sexual functions of her mother's wifely role; indeed, in important ways Pamela becomes a surrogate-wife to Mr. A. at the same time that Sheila becomes Pamela's surrogate mother.

In all instances, the children's individual needs or interests are subverted to the primacy of Mr. A.'s illness and death-provoking behavior. Granted, their individual proclivities, developmental phasing, and personalities are permitted some expression and gratification with respect to choice of role and identity within the family. But little is done to set limits on role emersion, nor is genuine choice or flexibility in role modeling, experimentation, and performance permitted. To the extent that rigid role conceptions and attitudes toward self are internalized, personality patterns, hypertrophied in some directions and atrophied in others, are firmly established.

Anticipation of future events and circumstances for the A. children are then minor matters. They are considered little. It becomes an empirical issue whether the distorting effects of interaction in the A. family could be readily shed if different or more favorable interpersonal patterns were encountered or made possible. Most clinicians would not be optimistic in this regard.

In sum, the A. family has a "futureless" feel. Like Mr. A.'s heart problem and surgery, the future is not acknowledged or discussed among the family members. Life seems suspended and unplanned.

The Fate of the Future

A Rare Exception to Its Noncontemplation

By actual count, less than 2½ percent of the A.'s 937 interactions take account of a time span extending more than one week into the future. It is of more than passing interest to realize that one of the rare occasions when future plans are discussed is also one of the few occasions when joy and pleasure are experienced by them all. The occasion is the eleventh home visit, which occurs after Mr. A.'s hospitalization for heart tests, but before his surgery. The highlight of the visit is the interaction engendered by a phone call from Mr. A.'s sister, who has herself just undergone successful surgery. The significance of this surgical success as a double entendre needs no elaboration. All that needs be said is that the following episode accounts for fully one-half of all the references to future happenings (Future is defined as something a week or more away) made in the course of the observed interaction.[1] This interaction also accounts for a sizable portion of all recorded joyful initiations. It is one of the few instances in which the A.'s openly display cathartic affects and relief to each other, and the single occasion during which they freely expose their private hopes. The transparency of their private and mutual fears is nowhere more evident than in this exchange. Nor is their hope for man's supremacy over natural odds at any time clearer. It is as if each A. has had a singularly personal nerve touched by a common stimulus, only to suddenly find that

---

1. In other words, for 1¼ percent of 937 interactions.

their private terrors were not so much singular as publicly un-shared. The reactions of each feed those of another, and ultimately each takes off in his own direction.

Home Visit 11, February 13

At this point Mr. A. returned from the kitchen and his phone call. He came in beaming. Mr. A. indicated that his sister had called to say that her brother-in-law in Oregon was sending her to Jamaica for eight weeks. He was sending her all expenses paid and with enough money not only for tickets and hotel, but also enough to buy a whole wardrobe. Mr. A. then turned to me and explained the situation, though he seemed to talk as much to his family as to me. He said that his sister had been quite seriously ill in the hospital and she had undergone surgery less than two weeks ago. She had had a stormy postsurgical course and it had been "touch and go"; today she was told she could go home. She seemed much better according to the doctors and her brother-in-law who lived in Oregon was now sending money so his sister could take a trip to Jamaica to recuperate.

Mrs. A. said her sister-in-law had called earlier in the day—about noon—with the news that the doctors said she could go home this week. She had not mentioned the trip to Jamaica then so probably hadn't known about it at all. Mr. A. said his sister had just found out. She got the call from Oregon and then called Mr. A. right away to tell him about the trip.

The family now became more animated than I had ever seen them before. They interacted more in the next few minutes than they had in the ten previous visits combined. The interaction was so animated, fast, and great that I had difficulty following what was going on. In effect everybody became involved in fantasies about trips to Jamaica and Florida and how wonderful it would be to have people pay their way and their expenses. Everyone was effusive and seemed to talk at once.

Mr. A. began by saying that his sister's brother-in-law in Oregon was loaded with money, that he owned a number of ranches, and lived in Eugene. They have lots and lots of money. Ricky immediately became involved and wondered if they were millionaires. Deedee ventured that they must live in a house like the Beverly Hillbillies—in a mansion. Ricky picked this up and mentioned four or five times that they really must be the richest people in the country and live in a mansion like the Beverly Hillbillies. Mr. A. said no, that they weren't by any means the richest people in the country and that there were many people richer, and that there were billionaires and trillionaires, but he did say that his sister's in-laws had a great deal of money. Deedee then wanted to know how soon the A.'s would be going to Florida to visit Mrs. A.'s sister. Mrs. A. said they would hope to go down for a long vacation next Christmas, but this may be doubtful. But she said she didn't know in view of the weather if she could hold out until next Christmas.

The family then began a vigorous and extended discussion of just what they would do on their vacation next Christmas, who would pay for it in part or total (an aunt in Louisiana was mentioned, also a cousin in Phoenix, Arizona), how they would enjoy themselves in Miami, or on the Cape, when down in Florida. The A.'s mentioned numerous relatives who seemed to be settled in all sorts of convenient places in Florida. Roscoe got very excited and talked about how they could watch rockets at Cape Kennedy, maybe see them take off at night, maybe even see and meet some of the astronauts. Mr. A. picked up the theme. He talked of "visiting" and "saying hello" to some of the parts his company made for the space industry. He would show the family how they fit in the rocket.

Mr. A. began his description of rockets at the table. But now no one was really listening. Mrs. A. was talking in run-on sentences about having a whole new wardrobe for the vacation, getting rid of all the worn stuff she had now and starting clean and fresh. "What a treat that would be," she said. Sheila, for her part, talked about breathing clean sea air and warm weather and no school. Ricky liked the idea of no school, and he wondered about moving to Florida as a family next year if they really liked it. Pamela watched television for the most part during all of this euphoria, but in a couple of instances she got caught up in the excitement and talked about playing on the beach and Marineland.

It was Mrs. A. who finally restored present-day reality. Seeing the dishes still on the dinner table she asked Deedee to clear them. Deedee, still contemplating the joys of next year's vacation, did not respond. Mrs. A. nudged her and Deedee still didn't respond. She said she was going to sit there and continue the discussion as long as she wanted to and that she would get around to the dishes when she felt like it. Mrs. A. had to keep urging her quite harshly and authoritatively, and finally Deedee, with obvious disgust, began clearing the table. . . .

The Fate of the Past

Evading the Persistence of Memory

With the single exception of the wish-fulfilling, fantasy material just cited, the A.'s were virtually unable to contemplate the future as a group. They were even less able to think of the past. In one sense this is hardly surprising since the past is so minimally valued in middle-American society. Innovation and change are our keynotes; our lack of tradition or veneration of the past is dismissed with the off-handed statement that we are too young a nation to have a heritage anyway. If we admit the past to consciousness at all it is commonly in the form of nostalgia, but even nostalgia is often dressed as novelty and confined to "trivia of the arts" where one can afford a backward glance because it costs nothing of value.

Yet, from another vantage point, it might be reasonable to expect the A.'s to value their past in view of the fact that they evade the future so assiduously. This is emphatically not the case. To value the past not only requires a cultural traditionalism as context but also necessitates a certain measure of pleasure or comfort in that which is remembered. The A.'s have none of the first, and mighty little of the second. True, Roscoe, in a treatment hour cited earlier, reminisces about the prestressful days of family life in Colorado. But the reminiscence is prompted by Mr. A.'s open heart surgery. Unfortunately, so are other memories of the past, and they are less happy.

Like a magnet that attracts iron but not copper, wood, or other materials, the awareness of Mr. A.'s cardiac condition serves as a nodule for selecting and organizing certain relevant reminiscences. More benign or pleasantly irrelevant memories are screened. Thus, what is remembered is seldom remembered easily, and when remembered is directly tied to Mr. A.'s precarious condition.

Home Visit 13, March 4

Roscoe looked through the drawers of the desk again and found two more drawings of boats he had done that day. He brought them over to me and began explaining them to me. He said he did not want to color them and preferred to leave them as line drawings. He then said he had made a model of a boat this week, and he went down to get it from the basement. He brought it up and showed it to me.

Mrs. A. had been listening to the conversation between Roscoe and myself. She now broke in. She began by saying that Roscoe's interest in boats was not new, and that in fact her side of the family had always been interested in boats and ships. She mentioned her father, and said she had had an uncle who had done nothing during his whole life but draw and build boats. It was both vocation and avocation for him. She said that he had drawn a number of pictures of boats in pencil without color and that she had acquired some of these upon his death. She had had them fixed with some kind of fixative so they would last, and she had them framed and covered with glass. She said that these were impressive drawings and that Roscoe had always liked them and had copied them in the past.

She continued to talk about this uncle saying that he had been so fascinated by boats that he had arranged his entire basement as if it were a bridge on a boat. On the walls he had painted very elaborate scenes of harbors, ships, and lighthouses as seen from a bridge . . . she said she was fascinated when visiting him and that Roscoe had seen this basement. The uncle had set up bells and whistles and a steering wheel in the center of the basement, and you could ring the bell or blow the whistle to indicate the time of day. Roscoe was caught up and enthused with this description.

Mrs. A. then pointed out that her uncle had worked for the naval engineering department of a university in the Boston area. He had been responsible for building model ships to scale from blueprints. These were working models of various

kinds of ships—for example, old time whalers or modern sub-
marines used in hydro-engineering experiments and testing.
She explained in some detail how he made these objects, how
he tested them in the tank of water that they had in the naval
engineering building, and she explained how they could create various kinds of turbulences in the water to simulate real
life stress conditions at sea, and thereby test principles of
naval architecture and construction. She said she really did
not know much about it, but as a child she had always enjoyed going up to the laboratory. In fact, her uncle would put
on demonstrations for her grade school class year after year.

Roscoe was getting increasingly excited about all this and
began agitating to see if his mother would take him up to
Boston to see the labs and tank. I volunteered that I had been
up there recently and had seen some demonstrations, but said
I did not know how regularly they were put on. Mrs. A. herself did not know but commented that she had never thought
about taking Roscoe up there. But since he was so interested
in boats maybe she should. She ruminated two or three moments on the reasons she had never taken Roscoe up there.
She then mentioned that she had tomorrow (the next day) off
from work and maybe would take Roscoe into Boston. Roscoe
immediately said he would like to go. Mrs. A. expressed some
hesitation and doubt. Still, Roscoe got very excited and assumed they were going. Mrs. A. never indicated otherwise.
Roscoe asked if Ricky could go along since Ricky is also interested in boats. Mrs. A. said "Sure." Roscoe ran into the living room to tell Ricky. Mr. A. throughout this time said nothing, being occupied in watching television.

Mrs. A. now pursued the whole topic of her uncle and his
occupation and said that her uncle was very devoted to his
job and to his hobby, and in fact that was the way he died.
She then related the story of his death, giving quick glances
to Mr. A. who began to listen some to what was being said.
On a couple of occasions Mrs. A. glanced at her husband and
found him looking at her. She described that her uncle had
had a heart attack—a couple of attacks in fact—and that he
had been told not to work too hard because of his heart condition. He was told he should not do any heavy work. However, Mrs. A.'s uncle was a man who was not happy and did
not feel he was living unless he was doing the work he loved

best—building boats. Against medical advice he returned to work at the laboratory. He had his final, fatal attack on the job following his return. Mr. A. did not comment on his wife's story. He went back to watching TV.

Needless to say, Mrs. A. never took Ricky and Roscoe to the naval engineering laboratory. The attendant memories were too evocative of present crises. For Mrs. A., as for the other A.'s, reminiscing is no narcotic for current psychic pains. References to past events—past defined as happenings a week or more old—occur in but 1 percent of all the coded interactions in the A. family. The preceding vignette accounts for most of them.

The Uses of the Present

A Mooring in Time

If the A.'s are not oriented toward the past, and if they are ill-at-ease with the enculturated future orientation, it follows that they endure cultural strain and anxiety by orienting themselves primarily to the present. The ordering is notable not simply because it runs counter to the usual emphasis of middle-Americans, but because of its extreme character. More than 96 percent of all interactions in the A. family have neither a past nor a future focus. But the conclusion that the A.'s reside almost exclusively in the present must be derived with careful qualification. While it is true they appear present-oriented, such a conclusion is not entirely consonant with the way Kluckhohn (1956) or Spiegel (1971) construed this orientation:

> Little change is expected; the past and future are both interpreted in terms of the present. Life is seen as a cycle of familiar events: the seasons, the holidays or fiestas, birth, maturation and death, comedy and tragedy are expected to occur in the same way year in and year out. Therefore, there is no need to plan ahead, and children are trained to attune themselves to the natural patterns which always have been and always will be. . . . (Spiegel, 1971, p. 374)

While the A.'s are all too prone to interpret both past and future in terms of the present, they are far from accepting or resigning themselves to the cyclical quality of human and natural events. Their suppressed dominance-over-nature and future orientations exert a powerful counterpull. They are trapped in the present, marooned in time, for quite other reasons. Then too, family energy and resources are expended mainly on seeing each day through to a finish, on merely surviving. It is basic insecurity, not resignation, that causes them to adhere to a joyless present.

Chapter 8

Cognitive Dysfunction as Family Style

Bewilderment as Virtue

Death Adience, Insanity, Psychic Escapism, and Cognitive Dysfunction

When the A. family contemplates the future or the past, they do so in a way that is intimately linked to their present fear—Mr. A.'s imminent death. Their projections of what is to come or their reminiscences of what has occurred inevitably flow to or from this concern. Their preferred way of handling the duress is to avoid it, and the A.'s do not think about future or past, except in unguarded moments. Their vigilance assures that lapses are few. They live very much in the present; what is current cannot be so readily avoided. Nevertheless they try. Even the things they attend to in the present are highly selected, emanating from their unspoken but central preoccupation with themes of death and what death can do to the survivors.

"Death adience" would be an accurate diagnosis for the A.'s. Like entranced individuals, they are unwillingly but irresistibly drawn to the very horror that terrorizes them. They cannot look away. It follows them wherever they turn. Everything speaks to them of their plight. They see and hear almost nothing else. The adience demands that they engage in many of the mechanisms that have thus far been described. It requires metaphoric communication, vast silences, embarrassed retreats, blatant denial. And yet the specter haunts them, cropping up anew each time they have to alter their perspective, encounter something different, or absorb a piece of Mr. A.'s counterthanatophobic posturing. Hence, their vigilance cannot be relaxed with respect to the present either. In fact, the bombardment created by the adience is so persistent as to require additional defensive maneuvers as the A.'s are attracted time and again to the very thing they most seek to avoid.

Home Visit 14, March 27

I arrived at the A. house a few minutes early. As I came up the front steps Mr. A., who was on the phone, saw me and signaled me to come in. I did so without knocking and entered the living room. Mr. A. waved but said nothing. Deedee, who was sitting in the living room next to the stereo set, was polishing her fingernails. She was putting on white polish and did not look up or say anything to me by way of greeting. Mr. A. interrupted his phone conversation to tell Deedee to get up and take my coat and hang it in the closet. Deedee was hesitant to do so, complaining that she couldn't do it because her fingernails were all wet with nail polish. I motioned to her not to trouble herself and hung the coat up myself.

Mrs. A. was out in the family room setting the table for dinner. I said hello, crossed the room, and sat in my usual place. Mrs. A. had hardly heard me, and did not acknowledge my greeting. Nor was she really very much involved in setting the table. She was leaving this mainly to Sheila and Pamela. She was glued to the television set. She would set one utensil on the table without watching what she was doing, keeping her eyes on the TV set. Then she would remain motionless for some minutes looking at the TV screen.

The program she was so involved with was a movie—*12 O'Clock High*. It is a post–World War II film with Gregory Peck, one that deals less with action and more with emotional disturbance and the strains of command. American bomber pilots based in Britain are sent on near suicide missions in the bombing of Germany. Losses are very, very great. Gregory Peck acts the part of the commanding officer who finally cracks up. The concluding segments of the film were on just as I arrived.

At a commercial break Mrs. A. finally said hello to me and apologized for not having done so earlier. She explained to me it was because she was so intensely interested in this film.

She said it had been on for two consecutive days at this time —5:00 to 7:00 P.M.—because it was such a long film. She had watched both days and now she "just *had* to see the conclusion."

The final sequences of the movie depicted Gregory Peck as the Air Force commander going through all sorts of emotional stress and strain until he finally broke, suffering shock, hallucinations, and psychosis. Mrs. A. watched these last scenes intently, as if they spoke directly and privately to her. She did not move a muscle, and hardly seemed to breathe, so intense was her engagement with the television.

During this period Mr. A. finished talking on the phone, and he quickly hurried in from the kitchen, brushing Sheila aside in the doorway, to watch the film with Mrs. A., though he sat himself down in his customary seat at the head of the table and watched from there. It was clear the phone call had interrupted his viewing of the film and that he had been as engrossed as Mrs. A. Another commercial break occurred. Mr. A. asked his wife to fill him in on what had been going on, what had he missed? Mrs. A. was almost entirely unable to verbalize what had happened. She could only manage that he (Gregory Peck) had gotten sick and she at least communicated to Mr. A. that she could not fathom the reason why nor describe in any detail the kind of illness he had. This despite the fact that Mr. A. continued to ask questions of this type: Was it a sudden illness? Intestinal? Appendicitis? What? Mr. A. wanted to know. Mrs. A. completely avoided talking about the emotional aspects of Gregory Peck's illness in the movie, almost as if she were entirely blocked by the events. She described everything but the most salient issue—the emotional stress. When the film returned, Mr. A. was no better informed of what was occurring than he had been before the commercial break.

He now sat there watching Gregory Peck's primitive reactions on the screen. He could not fathom what was going on. He betrayed his inability to comprehend by continually asking his wife what was happening. She could not give him any answers other than the statement that "he (Gregory Peck) looked ill." She stated that she did not know why he reacted this way, despite the fact that she and Mr. A. were intensely caught up in the proceedings of the film, a film they had watched over the course of two days, a film they had obviously discussed. They could neither understand it nor could they consciously deal with the emotional impact it made on them. It was as if all family activity and function had stopped or been suspended while Mr. and Mrs. A. indulged a need by maintaining ignorance.

It should be apparent from the events just described that people can be moved to use cognitive dysfunction in the face of a conflict driven adience. By extension, it follows that one can unintentionally model "ignorance" as a preferred, or at least useful, problem-solving device. People need not be innately stupid or thickheaded; nor need they be "culturally deprived." Psuedo-stupidity can be learned with great effectiveness in the sanctity of the family circle where, under the auspices of parental example or permission, the participants— teachers as well as learners—are not likely to have any cognizance of the ramifications of their erosive interactions. Thus, five or ten years from now, teachers and peers may genuinely wonder at the predictable bewilderment an A. child manifests in response to the most innocuous inquiries; and, one can be fairly sure the A. offspring will not be able to provide data relevant to the "why" of his cognitive flustering.

Home Visit 7, January 9

After dinner Pamela was briefly occupied with a bird house that Roscoe had made in school that day. When Ricky came by he cautioned Pamela to be careful handling the house since it had "just been glued together," and "maybe wasn't dry yet," and "could easily fall apart." Pamela set the bird house on the desk with some gentleness, and Sheila, who had now completed her chore of clearing the table, asked Pamela if she would like to hear a story. Pamela replied yes with evident enthusiasm. Sheila led her to the living room so they could escape the noise of the TV set in the family room. I followed to see what would happen.

When I got to the living room, Sheila was seated on the couch waiting, a book in her lap. Pamela emerged from the bedroom area moments later. She had gone for her security blanket. She snuggled beside Sheila, clutching her blanket and sucking her thumb, which protruded through a hole in the blanket. Sheila read "The Three Little Pigs." Pamela listened attentively.

When Sheila read the part about the wolf huffing and puffing and blowing the house in, Pamela began to ask questions. She was especially intent on knowing what happened to the pigs when their houses fell in. Did they get hurt? Did they get scared? How did they get out and away from the house? Sheila was totally unable to provide satisfactory answers. It was, in fact, near impossible for Sheila to understand what Pamela was asking. Despite repeated questions and rephrasing of questions on Pamela's part Sheila kept responding as if she were asking how the pigs escaped the wolf. Pamela was not asking that. Rather it seemed obvious to me that Pamela was interested in how the pigs avoided being hurt in the destruction of the house itself. She pressed her inquiry each time the story situation repeated itself, and each time Sheila would say, "They went to the brother's house." Sheila never lost patience, nor did she ever understand.

By the completion of the story Pamela had visibly lost interest. The entire sequence was odd, because Sheila had demonstrated on other occasions that she was bright and sensitive. Yet here she seemed unable to comprehend the obvious. . . .

V

The Fate and Dissipation of Anger

Chapter 9

Father Absence

Four things, some already mentioned, may be noted about the expression of anger in the A. home: (1) It is almost never freely ventilated. People almost never rage, yell, explode, slam, pound, or hit out—at least almost never during the twenty home visits. Instead, they internalize and turn anger against the self or they ridicule, antagonize, plague, impugn, accuse, and blame. Significantly enough, they usually communicate these things as they communicate everything else—in hoarse whispers. Voices are rarely normal in volume and never out of control. (2) Anger is more frequently contained—especially by Mrs. A.—in the presence of Mr. A. In his absence, demeaning and belittling attitudes are more likely to surface. (3) With or without Mr. A.'s physical presence, Roscoe is the favored recipient for expressed antagonisms—he is the family scapegoat. (4) Ricky is licensed to do most of the scapegoating.

These four points, all relating to the fate of accumulated hostilities in the A. family, are so closely intertwined as to be of one piece. For expositional purposes they will be reviewed in two steps. First, we will consider the concept of family constellations; then we will seek to understand how the family behaves when Mr. A. is expected home shortly, and how by contrast they react to his having just left. Second, we will consider in some depth the phenomenon of scapegoating in the A. family.

Family Constellations and Gradient for the Expression of Anger

The redirection of pent-up hostilities is executed by degrees, and distributed along a gradient of displacement. The A. fam-

143

ily's cardinal premise seems to be that the expression of anger be manifested least in the presence of Mr. A., who is both its most legitimate target and presumably its most vulnerable object. To disturb or annoy him is tantamount to prodding death or acknowledging publicly and privately one's destructive wishes toward him. Hence, in his company rage is suppressed, internalized, and ultimately displaced. One whispers when he is around. During the twenty home visits, however, there were frequent occasions during which Mr. A. was absent. Some of the absences were due to his hospitalizations. Others were the result of his late arrival or early departure during the time of a visit. These occasions provided opportunities to see the family function without his physical presence, and they proved instructive on a number of counts—not the least of which was the partial transformation of family interaction and activity. The nature of this transformation deserves some elaboration.

Family Subsystems: Theoretical Background and Practical Significance

It has frequently been claimed by family theorists—most vociferously by the Palo Alto group of the 1960's—that to study anything but the total family is ideologically misleading and methodologically atavistic. Only through the study of the total family unit—parents and all offspring at once, and sometimes extended family—can one fully appreciate social system variables and functioning. Anything less invites contamination from intra-individual or subsystem biases. Without gainsaying the legitimacy of this argument, it must be recognized that exhortations of this type create a prejudice of their own. In the field of family study they discourage the conceptualization of the family as a complex of interactional subsystems composed of individuals, each subsystem bearing upon the other. In one of the earliest papers on family structure, Henry and Warson (1951) called attention to just this phenomenon, and suggested that "each one of these interactional systems (relationships) has a different emotional quality" (p. 60). They presented clinical evidence to demonstrate their contention that a household may be analyzed as a field of subsystems, and that "in each one of these systems each person in the household functions in a somewhat different way" (p. 71).

The notion is similar to that of subrelationships and subidentities developed some years later by Miller and Westman (1964), in which interlocking and reciprocal roles were credited with pulling varying behaviors from the same individual. According to this idea, a father may be a very different person depending on which offspring he is interacting with. Conversely, a child can and will respond very differently toward each parent. The individual's "total identity" is comprised of the interplay of all his "subidentities." Insofar as Henry and Warson (1951) are interested in the personality of the child who lives at the center of the many subsets of field forces, and thus in the child's various subidentities and his core identity, they do not emphasize the interdependencies of the interpersonal subrelationships per se.[1] Yet, these clearly exist. The forces at work when all seven A.'s are together in the same room, for example, are very different from what they are when five or six A.'s remain together. Moreover, the interaction among a constellation of five or six A.'s when father is missing is substantially unlike interaction among five or six A.'s when father is included but mother is absent. The significances of such larger subsystems—triads and tetrads—have been sorely neglected in the family literature to date, lost somewhere between the exhortation to study the "total family system" and the ease of study and accessibility for analysis of dyads.

The formulations of interaction patterns in the A. family, based on coded home visits (see Chapter 5), exemplifies one side of this issue. The number of possible constellations of interacting persons in the A. family is given by Henry and Warson's formula of $2^n - n - 1$, or $2^7 - 7 - 1 = 120$. However, for reasons of available modes of analysis, clarity, and space, we

---

1. Henry and Warson are clearly aware of the interdependence of systems, as indicated by their statement that, ". . . although each system has its own pattern of interaction and shared experience that is different from the others, all the systems affect one another" (1951, p. 67). However, they also say that, "Since guidance work is child-centered our analysis of the interactional systems will be done from the point of view of the patient . . ." (p. 64).

have had to content ourselves with twenty-one possible dyadic configurations; and even within these confines, the focus has been narrowed to some half-dozen salient pairings. Obviously, much variance is not accounted for. We simply lack the methodological and analytic tools for tackling the more complex configurations.

Nonetheless, it is important to keep in mind that such configurations exist and make a difference. For example, it is vital to the comprehension of events to know that Ricky is likely to behave differently toward his father when his mother is around than when she is not. Moreover, such configurations can and do impinge on one another in influential ways. Since Mr. A., through his counterphobic gesturing, holds the entire family at bay when they are gathered as a group of seven, it stands to reason that the remaining members of the family will capitalize on his absence to vent or display some very different attitudes.

Precisely because rules and norms shift in interdependent or compensatory fashion from one configuration to another, the analysis of *all* interactional constellations within the family becomes imperative. At a minimum, such an analysis promises a useful means for tracing the processes involved in mechanisms like displacement. It also could enhance the task of charting the path of gradients in the expression of certain affects, and could aid in the creation of formulas for predicting choice in matters like scapegoating, loyalty, dominance, subservience, patterns of compatible fit, or mutual aversion. Analyses of this type presently remain admirable but unaccomplished goals. They are much in need of attainment, though we can borrow the principles involved, and apply them to our cruder assessment of the A. family. For the moment, we focus particularly on the fate of hostility in this family.

Even here we are constrained by our data and methods. Principles will have to suffice because exacting, more finite analyses elude us on a number of counts. Not only do we lack the tools needed, but our sampling process—home visits done around the dinner hour—made the observation of most interpersonal subconfigurations impossible. For instance, Mr. A. was never viewed alone with Sheila and Deedee; nor was the triad of father, mother, and Roscoe ever observed as an entity—neither in the home nor in the child guidance center which was so concerned for their treatment.

But the opportunities to see the A. family with and without Mr. A. *were* abundant and provided some interesting contrasts, contrasts that were very much a function of how Mr. A. was absent. It made a great deal of difference, for example, whether he was gone with the expectation of imminent return, or whether he had just departed with his return not anticipated for some hours. The differences in family temper in each of these circumstances have already been rather graphically displayed in a few of the episodes drawn from the recorded home visits. Both circumstances, in their own way, are influenced by the psychological omnipresence of Mr. A.—even when he is not on the immediate premises. And both are, as well, a function of how things are when the full complement of A.'s—including Mr. A.—is present in the home. In brief, people's behavior in his absence is, in part, a consequence of the effect his presence has on them.

Effect of Father's Absence

Mr. A. Away, but on His Way Back

The tenth visit, made on January 30, and cited as an illustration of Mr. A.'s counterphobic insistence and flaunting (see pp. 112–114), is one of the two occasions—other than his hospitalizations—when Mr. A. was not at home at the time of my arrival. The other occurred at the beginning of the third visit. In a qualitative sense, the episodes are remarkably similar. Both involve Mr. A.'s unexpected tardiness for dinner, and both are seized upon by the older children as a rare but welcome chance to escape a tension-drenched family dinner. On both occasions, Deedee, Sheila, Ricky, and Roscoe successfully press Mrs. A. into reluctantly serving them or permitting them self-service of dinner prior to Mr. A.'s return. Their ostensible reasons for being unable to wait are engagement in "crucial" activities outside the home—specifically, skating parties. Yet these are the only two occasions among the twenty visits in which such extrafamilial "commitments" served to draw away three or four of the older children.[2]

Throughout both visits Mrs. A. tries vainly to exert a countervailing force. Her efforts are increasingly desperate as she seeks to keep her children—mostly at Deedee's instigation —from leaving the field and to keep her family from flying apart. As tensions mount in anticipation of the father's arrival, the children press their demands, and Mrs. A. is hard put to resist their chorus of pleas. Besides, she understands their wishes only too well. In despair she gives in. Her efforts to hold her family in check have the aspect of a woman trying to retrieve spilled groceries after her shopping bag has broken; for every item she picks up and clutches to her chest, she drops another previously retrieved. Her own concern, anxiety, frustration, and empathy for an attitude of flight ultimately get the best of her, and, dismissing the children, she steels herself to face Mr. A. with Pamela as her major support. The irony is that in neither circumstance does Mr. A. so much as inquire about the whereabouts of his children. Instead, he diverts himself by teasing Mrs. A. and indulging his counter-oedipal feelings toward Pamela.

Mr. A.'s absence in these two situations creates a moderately different atmosphere in the home from that observed when all seven members of the family are present. The difference does not obtain to the way in which hostilities consequent to impotence are handled. Suppression, denial, evasion, and turning against the self are still favored. Furthermore, Mrs. A. is as steadfastly committed to an instrumental-task orientation and a show of family solidarity as ever. The major differences occur in these two arenas: the nature of the familial alignments and splits, and the available choice of group defense. These two visits are virtually the only ones in which intrasibling cohesion exceeds intrasibling rift. Deedee assumes

2. During both the third and the tenth home visits all four of the older children agitated to be fed before their father's arrival, as well as to leave home prior to his coming. In the tenth visit all four—Deedee, Sheila, Ricky, and Roscoe—succeeded in leaving. In the third visit Sheila alone stayed behind as a favor to her mother. She cleared the table and washed the dishes and hence was home when Mr. A. arrived. Clearly, however, she had wished not to be.

uncontested leadership, Ricky and Roscoe suspend mutual antagonisms to join in following her lead, Sheila puts aside her psuedo-adult sense of maternal and familial responsibility— and all four make for the exit as a team. The teamwork is predicated on the possibility of realizing the group defense of "leaving the field," a defense totally unthinkable in Mr. A.'s presence. Its purposes are too transparent, its social buttressing too insubstantial, except, perhaps, for the teenage Deedee. In addition, its implications are too painful for and too badly handled by Mr. A. Mrs. A. will not tolerate the use of this defense to his face, and this is undoubtedly one source of her continuing battle with Deedee. Hence, when Mr. A. is home no one can comment on the roots of conflict and stress, nor can they physically leave the field (home). When he is not home commentary on the source of strain is still prohibited, but escape becomes permissible *if* endowed with the resolve of a group. The entire situation is remindful of the double bind. It is only somewhat less binding. There is after all the outside world, and the outside world is, as a consequence, invested with a positive valence that it might not otherwise enjoy.

Mr. A. Away, but Having Just Left

A very different set of dynamics unfolds in the wake of Mr. A.'s leaving his family for a few hours. The impact is almost the reverse of that experienced just prior to his arrival. In the latter instance the children unite, and Mrs. A. struggles to reconstitute her family. In the former circumstance group effort is decidedly undermined. There is a palpably dissipated concern on the part of family members with their presented selves, and there is withdrawal into private reverie. The outcome borders on cathartic relaxation.

In ways quite similar to Goffman's (1959) descriptions of public and private demeanor, the A.'s seem to react to Mr. A.'s leave taking as if their on-stage behavior were no longer required. The sheer exhaustion from having to maintain their steady vigilance and their presented selves causes them to retreat into individualistic, inner-directed, restitutive attitudes to regroup and reconstitute ego and self. Backstage behaviors appear. And, while no one comments on the whys and wherefores of their communal stress—the social taboo on death runs very deep—no one feels compelled to whisper any longer; rivalries emerge, territorial disputes occur, tempers flare, and no one, it would seem, is concerned with minding the collective store.

The fourteenth visit on March 27, used earlier to convey the quality of conflictual interaction between Mrs. A. and Deedee (see pp. 69–70), illustrates only too well the general exhaustion experienced by Mrs. A. Psychically burned out, she savors a moment of idleness and private fantasy—albeit programmed for her by television—only to pay for it by losing track of her familial and maternal responsibilities. The result is projection and free expression of rage aimed at Deedee. The explosion is sponsored and induced by Mr. A.'s departure. It is not an isolated instance. Mr. A. absented himself mid-way through a home visit on four other occasions. Another sample:

Home Visit 9, January 23

Mr. A. finished shaving and now came out into the family room. He asked after the whereabouts of the A. children. Mrs. A. said she did not know, and Mr. A. said he wanted them in the house. He asked had Ricky gone out or where Ricky was and Mrs. A. said she thought Ricky was downstairs in his room in the basement. Mr. A. said he wanted all the children inside, and then he put on his jacket and mentioned to me that he had to leave—a scout meeting he said. He then left.

Mrs. A., after Mr. A. had left, went to the basement stairs, very feebly called Ricky three or four times and got no response. She came back into the family room and sat down. She looked utterly without energy. She was haggard, and devoid of color, and more visibly tired than I had yet seen her. Her hair was disheveled and her dress rumpled and she lay slumped on the couch staring off into space. She remained that way for some time. Roscoe was alone at the dinner table eating dessert. Everyone else had left the table.

Roscoe was eating cherry pie. Mrs. A. was now watching him. Roscoe very carefully scraped all of the cherry filling out of the crust and began to eat this. Mrs. A. now watched him with interest. She sat watching him with an intensely hostile expression on her face, just waiting to jump. As soon as Roscoe had finished the filling and was about to push the plate aside leaving the crust, she pounced. She told Roscoe that he should not waste the crust, that he should eat it up immediately, that he had no right presuming he could get away with not eating it, and on and on. Roscoe, with no words or any kind of overt expression, in fact without even an indication that he had listened to his mother, proceeded to devour the crust.

Watching Mrs. A. watch Roscoe eat pie was like watching a resentful and very hateful animal watch a victim whom she knew she had trapped and whose movement she could predict. She just lay in wait for the moment of kill.

The increment in expressiveness and in ventilation of hostility is not confined to Mrs. A. on those occasions when Mr. A. departs the scene. But it must be acknowledged that she contributes the greatest share of open negativism. Her bitterness reflects a basic discontent with her lot in life. It also tones her children for a particular style of encountering adversity.

Home Visit 8, January 16

When I got to the family room Mr. A. was busy eating. He looked up, said hello, and explained that he had a meeting this evening and would have to be leaving at 6:15 . . . Just shortly after the family had seated themselves, and following some moments of total silence at the dinner table, Mr. A. finished eating. He got up to leave, turned to me and apologized for having to do so—something about father's and Cub Scouts —and he then kissed Mrs. A. goodbye. He was already opening the outside door when Pamela puckered and smacked her lips in a loud fashion. Mr. A. turned around and went back to kiss Pamela goodbye—he kissed her on the forehead, however, and not on the lips. He then left.

The rest of the family, with the exception of Deedee, was seated and eating. Shortly after Mr. A. had left Mrs. A. sat down at the table and requested that Deedee take over the serving of the meal. Deedee was in the kitchen throughout most of the rest of the meal making toast. Again, as on past visits, Sheila seemed to have all the responsibility for seeing that Pamela ate her dinner. Deedee did not sit down again until most of the others had finished eating. . . . When she did a ruckus started.

When Deedee finally did sit down at the table, Roscoe was already seated. Apparently his chair was somewhat too close to Deedee, and she could not maneuver her right arm well enough to eat. She gave Roscoe an annoyed look, but did not ask him to move his chair. Instead she simply reared back and jabbed him in the chest with her elbow, thereby shoving him over. Roscoe did not say anything, but simply moved his chair. Deedee gave him a dirty look which was obvious to all. A few moments later when Roscoe asked a seemingly innocent question Deedee reacted with evident disdain, did not answer the question, and in the haughtiest of manners labeled Roscoe "a creep" among other choice epithets.

For her part, Sheila, who was generally so quiet, was not so today. She made some annoyed and even highly angry faces at Pamela during the meal, particularly when Mrs. A. urged her to see that Pamela ate what was on her plate. I had the impression that Sheila was venting some long stored irritation at having to watch over her younger sister so closely. On a couple of occasions she actually force spoon fed Pamela, jamming food into an already full mouth. The acts were deliberate.

Pamela, on her end, was making frequent faces and complaining aloud a lot. Her grimaces and contorted facial expressions were calculated to provoke reactions from others at the table, especially her comments on her treatment at the hands of Sheila and the quality of the dinner fare. People always responded by looking at her, and often enough replied in words. Mrs. A., for example, took the bait and launched an attack or two on Sheila for her improper handling of Pamela. This led Sheila to deal more abrasively with Pamela and engineered the cycle anew.

Ricky took Pamela's communications about the food—chile con carne on toast—to heart and began bad mouthing the food, saying it tasted awful because Deedee cooked it, and chastising his mother for not having prepared and served the meal as she should.

Mrs. A. was also very critical of many of the things that went on during this visit. Most of her criticism was about picayune kinds of matters. She criticized the way Deedee was making the toast—that it was not getting dark enough. She criticized the noise from the TV set and urged that it be lowered or turned off. She got protests from all the kids. She criticized Ricky quite strongly—to the point of yelling—for trying to let the dog out the side door of the family room rather than the front door of the house. She was critical of Mr. A. in his absence for not having turned on the space heater in the room early enough so that it would have been warm during the meal. As already noted, she reprimanded Sheila for not getting Pamela to eat her food properly. She also made critical comments about the family room itself, and the flooring on the concrete slab, and said it was always cold, and needs linoleum or a carpet. She blasted the quality and content of the cartoons on TV that her kids insisted on watching. Virtually all her statements during the course of the meal and shortly thereafter were hypercritical.

Dinner itself was not very successful insofar as no one had a second helping, and Ricky, Roscoe, Pamela, and Deedee failed to finish even the first. This really sent Mrs. A. off the deep end. She accused each of the kids of trying to hurt her personally, demanded to know what each had eaten after school in order to ruin their appetites, and would not accept statements to the effect that they had eaten nothing. Fuming, she ended the dinner by sending all the children from the table. Deedee and Sheila went to the kitchen to do the dishes. What I caught of conversation in there was Mrs. A. being critical of the girls—they were not washing the dishes properly and were not putting things where they should be.

Further Formulations of the Meaning of Mr. A.'s Leave-Taking

In an assessment of the influence of various family structures created by father presence and father departure on interaction among A. family members, a number of factors can be mentioned:

1. *The press for semblance of group solidarity.* In father's presence both parents are intent on maintaining a semblance of solidarity and togetherness. They kid themselves that they are the all-American nuclear family—replete with domestic

bliss, the Ozzie Nelson's next door. There is a premium on role
fit and the articulation of effective reciprocal and cooperative
functioning and task accomplishment. Meals are served, de-
voured, cleared away, and completed in smooth, routine, and
unruffled—for the most part—fashion. All this may be construed as denial of not only what is, but of what some day, in
the near future, may come to pass as a hard actuality. In any
event, the maintenance of high degrees of control, the pro-
scription of angry expression or even normal degrees of asser-
tive behavior, the emphasis on a show of togetherness, the
tacit rule that all obey, which labels certain vital topics as un-
mentionable taboos, all act to lock family members into an existence that is, unfortunately, much too real in its psychological pretensions. Their on-stage behavior is given the lie,
however, because not even the A.'s can make a pretense of
warm, loving, demonstrative affect. Their pseudo-mutality
(Wynne et al., 1958) can only go so far, and pseudo-hostility
(Wynne, 1961) is either beyond their ken, or too real in its implications to suit their situation or style.

The insistence on a show of togetherness and accord in
the A. home is of more than passing interest. It trains a spot
light on still another aspect of the severe cultural strain endured by the A.'s. As before, the strain emanates from a competition of cultural value-orientations that under routine, non-
stressful conditions would not surface in rivalrous fashion.
Dread of death seems to make all the difference. The value-
orientation involved concerns the conception of man's relation
to other men—that is, the articulation of individual and group.
Does the culture with an accent on horizontal, group-wide
structuring of positions and power emphasize collateral relations? Or does the culture encourage lineal solutions in which
authority resides in a hierarchical stratification of group structure? Or, is a third alternative favored by the society—the alternative of individualism, where decisions are optimally made
by each person? In this last, the group, whether collaterally or
linearly arranged, is referred to secondarily (Spiegel and
Kluckhohn, 1954).

Middle-Americans are inordinately and indefatigably individualistic in their relational orientation. Possibly no society

in the history of the world has accorded such a primacy to individualistic goals as ours has. In ordinary circumstances, every attempt is made to foster autonomy of individual family members and to allow children great latitude in making their own decisions. Independence and self-reliance, it is presumed, form an integral part of the free enterprise, democratic, egalitarian ethos and children are socialized for entry into the system. A collateral relationship is, at best, a very distant runner-up and is looked to only in times of recreation—team sports—or crisis (Spiegel, 1971). Even then it is invoked reactively, as an escape or as a corrective to too much self-concern in times of crisis. In crisis, some tone of social structure or semblance of organization must persist for society to survive and perpetuate itself. This is what occurs in the A. family. Their very efforts at a semblance of group solidarity stands as a tribute to the genuine but disastrous and unreasoned triumph of the individualist orientation. Cultural ills prevail despite appearances.

It must be kept in mind that it is not simply Mr. A.'s cardiac problem that threatens the family, but his wholesale, "rugged individualism," and his and his family's unflinching allegiance to American values. No one seems willing to call him on his individual concerns and defenses; yet it is precisely for these that the family suffers. His individual preoccupations are treated as his national birthright. The group endures and tries to reconstitute and maintain itself in the face of the evident priority given Mr. A.'s self-indulgence. Their efforts at group solidarity are, in fact, attempts to mask the abusive extremism of his rampant American individualism. This exaggerated individualism threatens to make group functioning and the family obsolete for all the wrong reasons.

2. *From group solidarity to anarchy.* Once father leaves the home, the rules governing family interaction shift. Personae drop away. Family members recede into personal and self-centered concerns. Group endeavor comes apart at the seams; it is everyone for himself. While anarchy does not reign by any means—there is no mistaking that comparatively speaking—it is much more in evidence. When the psychic governor on the system leaves the scene, Mrs. A. assumes the role

of governor, and out of her own need to revitalize, escape, seek peace, and turn in upon herself, she abruptly delegates her leadership status. She assigns her instrumental task functions and her maternal responsibilities to her children.

From at least one perspective, she counts on the children to assist her in the defaulting of rule-setting behavior. From another perspective, she does the necessary thing and re-establishes the ground rules for interaction. Within limits, she promotes anarchy. She is not entirely unambivalent in doing so, but she permits a number of much required gratifications.

For a period of time, Mrs. A. acts overwhelmed and incapable of managing her flock. She descends, in part, to their level. She even takes the lead, albeit with little awareness or conscious intent, in modeling self-interest as a concern and projection and externalization as defenses. Who is to fault her unconscious wisdom? Routine meal times do not occur; children disappear or get lost on the very premises, but people lack the energy to search them out. If the whole temporary adventure were not so guilt inducing for each of them or so demoralizing of good role performance, it might even have beneficial effects.

Unfortunately, the adventure culminates in recriminations. To be sure, the recriminations are appropriate and in the interest of safety. But they also cause pain. Suspending rules also undermines efficient role functioning. There are limits on permissible anarchy, just as there are limits to affecting "mutuality." Mrs. A. checks the anarchy she invites with her criticism, blame, and anger, unwittingly producing conditions rife for insubordination.

3. *Release.* Insubordination occurs and hostilities erupt. Pent-up anger is loosed in displaced and petty fashion. No one dares to label or assign, let alone attack, the real object or cause, but semicathartic reactions do take place. People complain, bitch, poke, and shove. Voices are raised, and rage is sometimes vented.

4. *Circumstantial gradients.* Gradients for the expression of affects—and anger in particular—now become discernable. When Mr. A. with his heart condition and his counterphobia are gone, the overt manifestation of affects and hostility—

considerably circumscribed when its immediate object or source is present—is permitted within reasonable limits.

On a prorated percentage basis, one would expect approximately 11 percent of all categories of all behaviors manifested by each remaining member of the A. family—Mrs. A., Deedee, Sheila, Ricky, Roscoe, Pamela—to occur in those four half-visits when Mr. A. left midway.[3] This is not, in fact, the case for some telling categories. These six A.'s do not contribute 11 percent of all their "antagonisms" and "disapprovals" during these four half-visits. They contribute roughly 30 to 40 percent of these categories; nearly three and one-half times the amount expected on a prorated basis. Conversely, this means that instead of 89 percent of their "antagonisms" and "disapproving" initiations being distributed over the other sixteen visit-equivalents, a lower percentage is recorded. Indeed, when Mr. A. is present but 60 to 70 percent of these initiations are so distributed.[4] One must conclude that hostility is released far more readily in the wake of Mr. A.'s temporary departures.

Summing Up: Two "Families"

The limited sampling procedures of this study have provided a highly instructive glimpse of the A. family at home; they have, in fact, revealed the presence of two distinctly contrasting "families." These families exist successively in alternating and reactively compensatory fashion. Each "family" constellation possesses a character of its own and persists in the actualization of its unique dynamic power despite the fact that the individuals comprising both "families" are identical with but one exception. The six persons making up the father-absent "family" possess a pattern of interaction, a set of rules, a body of shared experiences and understandings that is not of a piece

3. Since Mr. A. left mid-way during four visits, it might be anticipated that the four halves would represent one-ninth or 11 percent of all eighteen coded home visits. This simple assumption is complicated somewhat by (a) the fact that interaction was more frequent during some visits than others, and (b) that one family member—Mr. A.—was absent during the times considered, therefore reducing by one-seventh the possibility of interaction.

4. This statement makes no attempt to take account of the visits when Mr. A. was not present by virtue of his tardiness (two occasions) or by virtue of his hospitalizations (three occasions, two of which were lost for transcribing purposes and hence not coded).

with the formalized, regular interactional system of the father-present "family." What one negates, the other legitimizes.

The discovery of the differential patterns was nearly fortuitous from the standpoint of data collection. The design of this study did not appreciate or fully anticipate the significance of subconfigurations in the family. One may be sure that others exist within the A. family that did not come to light during home observations around the dinner hour. There is even the reasonable possibility that the two constellations reported here are not even the most dominant or influential ones. All that may be asserted readily is that they are of interest theoretically and methodologically, and that, thematically and dynamically, they make a good deal of sense.

Indeed, they contribute meaningfully to the "construct" validity of the arguments being forwarded in this book. They suggest a particular predisposition on the part of all A. children to "act up" in the absence of an adult male figure or in situations where they are not terrorized by the specter of death. That at least one of the A. children should be a behavior or management problem in school classrooms managed by female teachers is then no surprise. That Deedee particularly should act out in flirtatious and sexually loaded ways that arouse suspicion and concern because of her flair for autonomy and manipulation, is also readily comprehensible in view of much that has been said about her relationship to her mother. In light of the severe restriction on warm and physical affective expression in the A. home, it makes sense that she be chosen as public exponent of this dimension of the family's conflicts. But that Roscoe should be chosen to represent to the world the A.'s problems with the expression of impotence and rage, is not at this point so evident. It requires explanation. To ask why Roscoe has been so chosen is also to ask why he is first choice for family scapegoat,[5] and requires yet further investigation of the fate of hostility in the A. family.

5. It is fully recognized that Deedee has great potentialities for scapegoating in the A. family, and that, in fact, she enacts the role and absorbs the abuse attendant on the role to some degree. But she is a distant second to Roscoe in the attribution of this status because she possesses some trump cards totally unavailable to him.

Chapter 10

The Uses of Scapegoating

If scapegoating is construed as the result of unresolved tensions between family members, the A. family provides fertile grounds for breeding prejudicial and malignant forms of scapegoating. This is most especially the case because each parent harbors deep fears about the spouse's behavior. These fears serve to hinder the parents from accurate prognostication of the other's response. They only surmise that the response may be damaging to the point of annihilation. The assumption that underlies the emergence of scapegoating as a neutralizing force in the A. family group is as follows: the tensions produced by the unresolved conflicts and uncommunicated, unverbalized terrors, are so severe in this family that they cannot be otherwise reasonably or satisfactorily contained, not even by the many and various mechanisms discussed to this point.

Evasion, denial, and cognitive dysfunction are devices which succeed in holding at bay overt recognition of the "family secret"—Mr. A.'s flirtation with death. They also, to some extent, countermand Mr. A.'s hypermasculine challenges to "fate" and the familial adience to the all-absorbing death theme. They are less effective in binding the rage that emanates from helplessness; they fail in the face of the experienced impotence; they are not adequate to the felt sense of responsibility and guilt. These pervade and threaten to spill over. Indeed, all that smacks of assertiveness in the A. home must be muted and rechanneled.

Questions about Scapegoating

It is an established premise, at this point, that scapegoating exists in the A. family and that Roscoe is the prime object. What remains unestablished are the "whys" of these assertions. A series of three questions is involved: (1) Why the need for scapegoating? Why are all the mechanisms thus far discussed insufficient to the task of dissipating the family's accumulated rage? (2) Why the choice of an insider as scapegoat, and not an external agency or object? A person or group outside the family could, and often does, serve in this capacity. Yet, the A.'s have selected one of their own. (3) If the selection of an insider can be explained with reasonable credence, then one must undertake to offer a reconstruction of reasons for the consensual perception that Roscoe—as opposed to any of his siblings—is the choicest victim. This last question requires some speculation about his symbolic and historic meaning to his family and parents, and most especially demands paired comparisons with each of his siblings in these regards.

The Need for Scapegoating

Duration and Intensity of Stress as Contributing Factors

It has been contended, both here and elsewhere (Vogel and Bell, 1960), that scapegoating is a consequence of the existence of tensions within the family system which have not been adequately resolved in other ways. The locus of the tension is usually assumed to be in the marital relationship. These conditions certainly prevail in the A. home. Yet, to stop here is to argue tautologically or to diagnose by default. Scapegoating results from the failure of other protective mechanisms; when one finds it, one assumes it was needed. When it is absent, one credits other defenses with success. We have argued that a number of group mechanisms in the A. family are at least partially successful: evasion, noncommunication, denial, displacement, turning against the self, externalization, and altered rules in subconstellations of the family. Cumulatively, they have nonetheless fallen short of full effectiveness. This is concluded by tautological definition alone. Scapegoating does exist. But to settle for this explanation is to argue from weakness, and to advance not at all our comprehension of what scapegoating is all about—at least as it occurs in the A. family.

Stronger, more cogent arguments with greater positive inputs are required. Thus, one might contend that it is not in the failure of other defenses per se that the roots of scapegoating lie, but in the overwhelming persistence and magnitude of the stress. When the stress is unrelenting and powerful, and lurks ominously at the surface of the group's awareness, then most defense mechanisms will not be equal to the task of affording full protection to its members. Scapegoating is then employed to take up the difference. This argument of duration and strength of stress in conjunction with failure of other modes is somewhat more compelling, but it too suffers in modest degree from tautological speciousness. Concretely, it suggests that if the A.'s had to endure a less intense and long-standing stress situation, they might have done without the mechanism of scapegoating. However, one can often only assess the magnitude of the strain by the presence or absence of the explanatory phenomenon.

Hence, while the foregoing considerations provide necessary conditions for the evolution of scapegoating within a system, they are insufficient to explain the phenomenon totally. At least three additional elements, each serving the interest of scapegoating, can be observed in the dynamics of the A. family. These additional factors supplement those already cited as preconditions to the emergence of the mechanism, and each in its own way complements the other. There is no reason to believe these factors exhaust the range of possible explanations for the necessity of scapegoating in the A. family, and certainly no claim can be made to having discerned new or undiscovered underlying principles of the scapegoat mechanism in general; nonetheless, the following points seem significant to a fuller comprehension of the "whys" of scapegoating in the A. family.

Scapegoating as Expedient and Corporate Defense

Scapegoating is a ready, efficient, and highly expedient corporate defense, handy to have around. In its discharge of aggregated hostilities, it enjoys a number of advantages over the defense mechanisms discussed thus far. All the defenses discussed to this point have been inefficient or have exacted a cost in particular ways.

Thus, counterthanatophobic devices are the prerogative of Mr. A. and the bane of his wife and children. Projection and externalization similarly tend to be used in personalized and idiosyncratic ways, even if employed by most of the A.'s. There is little control over their use to ensure they are employed in the same way and at the same time by various family members and, concomitantly, there is the danger that each member of the family might unpredictably become a target for another member. There is a cost for this because it undermines willing and effective role performance via its deflation of morale.

Other of the defenses that have been thus far discussed are situation specific—they are good in some contexts but not in others. They therefore incur penalties in terms of relentless demands on memory storage, vigilance, flexibility, preparedness, and adaptability. Changing the rules of interaction each time one or more family members leave or join the group is a case in point. One must readjust and reorient, each time at hazard of possible error or misjudgment.

Finally, many of the other defenses are so intrapsychically burdensome that they damage effective group functioning. Denial obliterates whole pieces of reality, and therefore its use must be kept within limits by the group. Leaving the field assists the individual, but destroys family functioning by leaving role slots vacant, however temporarily. And the compromise formations—suppression, evasion, and turning against the self —inhibit not only hostility but the assertiveness and normal degree of aggressiveness needed for routine task accomplishment as well.

In part because of these specific limitations, and because none of these defenses can be applied generally, scapegoating becomes an important supplemental defense. Scapegoating can enjoy general and nonsporadic use. It permits the greatest gain to all with minimal expenditure. It resolves the problem of ego dividedness, pent-up hostilities, and experiences of self-recrimination and guilt. One can disown unwanted aspects of self by projecting them to the victim and then righteously attack those elements in the scapegoat. Hostility is discharged under the guise of moral uplifting. The experience of internal integrity is seemingly enhanced. Most significant, though, scapegoating permits low-risk, error-free discharge of group or commonly experienced tensions; moreover, it does so with a modicum of confusion, hesitation, effort, or noise in the interpersonal communicative channels. Teamwork takes place smoothly; people do not have to fear one another or worry about surprises; procedures are automatic. Anger, by mutual consent, is oriented in one direction and is uncontested so that in moments of surprise, change, or frustration one need not sort out the situation. Instead one can react with alacrity. In this way scapegoating becomes a true group defense, a shorthand, a cardinal rule under which the family discharges hostilities.

Reign of Terror as a Modus Operandi

Scapegoating is the institutionalization of a reign of terror against someone. As such, it fulfills a purpose that other modes of defense cannot. It organizes the terrorizing group into an entity. Unity of purpose, togetherness of mind, alignment against a common target, are both its trademarks and the measures of its effectiveness. These features are not by-products of scapegoating but are instead essential ingredients for its use. If the unity of a group is not threatened, or if a group is not in need of welding, it is unlikely that scapegoating will surface as a modus operandi, for its significant feature is its contagion, through which all members of the group become bound in its organization. As Vogel and Bell (1960) state, "From the point of view of the family, the primary function of scapegoating is that it permits the family to maintain its solidarity" (p. 395).

The severe strains that so threaten to rip the A. family assunder are thus suggested as a necessary condition for the emergence of scapegoating as a group defense. For a family so intent on maintaining its public and private image as stable, cohesive, and unchangingly anchored in time, scapegoating is, indeed, a logical and tactically sound rallying point.

Scapegoating as the American Way: Affixing Blame

If we construe the A.'s as a typical middle-American family, struggling valiantly against the odds to uphold the values of the milieu they represent, and scapegoating as the nearly inexorable outcome to their dilemma, it is as much to say that scapegoating, under certain conditions of stress, is the American way. The point is best underscored by a return to Florence Kluckhohn's formulations of cultural value-orientations (1958). In considering man's relation to nature, she suggests that the American middle class characteristically prefers to dominate and subdue natural forces. This is the posture sought by Mr. A. As we have seen, this is not a value-orientation which admits readily of failure. This is especially so when human control is baffled, as it is in Mr. A.'s case by a severe cardiac condition and imminent death. Protest is, in fact, Mr. A.'s response—much to the psychic distress of his family.

If we now turn to consider another value-orientation which characterizes middle-Americans we may further increase our understanding of why the A.'s are partial to scapegoating. Kluckhohn describes one more dimension, not previously discussed but of some relevance at this juncture. It concerns man's conception of innate human nature—is man predominantly evil, a mixture of good and evil, or basically good? And, regardless of his innate qualities, how mutable is he? According to Spiegel and Kluckhohn (1954), middle-class Americans prefer to see man as a mixture of good and evil. Nevertheless, they frankly acknowledge that assignment of a dominant position along this dimension is more problematic than was the case for the three dimensions of value-orientation previously discussed. Their greater caution occurs because Spiegel and Kluckhohn consider the American middle-class family to be in a state of relative transition. The Puritan view of man as basically evil, but perfectable through strong effort, will power, vigilance, and good deeds is only now gradually giving way to the more modern, social-scientific view of man as both good and evil. The wider implications of this are, of course, many, but for the present purpose we need only register that as staunch supporters of middle-class values, the A.'s are prone to view some persons as essentially good or redeemed and others as innately evil or corrupted.

The point is an important one, and of more than academic interest, for it underscores another precondition of scapegoating. A group that is not inclined to view man as inherently good finds scapegoating—involving as it does blame and disparagement of some while others are exonerated—an alternative to which they are eminently suited. To see man as basically good, in the best Rousseau tradition, would preclude any possibility of adopting such a mechanism.

But the impact and the lesson to be taken from this point involve substantially more: a tendency to see man as either good or evil does not prevail in isolation but is experienced in concert with other value-orientations—with staunch individualism, and a "technological driveness" (Henry, 1963) which demands that nature yield. This concatenation of mutually reinforcing American culturisms produces an obsession with externally judged performance, accomplishment, achievement, and planning for the future. Precious little room is left for lamentation over unhappy or unfortunate events. Accidents, in fact, don't happen and the successful "make their own breaks." "Competition is the spice of life," each man is the "master of his fate," and "the captain of his soul." Long-range planning, delayed gratification, and exquisite self-control ensure that "nothing succeeds like success" through good works.

Such a system provides poor tolerance for failure, though large doses of failure are an inevitable by-product of it. Another by-product is the compulsion to assign responsibility and to afix blame. When things go wrong or badly someone must be held accountable. The culture so narrows the degrees of freedom around these matters that scapegoating in times of stress is nearly compulsory. It is not that way in every culture. The A.'s are drawn to scapegoating because they are good Americans.

The Choice of an Insider

Why the choice of an insider as scapegoat, and not of an outsider? This question has not been extensively addressed in the literature. There is an extensive literature on scapegoating and the nature of prejudice, but mostly as it relates to the treatment of one racial or ethnic group by another. There is also a small, neonatal literature on scapegoating within family systems, but it assumes a closed family system and does not tackle the reasons outsiders are excluded as victims—if indeed they are excluded.[1] Data on the correlation between internal and external propensities for scapegoating are not abundant. Neither body of literature touches specifically on the issue raised here. The closest one gets are discussions of within-group prejudices, the anti-Semitic Jews, or anti-black Negroes, who in the interest of "passing" or experiencing a sense of belonging to or with the majority reference group, are believed, via identification with the aggressor, to consolidate negative identifications with their own membership group. This hypothesis has little application to the present concern which is a situation precisely the reverse—the majority defines one of its own as scapegoat, outsider, and destroyer in preference to a genuine outsider. The possible reasons for this phenomena, advanced here, are based on observations of the A. family. As such, they are very speculative and are best regarded with some caution.

Idiosyncracy in Family Problem and Choice of Victim

Scapegoating of a family member rather than an outsider is likely to occur in a situation where all family members are dominated by a common concern involving conflict and guilt which is, in some sense, unique to them in its intensity, character, and/or content. This is to say, other families in the community do not experience the problem or conflict in quite the same way. The social modeling, support, sharing, and facilitation for identifying, socializing, and institutionalizing a common external scapegoat is thereby simply lacking.

As popularly conceived, scapegoating of an external object or organization requires public bondedness and a shared premise. Moreover, it generally has the benefit of lifelong prejudices to buttress it. Thus, in times of economic depression when many families share the crisis of unemployment, they are

---

1. The growing child abuse literature is not construed as part of this, though it might be. But strictly speaking, scapegoating and child abuse should not be considered synonymous. Child abuse does not necessarily entail assignment of responsibility and guilt for particular failings or frustrations. By the same token, scapegoating, psychologically injurious as it can be, does not necessarily involve physical punishment.

likely to pool their woes in the scapegoating of a minority toward whom they were trained from childhood to feel an antipathy. While the A.'s may share with others training in given social prejudices,[2] they do not share with other families a commonly experienced crisis; in fact, the crisis the A.'s are facing is one the rest of the community—including its helping agencies—would rather not even hear about. Finding an unreceptive community, and finding it nearly impossible to articulate matters among themselves, they are, per force, pressed toward the choice of an inside victim. Even more, however, seems to be involved.

Choice of Victim and Reality Testing

The A.'s are a lower middle-class family, living in an old, established, middle-class residential neighborhood. Contact with and accessibility to traditional groups for scapegoating— Blacks, Jews, Chicanos—are limited. This proves true of both Mr. and Mrs. A.'s workplaces, and the children's schools. Extensive distortion in reality testing would, therefore, have to occur for the A.'s to comfortably adopt the scapegoats usually employed by society. In addition, it is not clear how these groups could be meaningfully implicated as causative or blameworthy agents in the A.'s' difficulty. Granted, scapegoating generally involves specious cause and effect, but the connections are seldom of a visibly tenuous quality. Unless the A.'s chose doctors, researchers, or the technological world as their scapegoated target, their selection of an outside party might bear an unacceptably tenuous relation to their central problem.

Actually, they are too much a part of and too wedded to the creed of a technological society, and too reliant on medicine and its research prowess to disparage and fault them at this time. Besides, the resultant rift in the A.'s' already strained value system would be insuperable and devastatingly disorganizing. In addition to community support, the choice of an

2. It is by no means clear that they do. There was no hint in any of the visits that the A.'s viewed any out-member group pejoratively or with disdain —other than perhaps school teachers.

outside scapegoat must be consonant with the value system of the family. Further, it must hold forth some potential for a cause and effect relation to the experienced problem.

Scapegoating and the Need to See Results:
Demoralization as a Dependent Variable

Still another factor guiding the choice of an in-member as opposed to an out-member, is the experienced need for control and effectualness. Scapegoating as a mechanism is typically a means of elevating someone's self-esteem. This can be done vicariously and at a distance. Scapegoating outsiders is usually done at a distance. One feels elevated to the extent that one is convinced certain others are less deserving, or to the extent that they can be held responsible for one's grievances. This process does not necessarily invoke face-to-face disparagement, nor does it put one's convictions to the test. Scapegoating an outsider is a mode of prejudice often reserved for frustrated classes of persons who do not genuinely expect their situation of low or poor status to change for the better in fundamental respects. The value of the scapegoating is experienced at psychological levels, but not accrued through direct or overt action. Control of the scapegoat's behavior is remote —though undeniably real in its contagiously aggregate and cumulative effects.

In other instances, however, where control of behavior, a sense of effectiveness, and direct feedback are sought, selection of a victim or victims from within one's own membership group is the better device.

Sheer convenience is a prime consideration. A group member is usually around and available, while an out-group person would not be so handy.

Efficiency and economy are equally potent factors. Since all members of the family share a common conflict and common guilt they can deposit their identical burden and foster encapsulation of the central problem, with all its attendant anxieties, in the single victim. There is little waste involved in this process. This is especially so because the victim can be highly specific in *his* role playing and reactions. With practice, he can enact the very kind of scapegoat the particular family requires or is intent on having. It is difficult to imagine an outside agency so docile, willing, and accomodatingly pliable. The choice of an insider assures maximum efficiency.

In principle then it is better to grow your own scapegoat. The degree of experienced mastery is greater, the rewards more frequent, the surprises fewer, and the discrepancy between stereotype and reality smaller. It may be conjectured that by the time the indoctrination and training are accomplished, the stereotype will be real enough to convince all parties involved—the scapegoating and the scapegoated.

Some Luxuries of Scapegoating: Expendability and Choice of Victim

Perhaps the most important determinant in the choice of an in-group member as scapegoat is the sheer availability of a household resident—usually a child or elderly person, both being low in status and disenfranchised—to serve as a repository for family members' projections of despised aspects of self. This factor embodies a number of further assumptions. It posits, for example, the notion of expendability.

Expendability implies the presence of an individual whose existence in his own right is of no consequence to anyone in his family. He is a person whose unique endowments, needs, aspirations, or potentialities are ignored in favor of saddling him with an identity that is not his own, that he did not earn. Moreover, it is assumed that he comes to symbolize a piece of someone else's harried or traumatic childhood, a piece of someone else's terrifying guilt, a piece of someone else's unconscious. He may be and probably is a receptacle for a parent, who himself having felt abused or scapegoated as a child, now brings to bear in the form of latent learning long-dormant notions of how to practice parenthood. The point is the scapegoat is denied his own existence.

Expendability has another connotation, that of luxury. Families are social systems and must perform certain functions that depend upon the articulation of interlocking role assignments. The creation of an in-system scapegoat assumes sufficient personnel or talent elsewhere in the organization to carry out basic group functions—economic, child-rearing, household maintenance—because creation of an internal scapegoat most often entails a degree of ostracism and alienation for the victim. A member of the group is made to feel peripheral, and becomes an outsider. In addition, the role is contingent on humiliation and demoralization; it therefore cannot be expected that the scapegoat be entrusted with the performance of essential functions such as earning money, socializing children, or maintaining the home. The inside scapegoat's crucial function is not to do any of these things himself, but to psychically free others so that they might perform their key roles effectively. But because he does not contribute in the traditional or typical ways, the family is sacrificing potential manpower. An in-house scapegoat is a decided luxury, a luxury that not all families can enjoy. At a minimum, the existence of an in-house scapegoat implies that others have the skill to take up the slack or that the family is large enough to contain an expendable member. Just why Roscoe A. is such an exquisite selection for the scapegoat role remains to be discovered.

Sorting the Candidates

Why the choice of Roscoe? This is a two part question. It entails knowing why other members of the A. family are less eligible, and what about Roscoe makes him so eminently well-suited. The answer to the first part concerning eligibility is complicated. It is predicated on the inexpendability of other A.'s.

Mr. A.: Immunity on Three Sides

Mr. A. is, on three counts, inviolate as a potential victim. In the first place, he is already a cardiac victim, but one whose psychological defenses require he be seen as anything but a heart patient. The family accepts this premise because it is consonant with their cultural values to do so. They, in their own way, cannot construe him otherwise. Nonetheless, they treat him with kid gloves. He is not the target of emotionally loaded or evaluative initiations. A compromise is struck. Secondly, Mr. A. is already the legitimate object of much, if not nearly all, of the family's frustration. Angers, if on target, would be most properly directed at him. But patricide is a heavy price to pay for momentary relief of tension. He is therefore safe-guarded on this count as well. Finally, he is the family bread-winner and enjoys real and deserved status for being so. It is not reasonable that his family should jeopardize his contribution by aiming a process of demoralization at him. Quite the contrary. They provide him free reign to help him maintain his masculine prerogatives and his prowess as wage earner.

Mrs. A. as Mother Courage

Mrs. A. is exempt from the scapegoated role on grounds very similar to those exempting Mr. A. Her continued functioning is the life-line of the family's continued existence. It is obvious from all that has been recorded thus far that her performance, even so, is quite below par and often ineffective. It is also clear that she is so taxed psychologically as to border on perpetual exhaustion and "mental collapse." Yet, impaired as her functioning may be, she is the glue welding the A.'s as a unit. Power resides with her, and to her all A.'s look for leadership. One may be sure that the family is fully appreciative of her value as instrumental task leader, money earner, and organizer of family activity. They are not likely to risk further overloading her psychic capacity for endurance by subjecting her to humiliations.

Deedee: A Delicate Balance and an "Also Ran"

Deedee's situation is more complex than that of the other candidates. She is, to be sure, of scapegoating potential being on the periphery of the group. While she could easily be construed as an outsider, she marginally escapes assignment of the role because of her age, her peculiar entanglements with and significance to her mother (as outlined on pp. 66–73), and because Roscoe possesses still better qualifications. Even so, the vignettes cited revealing her relationship with her mother suggest the ease with which a scapegoating function might take root and spread. What appears to prevent the process from gaining more than a foothold is Mrs. A.'s need to keep Deedee in the family circle in the face of Deedee's countervailing press toward leaving.

Deedee, who is precociously sexual, acts out this side of the A.'s suppressed affectivity and has established peer associations that are already—at age thirteen—competitive with her links to the family. It might be said that Deedee's attributes are most compatible with those of her peers. It is to them that she is attracted, while she is held back and contained within the boundaries of her family unit by legal barriers of dependency and by dwindling sources of compatible matching to her mother's needs. In a word, her connection to the family is tenuous. It has the delicate balance of the orbiting object impelled outward by centrifugal forces but contained by gravitational ones. The move toward dominance of the external pull is steady and inevitable, and it is a matter of short time before Deedee—as the oldest—physically leaves the system.

Largely for this reason, she is not a more focal object for family-wide scapegoating. Contagion does not set in. It may be also speculated that she is exempted because it would take so very little in the way of communal disparagement to tip the scales in favor of premature separation, with Deedee opting to become an "adolescent runaway" or a "teenage bride." [3] Conceivably, she could do both and earn herself abiding animosity as the "black sheep," or the "bad woman"; she would, however, then lack the favorable qualities of an in-house scapegoat that we listed.

We should additionally bear in mind that the sampling of the A. family's interactions are time bound, being confined to the space of one year—the time when Deedee went from thirteen to fourteen. As a consequence, there is no immediate means of determining whether Deedee was not, in fact, a more favored object of belittlement when she was younger. Similarly, we can only guess that by increasing her "comparison level of alternatives" (Thibaut and Kelley, 1959), by widening her peer contacts, Deedee has become less available to her family. Concomitantly, we may assume that Roscoe has, by degrees, been made to assume her vacated role.

Sheila as Surrogate Mother and "Dove"

Sheila is indispensable to the A. family. By virtue of her assumption of maternal, peacemaking, and mediating functions

---

3. A foretaste of the postscript: despite her mother's efforts, Deedee opts for the latter, marrying at age sixteen.

she is immune to scapegoating. It should be apparent from the analysis of Roscoe's interactions with other A.'s that Sheila's dove-like characteristics have nothing to do with this immunity. Rather, she owes her sacrosanct position to her enactment of the vital mother-surrogate role: she keeps Mrs. A.'s head above water and thereby aids immeasurably in keeping the family afloat; she is identified with traditional "good female" values; she resembles the acceptable aspects of Mrs. A.'s identity. Despite an evident dourness in demeanor she is well regarded and unbothered.

Ricky: Folk Hero and District Attorney

Ricky's special status in the A. family cannot be meaningfully discussed in isolation from his intimate reciprocal relation with Roscoe. The two are alter-egos and are careful not to occupy the same social space. Detailing the dynamics underlying this relationship will be deferred to the discussion of Roscoe's special requisites for the role of scapegoat. It will be understood in that context why Ricky is unavailable. For the moment, we need only mention Ricky's position as oldest son in a culture bound set of family values. We infer his sanctity. As oldest male child it is to be expected that he, if any of the death terrorized A.'s, will become the standard-bearer for the family, their "glittering star" to the outside world. Ricky is the son who shares his father's values, partakes of his father's activities, emulates his father's characterological modes. Ricky also "plays over his injuries" and prevails over adversity.

Home Visit 1, November 14

Mr. A. asked Ricky how his injured thumb was. Ricky had apparently injured it some days earlier in football. Ricky said that it pained him some, but that he was still able to play football. And, as a matter of fact, they had had a contest in school that day which he—Ricky—had won by throwing the football some seventy feet.

While, for the time being, no one in the family can afford to manifest great concern for his or any of the children's futures,[4] Ricky occupies a basic role in the family network. It is so basic that, barring any unforseen circumstances, it should stand him in good stead as a training experience throughout his competitive years. His future seems assured despite the family's suspension of its contemplation.

In addition, Ricky is the least likely of the children to be scapegoated because, as was seen earlier, he is the most feared and most powerful of all the offspring. All the A.'s are afraid of him. It is his assignment to prosecute, to implement scapegoating. If anyone may be designated the family "hope," the child most equipped to "make it" in American society, it is Ricky.

Pamela: The Flower of Innocence

We have already seen in the discussion of Deedee's insulation from scapegoating how, as a useful and convincing device for affixing blame, scapegoating is inextricably tied to developmental phenomena. In Deedee's case, the mechanism is compromised by her having developed viable alternatives to relationships in the home. In considering Pamela's availability we are at the early end of the developmental scale. As a consequence, we must attend to the matter of credibility in the assignation of responsibility and blame.

Scapegoating, to be effective, assumes the end of innocence in its target personage. Pamela is just now reaching that stage. At age four, cause and effect and culpability are newly palpable concepts for her. Because they are so new, and because the roots of the A. family strife are years old, it seems unlikely that her victimization could be justified at this time. It would certainly stretch the credulity of all family members, particularly since she was born at the time of Mr. A.'s first heart failure.[5]

This does not mean, however, that she will continue to

4. For an example of how even Ricky's achievement orientation is blunted by present stresses see excerpt from fourth home visit, December 5, on pp. 64–65.

5. It is, of course, quite conceivable and often the case clinically that a parent will ascribe malevolent motives to a child much younger than age four —say a child of two, recently launched into his battle for autonomy. This does not seem to have been the situation with Pamela, who is still very dependent at age four. The fact that Mrs. A. has worked throughout most of Pamela's life also has considerable meaning in this regard.

enjoy ineligibility. She has now reached the point in development where she is fair game. The contiguous relation of her birth date and Mr. A.'s cardiac arrest make Pamela, in fact, excellent game. However, in view of certain role functions she has already assumed, it seems probable that she will be permitted further immunity—at least temporarily.

Previously cited as primary among her role assignments is that of being surrogate wife to Mr. A. Her oedipal relationship with her father is hypersexualized. Whether Pamela is also replacing or being groomed as a replacement for Deedee as father's counter-oedipal object, is not entirely clear. One suspects she is. This is particularly so since Mr. A.'s current relation to Deedee is so muted. But Deedee's sexuality is so blatant that one cannot help speculating on Mr. A.'s role in its origins. At any rate, there seems no disputing that Pamela is, at age four, doing her part for the cause of family stability. It is hardly fortuitous that Mrs. A. dates the onset of her sexual revulsion to Pamela's birth. By relieving Mrs. A. of a large part of her sexual responsibilities she assists in releasing her mother's energies for group leadership tasks. She also guarantees herself continued freedom from the role as scapegoat in the process. In any event, given Roscoe's head start, and his suitability in the scapegoat assignment, it is unlikely that Pamela could have succeeded in dislodging Roscoe. As can be seen below, he has the role sewed up for some time to come.

The Victim as a Young Loser

Creating a Scapegoat: The Saga of Roscoe

The creation of an in-house scapegoat is not a simple matter. It proceeds in elaborate stages that require a multitude of daily repetitions, hourly reinforcements. It takes years to accomplish. While there are many subtleties to the manufacturing process, it may, for expository purposes, be roughly divided into two major phases. First, the premise of the expendability of one family member must be established; second, blame must be so convincingly ascribed to that member that it becomes incontestable family lore. Both tasks may be further subdivided into phases involving selection and induction. The expendable one is selected, and brought to the point of believing in his nonexistence; then, under the pressures of family crisis, he is reidentified as the vulnerable one and given the yoke of family guilt.

The sequence unfolds as follows: the family—primarily the parents—recognize early on the greater expendability of one of their children. Convinced of his superfluousness, his essential rolelessness, his lack of significance for them, they labor to make him believe it too. The achievement is a painfully grim one. It entails alienating the child from his internally experienced self and replacing that self with a sense of inner estrangement and distrust—estrangement from his own being, distrust of his own capacities and sensibilities. When the child is present his presence is not acknowledged. When he is gone he is not remembered. When he speaks he is not responded to. Ultimately, given enough time and diligent effort, he is mentally transformed into a nonentity: he does not exist for others or in his own right. His expendability is now manifest in his psychologic nonbeing. Jules Henry (1963) has called this the process of "pathogenic metamorphosis." It bears more than faint resemblance to brainwashing in the renunciation of self, the becoming nobody that leads to "pathological acquiescence," that "bizarre suicide of the soul" (Henry, 1963, p. 367) which is the ultimate in conformity.

The tacit belief in and overt evidence for nonexistence and acquiescence constitute a package in dehumanization. Yet this package is only a prelude to the second transformation that remakes the child, under the strains of family duress and threatened disintegration, the embodiment of collective guilt. The child who was once someone, and who was made into nothing—is now made into something he is not. And having been inessential, and hoping against hope for gratification and rekindled selfhood, he readily submits himself to greater humiliations. He acquiesces to the new designation. He does so on the premise that it is better to be somebody than nobody; that it is better to have unreal but attributed power than no existence. He believes that it is better to share the illusion of aliveness and interpersonal effectiveness—to be of some use—

than to be totally and irrevocably psychologically dead inside and out. Let us turn to a consideration of the particulars of Roscoe's transformations.

On Being an Out-Member of the In-Group: Selection

Roscoe was conceived and born behind the eight ball. He was an unplanned child. He was also unwanted. Most of all, he was a decided shock, and his birth may well have signaled the temporary cessation of a long-standing struggle between Mr. and Mrs. A. At a minimum, his arrival seems to have been an event that denied Mrs. A. a life-style to which she had long aspired. Her course was now redirected.

By early training Mrs. A. was cut out to be a housewife and mother. But, as with many American women, it was and is a destiny about which she has great ambivalence. The roots of the ambivalence are decidedly cultural. Mrs. A.'s mother was impelled to escape the house and go to work when her daughters were thirteen and ten and her son age five. She served as model for Mrs. A., as Sheila now replicates her mother's experience. Mrs. A.'s earliest and most basic training was in home maintaining and child care. Unfortunately, and as is the case today with Sheila, this early training was so intense, so all absorbing, of such long duration, and so blatantly by default—and not by choice—that concomitant with the development of fine skills in the role, she developed real antipathy for the activities.

She also developed an antipathy toward a mother whom she perceived as exploitative. Like her mother before, and Sheila after her, Mrs. A. experienced herself as drab, a spiritual spinster. By adolescence she found herself friendless, without girl companions or male dates. The upshot was an attempt at negative identity formation in adolescence. In the midst of rekindled oedipal feelings, and in the absence of a network of peers to influence her otherwise, she overthrew the feminine-maternal commitment and sought solace in a reactive identification with and allegiance to her father. She was his companion; she learned to navigate and operate boats, and became a mechanic. Her overt values were those of middle-class American men—devotion to the machine, defiance and conquest of nature. She met and married a mechanic, a man who raced motorcycles, a man of her father's persuasions. On the surface, it was a clear case of narcissistic object choice, but on the surface only.

In her reports of how she met Mr. A., Mrs. A. is quick to emphasize his emaciated look and her reaction of pity. The mate selection initially proved the best of all possible choices. Mrs. A. indulged her maternal tendencies, derived from pre-adolescent experience, and, at the same time, found a soul-mate in technological-machine worship. What was unforseen was that the match contained the seeds of continuing conflict.

The competition inherent in a narcissistic object choice erupted early. Mr. A. insisted his wife give up her active participation in boating. Mrs. A. did so reluctantly. Mrs. A., however, continued to work outside the home over her husband's protests. It was, he insisted, not financially necessary for her to do so. She risked the implicit assault on his sense of masculinity by working after the birth of each of her first three children. She utilized babysitters, child care centers, and nursery schools for working mothers to release her from the home. While still in her mid-twenties she had three children under four and was employed full time.

Deedee was nearly four, Sheila two, and Ricky barely six months old when Mrs. A. recognized she was pregnant for a fourth time. Needless to say, Roscoe was an unwelcome child. Mrs. A., who had worked through her marriage and first three children, reluctantly surrendered to maternal demands and returned to the home full time. The birth of Roscoe was a piece of reality that had negated Mrs. A.'s life-style and a fundamental aspect of her identity. Years later, Mrs. A. said of the mere eleven month discrepancy between Ricky and Roscoe's birthdates, that it was "like having twins." She was not drawing an idle comparison or talking figuratively. She stated that as soon as she could "reasonably" do so—that is, when Roscoe reached a developmental milestone such as sleeping through the night, or eating solid foods, she raised the boys as if they were twins. She began dressing them the same, feeding them the same foods, had them on the same schedules; she even admits to having reacted to their behaviors in the same fashion. And when Roscoe began to walk she began to measure them by the same yardsticks of achievement.

The Annihilation of Selfhood via Invidious Comparison

Mrs. A.'s claim that she dealt with the boys as if they were twins is certainly one possible interpretation. However, another is that, as the first male child, Ricky was born with a silver spoon in his mouth, while Roscoe was denied existence and invalidated from the outset. It was as if Mrs. A., deprived of a major piece of her own sought-after identity, responded in kind by denying Roscoe any opportunity to launch an identity of his own. A special irony attaches to this since Mr. A. claims that with Roscoe's arrival Mrs. A.'s employment was, for the first time, an economic necessity for the family.

To be reared in the long shadow of an older sibling, and to be quite literally evaluated in the light of his capacities—capacities which, all other things being equal, are bound to be considerably more advanced—is hardly an unusual circumstance. To be raised as a twin of an older sibling, who by definition and parental favor is certain to outstrip all but the most extreme bits of precociousness, is in degree, if not in quality, an entirely different matter. It portends an experience of self that is full of the most persistent failure; it offers a life comprised of almost relentless humiliation and a force feeding of felt incompetence that is nearly without interruption. Faith in one's capacities, sensibilities, and perceptions are bound to be undermined. The internal thermostat that guides self-regulatory feedback is thrown out of balance by public, parental evaluation. In Roscoe's case, the self was all but deprived the opportunity to develop. It was threatened with annihilation at its inception.

On Being Mistaken for Your Uncle

Still another not insignificant factor, which derives prominently from Mrs. A., should be cited in this regard. It seems clear from all presented that Mrs. A. is working out many of her central childhood conflicts. We noted vis-a-vis Sheila, as well as Deedee, that her history of employment reflected similar efforts at conflict resolution and need gratification. The same press can be discerned in her relationships with the boys. It is suggested that Mrs. A. treats her sons as if they were aspects of her younger brother. That she raises them as twins enhances the possibility that she may treat Ricky and Roscoe as "transferred sub-identities" from her younger sibling. The intense ambivalence she must have experienced toward her brother, whom she cared for throughout her post-latency and pubertal-teenage years, she can now manifest, in the form of a split transference toward her two sons. Ricky is seen as the demanding but competent, responsible, socially outgoing, achieving, favored part of her brother—the part that she sanctions and relates to warmly. Roscoe is preceived as the despised, resented, incompetent, annoying, and rejectable part. He is treated accordingly. He absorbs all the suppressed anger and neglect that had Mrs. A.'s brother as its original target. In yet an additional manner, Roscoe is never his own person. Again, he is effectively annihilated before the beginning of his time.

Choosing One's Mode of Suicide

Roscoe's alternatives are three: (1) He may surrender to namelessness and to a paradoxical existence as a nonentity, a resolution in favor of autism and psychosis. (2) He may pursue the path of buffoonery. Since he cannot hope to be competitive with Ricky, his efforts and presence are at best incidental and at worst a laughing stock.[6] With little effort he could play the clown. (3) He may reactively shape his identity in a direction that shows minimal overlap with that of his brother.[7] All three alternatives entail humiliation and acquiescence. They also evoke a strange kind of hope. As Henry (1963) points out, acquiescence "is presented together with an illusory promise of gratification, in order that the person . . . may stifle [his] sense of humiliation and alienation by presenting the promise [to himself] in a vivid and satisfying way. One might say that

6. See p. 89 for the baseball episode of visit number sixteen on May 1.
7. There is a small, but growing and quite provocative literature on the development of identities and role skills in the nuclear family. It demonstrates empirically that two persons in the same household generally do not occupy the same psychological space at the same point in time; they seek instead to maximize complementarity and differentness. For theoretical discussions of this point see Miller (1963) and Jackson (1965). For two recent examples of empirical research along these lines see Kent (1970) and Warren (1971).

in suicidal acquiescence illusory promises of gratification stand forth in the blinding glare of frightfulness" (p. 367).

In this oddest of ways, Roscoe emerges as the most optimistic and joyful of the A.'s. He succumbs to any hint of evoked or spontaneous interest in him, his existence, or his life space.[8] It matters not that his hopes are exploited and doomed to the keenest of disappointments time and again. He renews and revitalizes them each time. But the three alternatives do differ in the kind of renunciation of self they require. The first two, namelessness and buffoonery, negate dignity. The third permits its retention, albeit against formidable odds. Roscoe has chosen the third,[9] and it is perhaps because of this choice that outsiders—teachers and mental health professionals—accord him concern, warmth, and commitment. His unflagging dignity manages to shine through his most destructive and murderous of acts as a matter of self-preservation.

The Victim as an Artist and Naturalist

Perhaps Mrs. A. has stated it most accurately. She says she cannot understand how she could have raised two boys so identically and have had them turn out so differently. Roscoe has opted to become the negative image of Ricky. Where Ricky is masculine, Roscoe is not. Where Ricky is purposeful and industrious, Roscoe is not. Roscoe is not a hunter, not a fisherman, not an athlete. These domains, and all the middle-American value-orientations that belong to them—orientations that the A.'s endorse as signposts for directing their lives—belong to Ricky. Roscoe has instead, as a matter of displacement and survival, embraced the variants of these orientations. He is a naturalist, an "amateur ornithologist," a lover of all animals. He seeks to live with nature and not to subdue it through technology or the hunt. Indeed, he identifies himself

8. Again, the reader is referred to vignettes cited earlier. Roscoe's hopefulness and renewable trust may be evidenced in the thirteenth visit on March 4, when Roscoe gets enthused over visiting the naval engineering department with his mother and Ricky (pp. 131–33) and in the fifteenth visit of April 10, when Ricky dupes Roscoe through a show of interest in his school friends (pp. 86–87).

9. As we shall see later and as we have already recorded, not all professionals are of this opinion. Some mental health workers who lack the vantage point provided by the home visits are inclined to regard Roscoe as "psychotic" or, at best, "borderline psychotic."

with victims in the man-over-nature struggle. He fantasizes being a bird, collects and cherishes feathers, while Mr. A. and Ricky hunt and kill birds.

Roscoe is also an artist. He is fanciful and imaginative, attributes his teachers like but his parents cannot understand. He is creative and original in his drawing, and despite never having had lessons or encouragement, is fond of music. But in a family system geared to striving and "doing" such activities are not construed as work. Instead, they are seen as wasteful self-indulgences, or they are recognized as nonpurposful diletantisms. Roscoe is not a blamer. His family finds the attribution of responsibility and guilt pivotal to its equilibrium, but Roscoe alone, and with less reason, is open to trusting others and believing in their good intentions—an outlook which others in his family find well beyond their ken.

What identity Roscoe manages to salvage his family does not comprehend—which is to say that they do not merely fail to esteem it, they do not accord it meaningful existence. In this regard, once again, Roscoe is functionless and expendable. His being is superfluous. He becomes an alien in his own home —and thereby a ready object for disparagement. These factors form the substrata for his selection as in-house scapegoat.

The Victim as an Upstaged Artist

Persuading the Candidate: Inducing Alienation and the Maintenance of Selflessness

> The biosocial function of social climax is that by compelling social recognition of children it convinces the children they are real. What convinces Homo Sapiens that he exists is not that he thinks, but that other people think, that they think of him, and that they express this thought in social relations with him. (Henry, 1963, p. 372)

According to this definition Roscoe has no existence in the A. family, at least he has no reality consonant with his chosen, but deviant, identity. Three means, at a minimum, are employed to demoralize his reality. First, he is unreacted to on his terms—unseen, unheard, unrecognized. This message is steady and consistent: Roscoe is a nonentity. When he seeks to assert his presence it is as if he were not there. Fully 40 percent of his initiations are ignored by members of his family, a figure that more than doubles that encountered by any other. Is there a more direct training device for nonexistence?

Home Visit 14, March 27

The family had by now seated themselves for dinner. Mr. A., Mrs. A., Sheila, Deedee, and Pamela were all seated and about to start eating when Mr. A. inquired after the boys. Mrs. A. directed Sheila to get up and find them. Sheila went out the family room door and a few minutes later came back with Ricky trailing after her. Ricky took his place at the table. Mr. A. asked Sheila where Roscoe was, and she said she couldn't find him. The family then began to eat without Roscoe.

The family was about half-way through the meal when Roscoe came in the door. He was flushed and red, and dressed only in indoor clothes despite the chilly weather. When he came in he hesitated, did not say a word, did not explain where he had been, but looked quite guilty and frightened. Nobody said anything to him, and he stood, sort of lost, in the middle of the room . . . finally after some minutes he merely sat down in front of the TV table.[10] He stared down at his empty plate in silence. He did not eat until others had finished.

Everyone but Roscoe had gotten up and dispersed. Finally, Roscoe got up and left even though he had not yet eaten. Mrs. A. seemed to realize all of a sudden that he had not eaten and she called him. He appeared and Mrs. A. suggested

10. Ricky and Roscoe did not always eat at the main dining table with the rest of the family. About one-third of the time they were seated apart at TV tables. Sometimes both, sometimes Ricky alone with Roscoe at the table, sometimes Roscoe alone and not Ricky. No clear explanation ever emerged as to why, when, and how such arrangements were struck. During my first visit, Mrs. A. noted my surprise, and was quick to comment that the children rotated sitting away from the table as there wasn't enough room at the table for all the children. Therefore, one child each night would eat by himself. Mr. A. added that the children liked eating at the TV table, and it was something of a special treat. Nonetheless, Ricky and Roscoe were the only children so privileged during the home visits, and then only one-third of the time. Most often all A.'s managed to sit at the main table.

he now serve himself and sit down to eat. Roscoe did so. Mrs. A. said he could now sit at the dining room table . . . Roscoe, however, declined to do so, and without a word or comment promptly resat himself down at the TV table. It had been some twenty minutes since he came in. He had been totally silent during that time, and the only person to talk to him had been Mrs. A. when she called him back to the family room to serve himself.

A second and related technique for indoctrinating nonexistence is to disregard separations from the family, to treat them as if they did not occur, and therefore did not need bridging. The foregoing illustrates a blatant form of the device. More subtle forms exist.

A middle-American cultural ritual occurs during an evening meal time when the family is reunited after having gone their separate ways throughout the day. The meal becomes an arena for discussing and exchanging events. It is expected that one will inquire of another how things went, and the intent is more than mere expression of interest. The ritual serves to blunt separation experiences; it permits remerging and allows for future departures; it enhances mutual identification. The exchange of information, for example, will permit a father who is at work to evoke images of how and where his son is spending the day at school. To ask after daily incidents is to manifest empathic concern and a desire to be with, not separated from, the other.

In the A. family Roscoe has the status of outsider because alone among the A.'s nobody inquires how his day has gone.[11] It may be deduced that none of the A.'s cares to accompany him psychologically through those periods of time when he is off and away. His lack of meaningful identity is further underscored. Roscoe's existence is discredited in his acutal presence, and even in his absence, his family accords him no credence.

But there is always the danger that Roscoe's alien identity might find more than a toehold in the family. This is, of

---

11. The usual fate of Roscoe's efforts to convey some of the excitement from his world to his family has already been illustrated. See the vignettes from Home Visits 11 and 12, February 13 and 27, on pages 88 and 89, respectively.

course, particularly threatening to the A.'s, whose entire value system has already been upset by Mr. A.'s cardiac problem. By negating or obviating Roscoe's identity, the A.'s can reify their sense of control and their belief system. They therefore supplant Roscoe in his own territory by allowing Ricky to usurp credit and gain recognition for the skills that are uniquely Roscoe's. The effect is to strip Roscoe, however momentarily, of a last shred of appreciable individuality.

Home Visit 6, December 19

Ricky was showing me some Christmas cards he had received that day. Roscoe in the meantime seated himself at the piano and began playing some Christmas carols. He played without reference to music sheets, apparently by ear or from memory. He played a number of carols in their entirety. He noted that I was listening and played a medley of carols. Mrs. A. called people for dinner. Only Roscoe responded. Everyone else remained in and around the living room. Ricky almost seemed to be waiting until Roscoe left. He then sat down at the piano and began to play. His playing was far inferior to Roscoe's though I gather it takes no great great skill to play these carols. Ricky played the same Christmas carols Roscoe had, though not nearly as well. He had to refer to sheet music which had not been the case with Roscoe. Mrs. A. came in and called a second time for dinner, and people began to move to the family room.

After dinner the family returned to the living room. On the way Roscoe confided to me that he wanted to play the piano again, but that he really did not know how to read music. He had learned from watching his mother play. Mrs. A. began to play the piano first. However, Roscoe very much wanted to play carols and began after some time to ask for a turn. This prompted Ricky to agitate as well. Mrs. A. turned the piano playing over to Ricky and sat down next to the piano, watching Mr. A. play with Pamela and Sheila while she sang. Ricky played for some minutes. It was difficult for people to sing along because of his frequent errors and stoppages.

Finally Roscoe got his turn. Ricky turned the playing over to him at Mrs. A.'s request, and not without some obvious unhappiness. Ricky immediately slunk behind Mrs. A.'s chair

saying he would sing from there. He did not and Roscoe
asked that he really sing. He had only been miming doing so
. . . Ricky now stood up and again moved his mouth to Roscoe's playing, but I was unable to hear any singing. His attitude toward Roscoe was again condescending. He made comments to the effect that Roscoe was not playing properly,
playing too fast, and that Roscoe did not know what he was
doing, that everybody knew how this tune went and that Roscoe couldn't play it, but he, Ricky could. Roscoe tried valiantly to play throughout this avalanche of condescending remarks. Mrs. A. said nothing and did not intervene. Roscoe
finally gave up. He left the piano, and Ricky took over after
he left. Deedee and Mrs. A. continued to sing on as if nothing
happened. Roscoe had disappeared in the direction of the
family room.

Home Visit 13, March 14

As I took my usual seat next to the TV set and to the left of
the desk, Roscoe approached me in a very friendly manner.
He rummaged through the desk and produced a number of
drawings of whaling ships which he had drawn in the last few
weeks. They were quite elaborate. There were three or four
such drawings, almost all of them identical. Roscoe explained
that these were whaling ships and said that the sails were
rolled up, and explained to me some of the other details in
connection with the ships. I commented that I liked the drawings very much, that I found ships fascinating, and that I
thought Roscoe had really done an excellent job rendering
them.

Ricky, who had been on the other side of the room, apparently overheard some of my conversation with Roscoe. He immediately came running over and said that he had done some
sailing ships too, and his were larger and more elaborate than
Roscoe's. He produced a couple from the desk. They were indeed elaborate and larger, though they were less free and less
creative than Roscoe's. I told Ricky that I liked his drawings
also.

I asked the boys how they had become interested in doing
drawings of ships. Roscoe said that he had seen Tom in
school do some drawings of ships and that he started doing
these drawings in school. Mrs. A. endeavored at this point to

get the boys to wash their hands for dinner, to sit down at the table. Roscoe, however, did not move and for a moment or two stood around aimlessly not knowing what to do, trying to stay in my vicinity, and yet feeling that he should leave and wash up . . . he pursued the conversation with me . . . He said he had seen Tom do these drawings in school, and he had decided he wanted to do them, and he had begun doing them at home . . . Ricky had then begun to draw ships too. Ricky's attempts, he made clear, had followed his own.

Home Visit 14, March 27

. . . as I came back into the family room I noted that one of Ricky's drawings of ships was hanging on the wall behind Mr. A.'s chair at the dining room table. It was a drawing of a ship on a piece of paper which I would estimate was 40 by 30 inches, and Ricky had more or less filled the entire paper with his picture of a ship. It was done in elaborate detail, and more compulsively than Roscoe's of two weeks earlier. In some ways it was also more ambitious than Roscoe's attempts, yet it was not nearly as good. The drawing was awkward, the masts were akilter and the perspective was often distorted and poor. Roscoe's drawings had been more accurate in terms of dimensions, if less challenging of issues of perspective. Ricky had tried to deal with some graphic issues Roscoe could not even try. Roscoe's drawings were not anywhere in evidence on the wall.

Later, I inquired of the boys why Roscoe didn't have a drawing of his on the wall . . . Ricky didn't reply and Roscoe only shrugged his shoulders. Mr. and Mrs. A. overheard my question, and I think it jarred them some. Mr. A. then excused himself, saying he had to shave and get ready to leave.

The Victim as a Young Killer

Collective Guilt and the Ascription of Blame: Propagation of a Family Myth

Having made the determined effort to persuade Roscoe that he was not what he seemed to be to himself, it remained necessary for the A.'s to persuade him that he is something he is not. With the creation of this misidentity the metagenesis to scapegoat is complete. The final bit of transfiguration involves the parturition and maturation of a central, organizing family myth—a myth that is predicated on Roscoe's special vulnerabilities and a sense of mutually shared culpability by family members. The myth forms the crux of the A. family homeostasis, and is the final, if supplemental, solution to their problems with death and dying.

Long ago Freud asserted in *Totem and Taboo* (1913) that in an ante-historical time "psychic reality, concerning whose structure there is no doubt . . . coincided with actual reality" (p. 161). This view, in concert with his inclination to construe violence as the repressed underpinning of social action (Reiff, 1961), led him to suppose "that once upon a time [man] had a primeval father and killed him" (Freud, 1939, p. 159). Once accomplished, man never ceased to regret it. The act of collective parricide—the supreme crime—begets collective remorse and guilt.

It matters not that Freud's anthropology is outdated and/or wrongheaded, or that his proclivity for identifying the point of social origin as father-murder to the exclusion of other possibilities—brother-murder, infant-murder, son-murder— serves to expose his scientism as narrow mythology (Reiff, 1961); he has succeeded in disclosing an abiding theme for humanity, and his speculations retain a pungent topicality for a family like the A.'s.

One need not conjecture about the supposed prehistoric identity of the A.'s psychic reality; the actual reality is genuine and contemporary enough for them. The demise of father is all too imminent. Freud's proposed myth of a terrified, guilt-ridden human existence has a palpable reality for the A.'s. It causes them to contrive their own myth. Succinctly stated, the myth is that Roscoe is a potentially dangerous killer—a destroyer of life—whose every move requires constant watchfulness. Most heinously he could perpetrate the death of his father.

Developmental Vulnerabilities: Setting the Historical Stage

Roscoe does not earn the protagonist's role in the family myth solely on the basis of his expendability in other regards. This is, of course, the most compelling factor, but the distinction of being the family "heavy" is awarded to him on grounds of developmental and circumstantial vulnerabilities as well. The critical year appears to have been Roscoe's fifth.

Already a well established nonentity by age five, Roscoe undergoes a series of stresses which heighten his susceptibility to psychic disorganization and desperate, pathological acquiescence in the home. The year is ushered in by the birth of Pamela; Mrs. A. is separated from Roscoe for the first time during her maternity stay in the hospital. Following her return home, Roscoe, who had little enough attention from his parents, finds himself even further dispossessed. Within the year he loses an even more substantial piece of Mrs. A.; she returns to work full time for the first time in five years. Her return is made possible by Ricky's entrance into first grade, and Roscoe's beginning kindergarten. Because kindergarten is a half-day program, Roscoe spends afternoons with a baby-sitter. His brother, however, from whom he had never before been separated, attends first grade full days.

Roscoe's loss is, therefore, manifold, as is his encounter with strange caretakers. He loses two steady alter-egos—mother and brother—and in a single stroke inherits a baby-sitter and a school teacher. Instead of relating to only four siblings, he now must deal with thirty classmates as well. Many of these stresses are part and parcel of the normal transition from home to public school, and, as such, are not terribly unusual for any five year old, though they may differ in specific particulars. On the other hand, they do suggest a modicum of vulnerability for all children who make such transitions. For Roscoe, who proceeds without an identity he can comfortably call his own, the hazard is greater. But, other things being equal, it should not prove unnavigable.

Two events of traumatically explosive force are probably decisive in making Roscoe's situation decidedly less than equal. First, Mr. A. enters the hospital for a hernia operation, suffers cardiac arrest, spends weeks in the hospital and months recuperating at home. Then, shortly after the father's hospitalization, Roscoe is badly scratched and frightened by a dog who attacks him. The assault warrants a visit to the emergency service of the very hospital in which his father is staying. One need not be a fanatic believer in the universality of the oedipal crisis to appreciate the significance of these events in their contextual surroundings. While precise reconstruction of these events and their psychological meanings cannot be recaptured, some conjectures seem warranted.

Reconstructing the "Crime"

Roscoe, a boy of five, who is likely competitive with and resentful of a highly competitive father (*a*) loses his major props, his mother and brother, (*b*) suffers displacement via the birth of Pamela, (*c*) encounters strange people in a strange setting— school—and, (*d*) sees the stability of his world crumble with the devastating incapacitation of his father. With the usual sources of surcease unavailable, Roscoe is left with a nagging sense of his own worthlessness and guilt. His phase-specific wishes toward his father, mother, or siblings are "realized" and repaid in kind. He is clawed by a Great Dane, and sent to the same fateful place—the hospital. The "talion principle" was seldom more literally played out. The deduction of self as a dangerous, malevolent force, and the experience of guilt and retribution are facile. Roscoe is ready to believe. What is more, he is not alone in this regard.

Each A. shares the same premise about himself in his own way. Each considers his own wishes in regard to Mr. A. somehow implicated in the father's heart arrest. The burden of felt guilt resides in all—most especially, one might presume in Ricky, who by age and developmental phasing is Roscoe's closest match. Nonetheless, it is Roscoe who is ultimately the repository of collective terror, who carries the mantle of family guilt, who stands as the accused, the perilous, the accountable one. As if waiting anonymously in the wings for an opportunity, Roscoe, at age five, sheds his nonexistence for a purposive identity. He dons the garb of killer and destroyer, and accepts the jeers of his family. By the time of the home visits some three to four years later, he has had plenty of practice and has the role down to a 'T'. By the age of eight he is typecast for life. Such is the beauty of a family myth.

Indoctrinating the "Killer"

According to Ferreira (1963), "family myth" refers to:

> . . . a series of fairly well integrated beliefs shared by all family members, concerning each other and their mutual position in the family life, beliefs that go unchallenged by everyone involved in spite of the reality distortions which they may conspicuously imply. It should be noticed that although the family myth is part of the family image, it often differs from the "front" or social facade that the family as a group attempts to present to outsiders. Instead the family myth is much a part of the way the family appears to its members, that is, a part of the *inner image* of the group, an image to which all family members contribute and, apparently, strive to preserve. In terms of the family inner image, the family myth refers to the identified roles of its members. It expresses shared convictions about the people and their relationship in the family, convictions to be accepted *a priori* in spite of the flagrant falsification which they may represent. (p. 457–58)

The behaviors and attitudes of the A.'s are consistent with the foregoing. To the exterior world they seek to present a public image of solid family, American virtue, and social normalcy. They would be horrified at any public disclosure or discovery that they possessed within their midst a potential killer. They would be equally appalled at the notion that they deliberately construed one of their own as a destructive force. Indeed, they would among themselves most likely refuse to acknowledge the existence of this belief system or the possibility that they scapegoat a member of the family. After all, they insist Roscoe has never been a behavior problem in the home. The myth ensures he will never be one. By fighting private as well as public revelation, they guarantee the continued life of the myth.

In the A. family, however, the myth is given the lie by the undiluted extremism in the contents of ascribed roles and prescribed behaviors, as well as by the fact that outside the home Roscoe enacts the very malevolence that is attributed to him by his family. The give away is that it is a malevolence he never manifests in their presence.

Like all such myths, this one serves the interest of family

stability, protecting the system against the threat of the chaos engendered by Mr. A.'s precarious physical state and counterphobic style. And because it prevents the family from destroying itself the myth is endorsed by everyone and surrounded by an aura of sacredness which discourages its challenge or investigation. The circle of believers captured by its contagion include its victim and scapegoat. By age nine, Roscoe is as convinced of its veracity as are the others. At least he no longer protests if indeed he ever did. It does not matter that the accusations and implied motives are mirages unbuttressed by reality; they are so relentless as to make participation mandatory.

Home Visit 1, November 14

Roscoe continued to push the airplane around the floor. Eventually he stopped and began fiddling with the fuselage of the plane, probing inside the model for the rubber band. He finally got hold of the rubber band and tried to pull it but at this point Ricky, who had been watching for some minutes, could no longer contain himself, and he blurted out, "What are you doing, Roscoe?" Roscoe tried to explain what he was doing but Ricky got down on the floor with Roscoe, grabbed the plane from him, pushed Roscoe aside, saying he wanted that rubber band in the plane and he wanted to seal and repair the fuselage. He said he would do this so destructive people could not get at the rubber band. Roscoe on two occasions made gestures to get the plane back from Ricky. On one occasion he murmured that the plane was as much his as Ricky's. No avail. Ricky simply pushed him aside, shoving his hands away, ignoring what he said. Roscoe at this point got up and began wandering aimlessly about, his hands in his pockets.

Home Visit 2, November 21

Roscoe wandered in and out of the family room and finally sat down next to me and showed me a bow and arrow set . . . He showed me the set and told me that the bow was a fortytwo pound bow and that while he liked to use the set, he had difficulty pulling the string of the bow back sufficiently to get much distance. He said he could not pull it back further than his nose, and he should be pulling it to his ear. He indicated where the arrow would sit, and attempted to pull the string back as far as he could. At this point, Ricky came in and began watching. Ricky was still wearing his safety-patrol belt from school, and it had, at 6:30 P.M., the aspect of a badge or uniform. He watched Roscoe explain the bow to me. Ricky then proceeded to demonstrate that he could pull the bow back further than Roscoe. He told me that Roscoe had broken a number of arrows and had broken the best arrow.

Home Visit 2, November 21

Roscoe showed me his sister Sheila's terrarium with assorted plants growing in it and he began to explain it to me. Ricky came over and corrected Roscoe a number of times. Then he cautioned Roscoe. He told Roscoe not to put the terrarium too close to the edge of the desk and said that he should hold it extra carefully so he would not drop it. It might, said Ricky, fall all over the floor if Roscoe weren't careful.

Home Visit 8, January 16

Ricky came bouncing up the stairs and shouted to Roscoe and asked Roscoe what he had done with the drawing paper and water colors. Roscoe indicated that they were on his bed. Mrs. A. then chastised Roscoe for having taken the pad of watercolor paper and set of paints to school with him. She said it was especially unnecessary for him to have taken the paints. He had only wanted to show them off, and he had broken a jar of red. It was lucky, she said, he hadn't broken them all.

Ricky appeared a few minutes later from downstairs and reported that he had nothing to paint with. Roscoe, he said, had lost the brush that goes with the paint set. Mrs. A. said Roscoe was irresponsible and careless and could not be trusted. Roscoe said nothing and did not acknowledge the comment his mother had made.

Home Visit 10, January 30

Mrs. A. talked sharply a couple of times to Roscoe. It was about having the dog, Flip, up on the chair next to him. The dog, she said, was shedding and had sharp claws. He was tearing the furniture, ruining it all. Mrs. A. said Roscoe was teaching the dog habits that were damaging and costly.

Home Visit 14, March 27

Roscoe got up at one point and went to the other side of the room and took out a large map of Hawaii which he started to unroll on the floor. Mr. A. said he should be careful, that it was a good map, from the *National Geographic*, and that he could easily tear it. Mrs. A. said he should not put it on the floor—it might get stepped on. Roscoe put the map away, leaning it up against the wall, and returned to his seat in front of the TV.

Home Visit 15, April 10

Ricky began inquiring about Roscoe's crab. Apparently Roscoe had found a crab near the house and had brought it home. Ricky asked about it in an initially friendly vein; he asked where Roscoe had found it, how Roscoe was keeping it, whether he had changed its water regularly, etc. Roscoe responded warmly and enthusiastically to his brother's questions. Ricky seemed to be expressing genuine interest in something Roscoe had done. Ricky then supplied the crusher. He had fooled Roscoe as well as myself. Ricky announced that the crab was in a bucket, but the bucket was not only full of water, but was filled with sand as well, and that the crab was going to die. Roscoe, he said, was killing the crab. Roscoe looked bewildered. How, he wanted to know, had the sand gotten into the bucket. Ricky said that was why he was asking him all these questions and that he knew how the sand got in there. He said that Roscoe put the sand in there and that he had done it in order to kill the crab. Roscoe denied the accusation. He said it must have been someone else. He mentioned a girl in the neighborhood named Holly. She might have done it. Ricky, however, was adamant. He continued to accuse Roscoe of deliberately attempting to kill the crab with sand. Roscoe looked hurt, frightened, and confused. He no longer defended himself. He looked from one family member to another. No one at the table said a word, except Ricky. He was now relentless. He pointed out the crab needs clear, fresh water and that sand would invariably kill the crab since the crab depended on breathing through its gills much like fish, and sand would get in the gills and the crab would suffocate. No one questioned his claim.

Under the barrage Roscoe did not respond, but now simply withdrew, and conversation ceased with Ricky's final and seemingly informed attack. Mr. and Mrs. A. had listened in silence along with the rest of the family. Finally, Mr. A. said to Roscoe he should take the crab back to the creek and get rid of it. That if it were kept in the house a kid or an animal might get at it and kill it. He said the crab was a mean looking thing, and ugly. He said that Roscoe was "supposed to be the animal lover" and "the nature lover" and that he should know better. Pamela picked up the theme. The crab, she chanted, was a mean thing, an ugly thing, and had biting claws, and that "Roscoe should kill it." She chanted on about this in the background of new topics of conversation . . .

Mr. A. called Roscoe back into the family room and told him he should get rid of that crab right now. Roscoe disappeared into the basement and a few moments later reappeared, bucket in hand. Mr. A. said that every minute he kept the crab around he increased its chances of dying, that it was Roscoe's responsibility, and if anything happened to it Roscoe would be at fault. Roscoe said nothing.

A few minutes later Roscoe could be seen from the windows of the family room walking with the bucket in his hand back toward the creek. Mr. A. at this point reiterated what a terrible looking creature that crab was, and how it would definitely perish unless it were taken back to its natural habitat. He said it had been foolish of Roscoe to bring it home. All animals perish outside their natural environment. All animals need their natural surroundings and die if away from home. What had possessed Roscoe he couldn't understand—especially putting sand in the bucket. Crazy!

Mr. A. then fell silent for a few minutes, and the two of us watched Roscoe through the window as he trudged back toward the creek. Suddenly, Mr. A. broke the silence by announcing that he would be entering the hospital on May 3—three weeks hence—for heart surgery. He said it would sure seem funny being away from home and work for months. He estimated he'd be in the hospital until July. He probably wouldn't work until the end of August.

Home Visit 17, May 18

Mr. A. was in the hospital during this visit. He had undergone surgery just days before . . . I asked Mrs. A. how Mr. A. was doing. She said noncommitally that he seemed to be doing "fine." She hoped he'd be home soon. Before my next visit, maybe.

Mrs. A. apologized for the chaos. She explained they were planning to go up to the hospital. She would see Mr. A. and might be able to persuade the nurses to let the kids visit him too. She had, therefore, bought hamburgers at a local drive-in. Dinner was to be brief and easy. They had just been shopping for shoes and clothes for the children so they would look nice in case they got to see their father. Mrs. A. looked haggard.

Ricky came in carrying his new shoes with him. He sat down at a TV table and proceeded to put on his new shoes which were shiny black and pointed. Roscoe also had a pair of shoes, but his were suede and light. Ricky immediately cautioned him about getting them wet. He could not do this because they were suede. Ricky concluded aloud that Roscoe was sure to ruin them. He was *so* careless. Roscoe put his new shoes on.

Sheila brought in the hamburgers and french fries. Deedee set places at the table. She set places for Ricky and Roscoe at the TV tables. Everyone seated themselves in their usual places to eat, and all began unwrapping hamburgers. Now the two boys hesitated. They seemed unsure whether they wanted to eat at the TV tables or at the dining room table. Ricky picked up his hamburgers and french fries and started toward his father's vacant place at the table two or three times. After deliberation and open conflict, however, he declared aloud that he was going to sit at the TV table. Finally he sat down and began eating at the TV table.

Roscoe, however, had also gotten up and with considerably less deliberation went over and sat in his father's chair to the left of Deedee at the table. There was silence. Roscoe had effected the move with haughty bravado. Deedee spoke first. She demanded with evident anger that Roscoe sit properly in his seat. He had rocked forward on the two front legs of the chair in order to lean over the table and eat. Deedee commented that the "chair is too big for you." Roscoe fixed her with a disdainful look, almost as if he were peering down his nose at her. He tipped his head back and looked at her with a hateful stare. He did not correct his position but continued to sit forward in the chair so that it balanced on its two front legs. Deedee said nothing. Sheila was busy helping Pamela eat, cutting up her hamburger, and generally mothering her. Mrs. A. continued to eat in silence. Everyone was silent.

Then Sheila asked to see Ricky's new shoes and Roscoe's new shoes. Ricky twisted around in his chair and lifted his feet in the air so all could see. Sheila said they looked nice. Roscoe showed his shoes. Sheila commented that they seemed "too large for him." Mrs. A. also said they looked too big. She got up and felt the toes of Roscoe's shoes and finally said, "They look like they gave us the wrong size, but I guess they are the ones you wanted." Ricky commented that they were suede and Roscoe was sure to ruin them in no time flat. Mrs. A. agreed. But, she said, they were what he wanted. She told Roscoe to sit up straight now and with some vigorous irritation said that if he couldn't manage to sit right and keep his feet on the floor in front of him he would have to move his seat. He didn't belong where he was anyhow, she added. Roscoe didn't move. The rest of the meal was consumed in silence.

Ricky: The Brother as Superego

In all these vignettes, not only is onus of destructiveness placed exclusively on Roscoe, but Ricky consistently has a major and licensed role as prosecutor. It is in the nature of a family myth that, on first glance, the myth appears to be focused primarily on a given member of the family—in this case, Roscoe as usurper and annihilator. In reality, however, the emotional factors that prompt and sustain the myth cannot properly be thought of as having their locus or expression in one individual—a whole system of family role designations is invoked. If there is a role slot for scapegoat, or victim, one may be assured the complementary role of attacker exists. Ricky is the sanctioned attacker, the elected representative of moral right and social order—in a word, the family's district attorney, the active, operative component of a collective superego. And he is a skillful and punitive agent. He holds parricide in check. By the same token, Roscoe is the repository of family transgression, aggression, destructive impulsivity. He embodies the paternal death wish. To him devolves the collective guilt. His acquiescence to this role and his metamorphosed identity make it possible for other family members to get off "scott free"; they can disown their share of self-recrimination over Mr. A.'s plight to the extent that Roscoe can be counted on and made to absorb it, and to the degree that Ricky can succeed in driving it home. In this regard, Ricky's acquiescence is every bit as great as Roscoe's, though it is not usual to ascribe acquiescence to the superordinate status. Nonetheless, Ricky has as little choice in the matter as Roscoe. Indeed, all the A.'s are unwitting, ultra-conformists who, in their collective fright, caricature the salient features of cultural codes—codes that all too often prove lethal.

VI
Sequelae

Chapter 11

The Immediate Aftermath

Shortly after the last home visit, Mr. A. returned to work and resumed virtually all his usual activities. He repaired motorcyles at night and raced them on weekends. He hunted, fished, played baseball. Within a matter of months, Mrs. A. was pregnant. Contacts with the parents became fewer as casework with Mr. and Mrs. A. had never really resumed to any extent following the initiation of the home visits. They came to meetings infrequently, and they remained silent and guarded in what hours they had with their social worker. Most often they did not come. Eventually, they stopped coming altogether.

Nonetheless, Roscoe did better in the child guidance center Day Treatment setting. His rage and aggressive outbursts subsided over the year the home visits were made. While his therapy hours never became greatly focused, they were often the arena for what hostile acting out he did. It was as if he succeeded in channeling most of his anger into the office. He returned to public school at about the time his father returned to work. He had been in the child guidance center school more than two years.

For some months, Roscoe continued to return for outpatient therapy appointments at the center, but transportation problems made his visits sporadic. He had to come three miles for his sessions. Buses ran infrequently, schedules were badly timed, and the winter months provided prohibitive weather conditions. Eventually, outpatient treatment was terminated. Because reports from the public school were consistently good, and because Roscoe's therapist was leaving the state, transfer of treatment was deemed unnecessary and unfeasible. He was ten years old at the time.

A Month of Wednesdays

One Year Later: Treatment Renewed

Within a year, Roscoe was back at the Yankee Child Guidance Center. He referred himself. He phoned from school during a lunch hour and said he needed help. He said he had been stealing, fighting, "running around with a bad crowd." Sometimes, he said, he did not go home. I arranged to see him that afternoon.

When he got to my office, he told me he had recently been arrested and detained by the Youth Bureau of the Police Department. He said he had been shoplifting and was apprehended in a local department store attempting to conceal a record and some candy as he left the store. He said he needed treatment and asked for regular appointments with me. I agreed to see him on a makeshift basis.

Arrangements could only be tentative because there were problems. First, transportation difficulties persisted. Roscoe lacked money and reliable busing. Second, his parents were unaware that he had reinitiated contact with the center. He did not feel they would be receptive to his renewed desire for treatment. His father, he said, would simply be opposed. Besides, the timing was poor. Roscoe explained that his mother was expecting still another child—her sixth. She was due any day.

I indicated that while I would be glad to meet with Roscoe, it would be necessary for me to work out plans with his parents as well. Roscoe agreed this was necessary but was skeptical of the outcome. I told him I would call his parents after he had broached matters with them, and that, in the interim, I would plan on seeing him weekly.

Roscoe spoke to his mother. He reported that his parents were expecting my call but that he was not hopeful. Mr. A. had received the news from Mrs. A. with a series of negative statements about the futility of the "talking methods" at the child guidance center. But because of Roscoe's involvement with the Youth Bureau, Mr. A. had indicated a readiness to talk with me.

I called the A.'s during a noon hour because Roscoe had

informed me his father was now working the afternoon shift and did not report for work until 3:15 P.M. Mr. A. answered the phone himself and explained, without so much as an inquiry on my part, that he had fully meant to call me sometime during the prior two-week period. Things, however, had been extremely hectic. Mrs. A. was to go to the hospital imminently, and with her being in the final stages of pregnancy Mr. A. had had to "take over" a lot of her activities. He had found no opportunity to call me. He said, in reply to my question, that he and Mrs. A. would be "real glad" to meet with me, but that things would have to wait since Mrs. A. was due "any minute." We would have to "wait until things settle a little." I said I understood, and that I would keep in touch with the situation via Roscoe whom I would be seeing weekly.

Despite his parting remark that he was "real glad" I had called, Mr. A. was quite cool and uninvolved over the phone. He did not sound pleased to hear from me and appeared impatient to get off the line. I neglected to ask why he had "been meaning to call" me for two weeks, but merely surmised that it had to do with Roscoe's apprehension by the police. In spite of his claim, I did not believe he would ever have called me, and I felt convinced he would dismiss my call from his mind within moments of hanging up the receiver.

Public School

For the next four weeks I met with Roscoe. He made it to the center with the assistance of his teachers. I had contacted them and, with Roscoe's endorsement, had enlisted their help. They proved more than ready to take turns as his chauffeur for they had been both concerned and puzzled by Roscoe's behavior in school. Most of all they were terrified of him.

Mrs. R. was Roscoe's regular classroom teacher; Mrs. D. was the "crisis teacher" in the building. They reported that Roscoe was capable of better than grade-level work, but that his motivation was variable. Some days he would not try and those were the days when Roscoe was invariably in trouble. They were the days "he did not belong in school." Both teachers described him as "extremely nervous." He used pencils or fingers to tap incessantly on his desk. Moreover, his dress was "peculiar." He wore a uniform characterized by "black shirt, black pants, black boots, and black leather jacket" to school day after day. Weeks would go by with not the slightest change in costume. Mrs. R. reported that she was "frankly" scared of him: "I am afraid to turn my back on him in class. I can always hear him tapping. I feel he may explode at any moment, and I don't want to have my back to him." Mrs. D. agreed. She explained that Roscoe was trying desperately to ingratiate himself with a "delinquent crowd" and that he would do anything to impress them. This had led to the recent episodes of stealing. She said, "He can't be trusted for a minute, and is capable of any action."

The teachers reported, and Roscoe confirmed, that he had stolen in school and in the neighborhood. On one occasion, he entered a house in which no one was home and made off with a motorcycle jacket. He wore it around the neighborhood, and so was caught some days later. Charges were not pressed. On another occasion, he apparently damaged a storm door as he tried to break in. In school, he was discovered with $40 on his person shortly after Mrs. R. had reported it missing from her purse. Mrs. R. said this was "a boy walking a tight rope" and that she was literally frightened of what he might do. Mrs. D. added it was sad.

Both noted that Roscoe was a contrast to his brother Ricky. Roscoe seemed the brighter, more talented, more creative and sensitive of the two; Ricky the more predictable, reliable, and conscientious. Mrs. R. expressed amazement at the difference. Roscoe, she commented, had a habit of calling her at eleven or twelve at night on some pretext or other, "just to say hello" and to chat, or to wish her "happy holiday." Ricky was much too sensible to do something like that. He was also less needful. Because he was so "needful," Mrs. R. and Mrs. D. took turns driving Roscoe to his appointments.

Sessions with Roscoe

I met with Roscoe four times over the next four weeks. He was friendly, highly talkative, and quite outgoing. He was also nervous and oddly cautious in his gregariousness. He spoke in a rush of words, in stumbling, driven, halting fashion. He became embarrassed and red-faced, but continued to press his words forward. For the first time in my contacts with him, a speech hesitation was marked. His teachers had already alerted me to Roscoe's recently acquired difficulty in this regard, but it was only in my second session with him that I encountered it in manifest form. We talked about it a good deal. Roscoe complained that it annoyed him greatly in school. He felt it made him an object of ridicule. It was, he said, especially bad when he was very nervous. He denied being anxious in the office with me; yet, his speech hesitation did not abate.

During those four weeks Roscoe and I also spent time reviewing treatment prospects. It was agreed we would continue to meet weekly until we had an opportunity to finalize plans with his parents. Roscoe expressed a hope for more frequent contacts—maybe twice a week. He responded positively to the possibility of family sessions when I suggested them as an alternative or supplement to individual contacts. But he registered doubts about his parents' willingness to cooperate.[1]

Other topics we talked over included school, friends and shoplifting, Deedee, his mother's pregnancy, and his father's motorcycle racing. School he described as a persistent trial. He could not sit still, found it hard to concentrate, was always nervous. His restlessness resulted in his frequent exclusion from the classroom. Roscoe recognized the good intentions of his teachers, but said he felt they did not like or trust him. He denied hurting other children, and ventured that he had made strides in the realm of self-control.

He described his friends in admiring tones. He was clearly in awe of them and in great need of currying their favor. He did not feel they were "bad" kids, but he did acknowledge that it was with them that he ran into trouble. Roscoe admitted quite freely that he had shoplifted and stolen money and possessions on a number of occasions. However, he could offer no details about the reasons or compulsions for such stealing. He was judicious in his care not to implicate partners

1. Yet Mr. A. had already given my name to the Youth Bureau. The Youth Bureau called me to verify my involvement following my second contact with Roscoe. I verified it to the extent that I could. I explained the unsettled, somewhat tentative prospective plans for treatment. The Youth Bureau seemed satisfied. When I told Roscoe about my talk with the police, he was skeptical. He reiterated his lack of faith regarding parental follow-through. He was, of course, all too correct in his judgment.

or friends. Roscoe talked most often about his sister Deedee and his relationship with her. This was something of a surprise in the light of the sparseness of recorded interchange between Deedee and Roscoe during the year of home visits. Times had changed now, and he and Deedee were perpetually at odds. They could not so much as walk past each other without a fight erupting. She was constantly poking and pushing him. The children had adjoining rooms, and at night he claimed to overhear Deedee taunt Sheila. Roscoe said she would take off her bra and show her breasts to Sheila while mocking Sheila's undeveloped state. Roscoe said it made him furious to hear this or see Sheila hurt. He never mentioned his relationship with Ricky, nor did he comment on how Ricky was doing.

It seemed relatively apparent that his empathic concern for Sheila and his antagonism toward Deedee were predicated on a perceived parallelism in relationships. I had the sense that at some unarticulated level Roscoe viewed his status vis-a-vis Ricky as similar to Sheila's with Deedee. I alluded to possible parallels on a number of occasions during Roscoe's visits, but he never followed the lead.

Roscoe did talk a bit about his mother and father. Mr. A., he reported, was extremely busy—working, repairing and maintaining motorcycles at night, and racing them weekends. His father's health seemed fine. No problems followed the surgery. Roscoe did a number of drawings of motorcycles as he discussed his father. The drawings were quite good, and we hung them up. Mrs. A., on the other hand, he described as always tired. She had left work some weeks earlier and was impatiently awaiting her baby. Roscoe talked about her, her pregnancy, and the prospect of a new baby without enthusiasm. He said he was not sure his mother, or for that matter anyone in the family except Sheila, really wanted another baby.

During the fourth hour, Roscoe reported that his mother had delivered the previous night. The baby was a girl and had been named Marsha.

Early Denouement: Incompletion of Treatment

After those four sessions, I saw Roscoe one more time. It was a difficult last meeting, and our parting was singularly distressing. His good-bye was given in silence. He was keenly disappointed and angry at my incapacity to persuade his father.

These events led up to the abortion of treatment: A few days after Roscoe informed me of the birth of his sister Marsha, I phoned Mr. A. We chatted at length about Marsha's birth, the growing size of his family, and Mrs. A.'s health. Mother and child, he said, were doing fine, and both were due home from the hospital in a day or so. We talked of getting together to discuss treatment plans sometime in the next two weeks. Mr. A. was reluctant. He did not complain that this was too soon as I thought he might. Instead, he objected in principle to meeting at all. I emphasized my feeling that the need was great. When Mr. A. continued to demure, I reminded him that I had been meeting with Roscoe for a month, and that I did not feel it fair to continue without explicit planning. Mr. A. sounded startled. He had not remembered that Roscoe was coming to see me and seemed genuinely taken aback. It was necessary for me to recount to Mr. A. our noon hour conversation of some weeks earlier. I told him that since Roscoe had been driven to appointments by his teachers, and since Roscoe came after school while Mr. A. was at work, I could see how he might be unaware of Roscoe's meetings with me. He had, after all, been involved minimally. I pressed the need for his involvement at this point.

Mr. A. immediately raised questions about fees. How much, he wanted to know, was this process going to cost him? I told Mr. A. that we needed to decide this mutually and with full discussion. I again urged we meet. Mr. A. acquiesced. We set a meeting time, one week after Mrs. A.'s arrival home. My next scheduled appointment with Roscoe was to precede that date by two days. He failed to arrive for the hour and did not phone with an explanation.

Mr. and Mrs. A. were on time for our meeting. I went to the center lobby to escort them back to my office. Mr. A. was engaged in an argument with the clerk behind the reception desk. He was saying that he could not possibly afford to come in or have Roscoe come in. It was, he said, entirely too much of a financial burden. Four dollars a week was "beyond question." Mr. A. was quite angry and flushed, and the clerk looked to me pleadingly for relief. I said hello to the A.'s and led them back to my office. Mr. A. greeted me with, "I can tell you right now I can't afford it."

Once in the office, we exchanged pleasantries, and Mrs. A. held forth for a time on the wonders of Marsha. Mrs. A. looked fatigued, and ended her discourse rather abruptly with a sigh. She was virtually silent thereafter.

Early in the meeting, I attempted to take up the whole issue of finances. In the face of Mr. A.'s insistence that he could not "afford" four dollars a week—a figure based on re-duced fees calculated on a sliding scale—I suggested the possi-bility of special aid which would reduce the cost to nothing. The special aid required a financial statement from the A.'s. Mr. A. objected vehemently. Nobody, he said, was going to snoop around in his financial affairs. He didn't want us med-dling around in his life, and he certainly was not going to ac-cept charity. I attempted to reassure Mr. A. that I knew his heart surgery and convalescence had drained the family's re-sources. Mr. A., however, remained adamant. He would not accept handouts, and he could not afford the cost of Roscoe's treatment.

I wondered with the A.'s if financial cost was the only or even primary cost they feared would result from treatment. I suggested they were concerned that treatment might incur psychological costs in the anxiety, the discomfort, and the pains of looking at some hard realities. They might be worried that the process would require readjustments in established patterns of behavior and interaction and would therefore en-tail degrees of stress. Mrs. A., speaking for the first time in a while, said this could be so. I said that in all honesty I could not guarantee the A.'s that the process would be easy or pain-less, but I said that it usually cost something to gain some-thing. I told them I understood their apprehension in view of the duress the family had been under for years, and I hear kened back to Mr. A.'s heart condition, his open heart surgery, the family's terror, and my visits to their home. I told them what I felt their long standing fears were already costing—especially in terms of Roscoe's welfare.

I reviewed with them my construction of their long-standing thanatophobia and told them I thought their struggle with death-terror had become their accustomed way of family life. I conjectured that it dated at least from Mr. A.'s cardiac arrest, if not even earlier, and reiterated that I could understand their fear and reluctance now. It was to no avail; I lost them right there. My timing was poor, and my declaration too frontal, too blunt. At another time, in another place, under other circumstances, it might not have proved so. And as things turned out, my efforts were misplaced and premature by only a matter of weeks. Just why this was so will become clear momentarily. For that moment, my attempt at confrontation was ill-advised.

Mr. A. responded to my construction of the situation by accusing me of "trifling." It was, he said, his life and his family and therefore his business, and no one else's. I had no right to meddle, and even though he felt I "meant well," he protested that I "was out of bounds." Good intentions, he pointed out, could hurt and do much damage.

When I attempted a rebuttal, Mr. A. flared to greater anger. He countered that his family was perfectly average, was not and had not been under any undue stress. Moreover, he insisted that Roscoe was not in need of special treatment. Quite the contrary. Roscoe had received three years of "talking" treatment at the center, and he was no better off now than before. Mr. A. emphasized various ways in which our techniques had failed, and offered the opinion that we did not know what we were doing. He said he would have no more part of it. It stirred things up and cost too much. He was perfectly capable of looking after his family and after Roscoe. In fact, he went on, he was sure that he could handle Roscoe better than we could with our talking methods. He could hold the boy in line with paddlings, and that, therefore, he would be quite willing to inform the police that Roscoe was his responsibility. His rage mounted as he faced the implications of Roscoe's delinquency. His sense of self-reliance had been assaulted. No one, he declared, had to tell him how to care for his son; and no one had a right to tell him what was wrong with the boy. It was rugged individualism and American independence to the last.

Mr. A. then launched into a commentary about Roscoe's

essential normality. He asserted that there are other children far more disturbed than Roscoe—children whose parents think them models of goodness. He concluded his diatribe by reasserting that Roscoe needed no help, that his family was fine, that he could manage his world, and that we should not tamper with the way things were.

Mrs. A. had said nothing throughout this exchange. She sat haggard and forlorn, and listened. Her eyes were red rimmed and wet with tears. Her contributions to the meeting had consisted of talking about Marsha, of allowing that psychological fears might be operative in the family, and of weakly asking her husband to at least fill out the forms to see if they might qualify for special financial aid. Further efforts on her part were not forthcoming. Further efforts on my part met with continued frustration.

By the end of two hours we had all three slumped into exhausted silence. There was no longer any tension. There remained only the futility of mutually acknowledged disagreement; compromise was not possible. When I closed the meeting by saying that I "truly believed we each wanted the best and that we all probably wished the outcome could have been otherwise," I meant precisely that. We had recognized our differences with respect to cost accounting, and had decided to respect those differences. We said good-bye with surprisingly little acrimony. Mr. A, who had kept Roscoe from his last appointment, agreed to send him for a final session.

I saw Roscoe for the last time two days later. I did all the talking. He refused to say anything, and spent the entire hour in silence. When I suggested to him that he felt betrayed by me and therefore angry at me, he nodded in agreement. He nodded only one other time. That occurred when I told him he must feel that I was powerless to help him and that must make him feel hopeless and sad. He left without a good-bye and without ever having removed his coat. I have not seen him since.

Mr. A.'s Relapse and the Use of
Behavior Modification

I was unhappy about my month of contacts with the A. family, and found myself wondering about alternative ways to help Roscoe. I finally decided to work through Roscoe's school. My earlier contacts with the school had led to my contracting with them as a mental health consultant to teachers. I continued to meet with the teachers in this capacity over the year, and Roscoe was among the children frequently discussed. There were substantial reasons for his being so. First, I was personally interested in his general welfare and progress. Second, he was, as already described, among the major problems experienced by the teachers. Third, within weeks after my last contact with the A.'s, Mr. A. suffered a severe cardiac arrest. It required hospitalization and culminated in his undergoing open heart surgery for a second time some weeks later.

Mr. A.'s Relapse

The school officials could not be clear about the circumstances of Mr. A.'s setback. It was reported to them by Ricky and Roscoe. Neither boy could provide details; neither had first-hand information or enough comprehension of the medical intricacies to make clear what was occurring. The school officials, for their part, seemed to have no knowledge of Mr. A.'s previous surgery. They decided to check matters out with Mrs. A.

Mrs. A. revealed little to them. She did confirm the boys' report. Mr. A. had suffered a "relapse" and open heart surgery was necessary. It had been scheduled for some weeks hence. She could not or would not offer more information, except to say at which hospital Mr. A. was staying and how often the family visited.

Neither Ricky nor Roscoe missed any school, although both were visibly anxious during the critical weeks. All family members were undoubtedly aware that the first artificial heart valve had failed, and all were likely conscious of the odds against survival the second time around. Aware of the success rate that obtained in the first series of surgeries, I decided to visit Mr. A. in the hospital. He was glad to see me and proved talkative. His fear of surgery and the long hours of waiting may have had something to do with the friendly reception he gave me. I saw him twice before his surgery, and once in the hospital subsequently. Miraculously, Mr. A. defied all odds and survived the second operation. It was as "successful as could be" and his postsurgical recuperation rate was once again remarkable. Mr. A. was discharged from the hospital on schedule. He returned to work thereafter, doing so decidedly ahead of schedule and within a couple of months.

Mediation through the School

Roscoe's problems in school have already been described. They consisted of restlessness, nervous tapping, stealing, variable motivation regarding school work, and running with a "delinquent" crowd. His difficulties were magnified by his father's relapse. He was now unable to remain in his classroom seat for more than three or four minutes at a time, seemed keyed to the point of snapping, annoyed others with his nervous mannerisms, and made frequent and oddly timed demands for attention from his teachers.

In a series of conferences with his teachers and based on my knowledge of Roscoe's background, his teachers and I were able to generate a series of interventions based on the selection of target behaviors, contingencies, and mediators salient to Roscoe. The target behaviors we chose were his nervous tapping, his leaving his seat, his lack of concentration on academic work, his association with "undesirable peers," and his late night calls to Mrs. D. or Mrs. R. We chose not to deal directly with the stealing, believing that if we were successful on other counts we would modify that behavior as well.

Generally speaking we were successful. Mrs. R. and Mrs. D. acted as behavior analysts, mediators of positive reinforcements, and utilized themselves as reinforcers. As behavior analysts they attended closely to Roscoe's classroom activities over a period of weeks. They kept accurate records of the target behaviors, carefully noting the antecedent and consequent events that bounded them. In this fashion they produced base-line readings. The very attempt also produced a kind of intervention. The mere increment in attention-giving had a salutary impact and a number of undesirable behaviors withered under the scrutiny of close observation. In many instances, the close-order observation seemed to cause the observer to reconstrue the target behavior. As a consequence, the teachers' perceptions and reactions were often as much modified as Roscoe's, and the results were invariably beneficial.

But not all behaviors succumbed readily. Some, such as restless moving about the room, lack of concentration, and association with predelinquent boys required the dispensation of designated reinforcers and subsequent shaping. Among the positive reinforcements used by Mrs. D. and Mrs. R. to shape Roscoe's behavior were personal forms of attention giving, responsibility for maintaining the classroom's "nature" and "ecology" bulletin board, the task of planning nature trips and organizing nature study programs, and the job of taking care of the pet menagerie maintained in the classroom. This last was particularly effective throughout the hospitalization of Roscoe's father. Roscoe worked hard to please and to earn the opportunity for care-taking during this period. He doted on the animals. Indeed, when a hamster died his teachers reported that Roscoe conducted a simple but moving funeral service before the class. The experience enhanced Roscoe's public esteem considerably.

Mrs. R. and Mrs. D. also made use of themselves as personal reinforcers. Mrs. R. permitted Roscoe to have lunch with her in the classroom on those occasions he earned it, and Mrs. D. arranged to see him twice weekly for an hour. Roscoe used these hours to make drawings of animals and nature and more rarely for cathartic purposes.

With all this expenditure of effort, Roscoe's public school situation stabilized in relatively short order. Toward the end of the semester, Roscoe was concentrating well in class, remaining in his seat, and more than holding his own academically. There were also indications that he was beginning to relate to "desirable" peers more appropriately and that his contacts with the school's local "black shirts" had diminished in frequency. The lunch hours with Mrs. R. and the twice weekly sessions with Mrs. D. had succeeded in substituting for Roscoe's late night calls, though these still occurred on occasion when Roscoe felt especially isolated and at loose ends after school. Indeed, after school hours continued to provide problems, since we had less control or access to potential mediators of reinforcement during that time. Programs, such as those offered by the YMCA, were tried, but with minimal success. The attempts came to little because of the shortage of funds, the unreliable transportation, and the difficulty of enlisting the cooperation of YMCA personnel as dispensers of rewards. A Big Brother–Little Brother program ran afoul because parental sanction was denied, and internal problems in the program itself made success improbable. Nonetheless, Roscoe's stealing, both inside and outside the school setting, stopped. More importantly, Mrs. R. reported with some considerable relief that she was no longer afraid of Roscoe. She was, in fact, so "unaware" of his presence in the room as an explosive force that she could comfortably and unthinkingly turn her back on the class in order to write on the blackboard. She stressed that one could not really appreciate the significance of such a small, routine event. It made, she said, "all the difference in the world." Unfortunately, she was only speaking for herself and her vision of the world. Having made it through this school year, she could look forward to the next. Roscoe was less lucky. For the better part of a year, we had created an artificial and unreal surrounding for him. His modified behavior could be expected to endure only so long as the reward contingencies we had arranged continued to prevail. When he graduated from the sixth grade and moved to junior high school, we lost control of this "world." Access to significant modifiers was drastically curtailed. Roscoe now had eight different teachers, each of whom taught five classes of forty children each. There was one counselor available for every 500 students. The orchestration of a behavior modification program seemed infeasible. I called the junior high school a number of times in the fall to inquire after Roscoe, but none of his teachers seemed aware of him or his potential problems. He had not "surfaced as yet." If he did "float to the surface" of their attentions, they promised me a call. I never heard from them.

Chapter 12

Recent History

It was not until more than four years after my last direct contact with Roscoe that I had the opportunity to reconstruct the events of the intervening period in his life. In the course of preparing a report on the method of home observation as a clinical assessment technique, I obtained the A. file, among other's, from the "inactive" record room of the child guidance center. The last entry in the file was my own, and it recounted Roscoe's final visit.

While the file was in my possession, a request for information on Roscoe came from a psychiatric facility in Boston. Contact with the Boston agency revealed that some weeks earlier, Roscoe, now aged fifteen, had been referred for psychiatric help by Mr. S., Roscoe's probation officer. I learned that Roscoe had been in a foster home in Boston for the prior ten months. During this time Roscoe had made some considerable gains, and Mr. S. felt he was now reaching out for further assistance. In brief, according to the record, Roscoe was requesting psychiatric evaluation and treatment "for the express purpose of better understanding his past difficulties as an aid to preventing their reoccurrence." The situation appeared to be anything but emergent. Roscoe's attitude was good, he was holding down a part-time job, and was completing high school course work. He had not been in difficulty with the police in ten months. His controls seemed good.

An evaluation was begun. Appointment letters were sent to Mr. and Mrs. A. and to Roscoe. Mrs. A. appeared alone for the first interview. Mr. A. did not come. Roscoe came once. Neither Roscoe nor his mother kept their second appointments.

From the reports of the social worker and the evaluating

psychiatrists at the Boston agency, there is every reason to believe that Roscoe was well-intentioned in his request for help. There was also some basis for believing Mrs. A. to have been concerned, cooperative, and guardedly hopeful. When Roscoe and his mother came for their initial interviews—each separately—they freely recounted Roscoe's history. In addition, Mrs. A. signed the needed release forms so that the evaluators could request privileged information from other social agencies and helping institutions with whom Roscoe had had contact. Mrs. A. did, however, explain Mr. A.'s absence by stating that her husband was unaware of the evaluation. She had purposely not mentioned it to him. She felt Roscoe's continued contacts with mental health professionals would further upset him and aggravate his heart condition. According to Mrs. A., he had had cardiac difficulty approximately once a year since his first open heart surgery. "He has some form of arteriosclerosis-thrombosis," she stated, and he "sometimes loses his balance." His most recent heart attack had occurred three months earlier. More than ever it seemed necessary to tread lightly.

Thus, Roscoe failed to arrive for his second appointment. When he did not call to cancel or reschedule, the agency contacted him. He refused to return. He said he was working and doing quite well, and he didn't feel it necessary to continue the evaluation or to seek treatment. School, he said, was fine and his adjustment in the community, "as good as could be expected." Mrs. A., for her part, called to cancel her appointment. She said there was no sense in going on with the evaluation since she and her husband were planning to sell their house and move out of state. Friends from the motorcycle circuit had offered him an opportunity in upstate New York. Mr. A. wanted to build a house and start his own motor boat–motorcycle–snowmobile repair shop. Roscoe was included in these plans. He would be returning to the family and reside with them. As a consequence, the evaluation remained "incomplete."

Chronology of the Dispossessed: Munificence of
Disappointment

Access to the information accumulated by the Boston agency enabled me to create a chronology of events in Roscoe's life following the home visits—events about which I had no direct knowledge. It is a lesson in the futility of well-intentioned effort, and an example of the absurdities that permeate our presumptions about how people function.

Roscoe was age five years, one month at the time of his father's first heart stoppage. He was nine years, four months old when his father underwent open heart surgery for the first time. He was nine years, nine months old at the time of my last home visit. The chronology below picks up from the date of that last home visit.

> *Age 10 years, 3 months:*
> Roscoe leaves the Day Treatment Program of the Yankee Child Guidance Center and reenters public school. He enters fifth grade.
>
> *Age 10 years, 7 months:*
> Roscoe's outpatient treatment at Yankee Child Guidance Center is terminated. He has been in psychotherapy almost three years.
>
> *Age 11 years, 3 months:*
> Roscoe is arrested for the first time. He and a friend are apprehended for shoplifting. He is also experiencing trouble in the neighborhood and in school. His sixth grade teacher is terrified of him. A "self-referral," Roscoe calls me and requests treatment. Charges of theft are not pressed. The Youth Bureau merely checks to see if Roscoe is reinvolved in psychotherapy.
>
> *Age 11 years, 4 months:*
> I meet with Roscoe on four successive Wednesdays. His sister Marsha is born. I attempt to engage Mr. and Mrs. A. in the support of Roscoe's treatment. Mr. A. is adamant in his refusal. The attempt to reengage the family meets with failure.
>
> *Age 11 years, 5 months:*
> I have my last direct contact with Roscoe. He is angry and bitter. He leaves the session after an hour of total silence.

Age 11 years, 6 months:
Mr. A. suffers a relapse. He is told he must undergo open heart surgery and a valve replacement once again. A date is set. I visit him in a Boston hospital as he awaits the operation.

Age 11 years, 5 months to age 11 years, 9 months:
I work as consultant to the Revere Public Schools and to Roscoe's grade school, and, in conjunction with his teachers, design a behavior modification program for him. His school effort improves, and he manifests greater controls, less tension. His teachers are relieved.

Age 11 years, 8 months:
Mr. A. undergoes surgery and, once again survives and makes a remarkable recovery.

Age 11 years, 9 months:
Roscoe graduates elementary school on time, with his own class and age mates.

Age 12 years:
Roscoe begins junior high school. He has left a grade school of 300 students for a junior high school of 1,200 students. He is lost in the crowd, and it becomes impossible to reinstitute an effective behavior modification program. He is unnoticed by teachers and school authorities.

Age 12 years, 2 months:
Roscoe is arrested a second time. This time he is charged with the theft of a portable TV set and radio. He removed them from the house of a "friend" and attempted to sell them. Charges are dropped and he is placed under the supervision of his parents.

Age 12 years, 4 months:
Roscoe is arrested a third time, on this occasion for stealing a guitar. Once more he is released to his parents' supervision. For the first time he surfaces as a behavior problem in junior high school—he is truant for a week.

Age 12 years, 5 months:
On two separate occasions Roscoe is taken to the emergency room of Revere Memorial Hospital—a local hospital across town. On both occasions he has had an overdose of LSD, and is kept overnight for observation.

Age 12 years, 6 months:
Roscoe is arrested a fourth time. He has stolen a motorcy-cle. He claims it is the third he has stolen, but only the first for which he has been caught. He is detained by the county and held over for a hearing. He is made a temporary ward of the court, and placed in the Hampshire Valley Residen-tial School for emotionally disturbed boys. He is to remain there six months.

Age 12 years, 10 months:
I encounter Mr. A. and Ricky in the parking lot of a shop-ping center. They inform me that Deedee has married and left home, and that Janet A. has been born. When I inquire after Roscoe, Mr. A. says he is living away from home with a friend. He does not tell me that Roscoe is in a residential school for boys.

Age 13 years:
Roscoe is discharged from the residential program to the custody of his family. He has made no gains during his six months stay. Reports from the school indicate he has made a poor adjustment to the school, that he has not adapted well to his cottage or his peers. They note particularly his inability to accept limits and his continual truancy. Also cited are aggressive tendencies. In addition, the reports state that he sometimes seemed confused in ideational con-tent and manifested some "inappropriate affective re-sponses." They concluded: "He appears to have made a schizophrenic-like adjustment, but with no further evidence of deterioration . . . his object relations are impaired and he is emotionally labile."

Age 13 years, 1 month:
Upon Roscoe's return to the community and to junior high school, a special conference is set up to specify guidelines and ground rules for Roscoe's behavior. Included are Ros-coe, his parents, the junior high school principal, and school counselor, as well as Roscoe's court social worker and probation officer. It is made clear to Roscoe and the A.'s at this conference that any failure on Roscoe's part to abide by the established rules will mean placement in either the New England Boy's Training School—once called a "reform school"—or a state mental hospital.

Age 13 years, 3 months:

Roscoe truants from school for three days. Hospitalization in a state mental institution is requested by the school and the court. The report reads: "Compared to his previous misbehavior, Roscoe has done relatively well in the past three months. At least up until the last three days when he has been truant from school. . . . The parents state that they are not aware of any misbehavior whatsoever on his part. . . . On one of the three days of truancy in question the parents say Roscoe was ill and at home, but on the other two days they were not aware of his absence from school. . . . While he was in school his behavior was relatively better. None of his usual, blatant, aggressive behavior has been in evidence." The request for hospitalization, therefore, "must be taken in the context of a firm stand by school and court authorities and certainly Roscoe's recent school truancy makes very questionable his ability to stay in the community and public school setting."

Age 13 years, 4 months:

Roscoe is given a preadmission evaluation at the Salem State Hospital. No clear-cut diagnosis is made at that time, but there is "some suggestion of a possibility of a mild, diffuse brain damage. Other than that, or on top of that, there is certainly a tendency for sociopathic behavior and also there are indications of possible marginal reality testing at times. . . ." Psychological diagnostic testing and an electroencephalogram are requested to further determine the diagnosis.

Roscoe is placed on the waiting list for admission to Salem State Hospital. He and his parents are told that, "should he return to public school during the waiting period and show exemplary behavior, he might possibly have his admission postponed." He is given Librium 10 mg. t.i.d. and released to his parents.

The very day following this conference, which Roscoe attended and the details of which he seemingly understood, he ran away from home. He was finally picked up in Albany, New York. He was detained in the juvenile home there for seven days until his court social worker brought him back for admission to the Salem State Hospital. Roscoe begins a ten-month stay in the state mental hospital.

Age 13 years, 5 months:

Roscoe is given psychological testing and an electroence-phalogram. The results of the electroencephalogram prove negative. The psychologicals point to a diagnosis of border-line psychosis. For further details regarding the diagnostic testing, see below.

Age 14 years, 2 months:

Roscoe is one of a number of boys who admit to stealing medicines and supplies from the hospital infirmary. He had been scheduled to leave the hospital on convalescent status in the near future. Roscoe's convalescent status is delayed. He is told to pay back the money he received from patients to whom he sold the supplies. He is also made to share in the costs of repairing the damaged lockwork on the infirmary door. In addition, he is placed in the quiet room for twenty-four hours, and then on full ward restrictions. His ground privileges are similarly removed.

Age 14 years, 3 months:

Roscoe obtains convalescent status and is returned to live with his parents. The convalescent status note reads as follows: "This was a first state hospital admission for this four-teen-year-old, white, single, ninth grader. He was admitted on a voluntary basis ten months ago. His determined diag-nosis was schizophrenia, childhood type. The main problem was anti-social behavior which, however, was felt to be largely a defense against a psychotic process."

"His overall course in the hospital was satisfactory. He went on leaves with his parents on many occasions, largely without any difficulty. He participated in many areas of the achievement program."

"He is not now on any medication. He is placed on conva-lescent status to return to live with his family. He will go back to public school in the fall. We hope to have follow-up and to move in the direction of vocational planning. Given his father's interests, we believe Roscoe might enjoy mechanics training."

Age 14 years, 5 months:

Roscoe is "discharged from convalescent status . . . as not mentally ill."

Age 14 years, 6 months:
Roscoe is again admitted to Revere Memorial Hospital emergency room. He is kept overnight for observation. Diagnosis: suspected overdose of LSD.

Age 14 years, 7 months:
Roscoe is arrested for attempted motorcycle theft. Once more he is placed in the county detention home. His parents do not take him out. Roscoe's probation officer places him in a foster home in Boston.

Age 14 years, 7 months to 15 years, 3 months:
Roscoe resides in a foster home. He makes good progress and experiences no further difficulty with the courts. He seeks to consolidate his gains by requesting an evaluation and treatment. He is brought to the adolescent service of a Boston psychiatric facility. He and his mother, most likely out of fear of or concern for Mr. A., abort the evaluation.

In his concluding note the social worker writes: "While it is unfortunate that the evaluation has not gone to completion, it is probably a good thing and a healthful thing that Roscoe has decided to rejoin his family. Mr. A. is embarking on a risky and new venture, one likely to be taxing and stressful to himself and his family. They will be newly located in strange surroundings, and the father will have to work with heavy machinery, engines, racing equipment, etc. Under the circumstances, Roscoe could serve as support to his father, a man in precarious health. The venture would serve the interest of consolidating a relationship between father and son. Most significantly, it would give Roscoe an opportunity to play a vital role in his family, perhaps for the first time. . . ."

Age 15 years:
The A.'s sell their house and move out of state. Mr. A. hopes to start a motor boat-motorcycle-snowmobile repair shop elsewhere. Roscoe goes with the family which once again contains five children. Deedee has married and Sheila has gone away to college in California. Ricky is sixteen and at home. Roscoe has rejoined the fold. Pamela is eleven, Marsha is four, and Janet almost three.

Reckonings: Roscoe A. at Age Thirteen

*Stability and Repetition: A Digression
on a Dilemma*

The chronology just given was purposely brief and intended to render Roscoe's history in terse, journalistic style. As a capsule documentary, the chronology could be abstracted to read: Roscoe A. can *only* go home again. His parents can *only* invite him back. Despite attempts, they know no other way. And somehow, involved throughout it all are mental health workers who seem charged with the task of repeatedly effecting or, at a minimum, repeatedly blessing the recurrent reunions. Our culture is loathe to seek or permit other ways. This chronology makes vivid the redundancy of experience and outcome, and the security as well as futility that redundancy creates. Though the A.'s succeed in suspending their awareness of time as a dimension in their lives, time passes and things happen to them. Great events, as well as small ones, occur to them as a family and as individuals; yet, things seem not to change. Six years make little difference.

The lack of change and the lack of altered circumstance are important factors in human affairs because they allow the establishment of tradition and social order, of interactional rules and ritual. Stability supplies the individual with a kind of certainty, a predictability of event. It negates surprise and strangeness and reduces anxiety. Thus, a guarantee of sameness is sought by a great majority of mankind. Stability has become the cornerstone of many psychological theories of personality, and a number of schemes for explaining both human motivation and animal behavior are organized about it and related principles (Festinger, 1957; Hebb, 1949, Lecky, 1951; Miller, 1963). So, too, are theories of conflict and defense. As social scientists, and as mental health practitioners, we are understandably prone to extoll the virtues of predictability.

Yet predictability, constancy, or unchangeableness in social affairs can signify a piece of ritualized human tragedy, and this we are less prone to acknowledge. We see less readily that the permanence of the most meager or most despicable things can bring comfort and gratification. It is a sad, if sobering, insight to realize that misery and degradation, self-negation, defeat, and cruelty can in their predictable recurrence have salutary effects, can come to connote pleasure. This is, of course, Roscoe A.'s predicament, and his family's.

But the problem of pleasure in stability, of security in familiarity, is a problem for mental health workers too, though perhaps in different ways. As would-be agents of change, as clinical researchers, as diagnosticians—as persons construing events and people, as persons mandated to see things as they are—mental health professionals, no less than those they endeavor to help or to research, are dedicated to locating stability, sameness, order, permanence, and predictability. Inevitably this dedication runs afoul of their mandate as clinicians and researchers. The mandate asks them to step outside cultural and theoretical biases, to construe things anew. But their human proclivities ask them to seek the sanctity of sameness. Their compromise may be suggestive of repetition compulsion, but they may prefer to label their own compulsions differently. They make the rules, so they are able to label their compulsions as theories or methods that have been validated by scientific means. Nonetheless, these theories are belief systems—personalized and shared constructions of how the world is made, how it fits together, how it works.

If results or methods are inconsistent with a mental health professional's belief system he is prone to disregard them or call them unscientific. More importantly, he does not even entertain those methods and ideas that fall outside the pale of his particular way of construing events—they simply never occur to him.

In the final analysis, one might properly inquire just who manifests the compulsion to repeat—the persons in need of help, or the persons seeking to help.

Obviously, the matters of stability and change, repetition and innovation, need discussion because they are, as phenomena, only too visible in the A. story. The story ends where it begins—in anguish, in fear, in mistaken assumption. Given the supposition that professional helpers are as inflicted as their clientele with the need to recapitulate the past, this can come as little surprise. Indeed, it may be supposed that many of the events documented in Roscoe's chronology, alone or in combination, might have served to spotlight the ultimate standoff. Any of a number of items might now provide a springboard for the greater expansion of this theme—any of a number could become the basis for its redefinition or illustration. We have chosen just one to make our point. It is the Salem State Hospital evaluation of Roscoe, done when he was thirteen years, four months of age. Conducted in completely independent fashion at a later time and by different personnel, and seemingly without any thorough-going or for that matter superficial awareness of the evaluation done six years earlier at the Yankee Child Guidance Center, this second evaluation fails to achieve even modest counterpoint with the first. Instead there is duplication and reiteration.

Excerpts from the Salem State Hospital Evaluation

Preadmission statement—reason for referral:

Roscoe A. is a thirteen-and-a-half-year-old, Caucasian boy, presently an eighth grader, though in a retarded learner program. He was referred here by Mr. F., a social worker with the juvenile court. The central problem revolves around a long-standing history of acting out misbehavior which has not satisfactorily responded to remedial efforts to date and in the opinion of the referring agency probably requires inpatient treatment.

History and current situation:

This youngster has a history of aggressive behavior, uncontrollable outbursts of unsocial activity of various kinds since kindergarten. His behavior included his becoming wild, reaching high pitches of activity, and, at that time, according to school reports, he alternately regressed to infantile behavior such as sucking, biting, crawling, and rolling. At that time it was noted that he seemed preoccupied with birds and butterflies, and in general there seemed to be a slightly bizarre quality about his behavior. This has extended and been noted off and on to date. . . .

According to the mother when Roscoe was seven he was seen for an outpatient evaluation at a child guidance center. The reasons for the evaluation were complaints from the school about Roscoe's behavior. The mother claimed that Roscoe was not then nor ever a behavior problem in the home and that she was surprised at the school's complaints. It must be noted here that these are very resistant parents, who refuse to acknowledge Roscoe's problems . . . They have been most resistant to acknowledging his anger and explosiveness. Time and again the parents have been called to school conferences, have seen psychological helpers, have had many dealings with the court and police because of Roscoe's behavior. They have stated that Roscoe is absolutely no problem at home, and they are further confused by the fact that they have had no problems whatsoever with any of their other children. The latter, indeed, seems to be the case. The other children have not had any school or community problems. . . .

Although a psychological test at age seven indicated an IQ of 124, Roscoe has not done well academically, and is currently operating three years behind his grade level. . . .

After increasing difficulty at school, with repeated fights and rebelliousness plus many contacts with the police because of stealing and destructive behavior, this boy was placed in a residential home for boys where he stayed six months. . . .

Indeed, there has been a quality about this boy's personality and thinking and affect that has bordered on the bizarre. His earlier evaluations in school and in agencies suggested he was a borderline psychotic youngster. School counselors and court social workers report an intangible kind of quality about him which seems to take him out of the usual characterological disorder category or sociopathic area. There is question about whether he is psychotic. Maybe it is this possibility the parents don't want to acknowledge, and maybe this is why they continue to insist on his lack of behavior outbursts. There has been hyperactivity and impulsivity noted all along. Yet, he has never had a psychological test specifically for organicity nor has he ever had an EEG to our knowledge. . . .

. . . Roscoe's recent school truancy makes very questionable his ability to stay in the community and public school setting.

Assessment of parents:

Although there is a certain paucity of warmth and evidence of some lack of cooperation and strong resistance by the parents in the past, there has never been any specific evidence of a good deal of pathology being present in either parent, and, of course, all the other six children are doing quite well. The parents have always seemed quite confused by Roscoe's misbehavior when in fact they may be seeking to deny their son's "bizarreness." The mother is definitely a rather cold, ungiving, uncaring, not spontaneous person. And the father is quite inflexible, perhaps somewhat immature and passive. However, no specific psychopathology has been evident in either parent.

Mental status examination:

Roscoe is a fairly nice looking, average sized, normally proportioned, blond boy. He was very cooperative, quiet, and passive. He answered questions in an appropriate manner but without much range of affect. At times he seemed to "blank out" a little and it was difficult to tell whether he was using this as a method to avoid questions or whether he actually was tuning out. He seemed to have little insight into the reasons why he was being seen, being very concrete and not seemingly aware on any meaningful basis of his behavior in the past and how it had resulted in his eventual referral here. . . .

He did not give much evidence in any way of other than low normal intelligence. Any attempts to bring out abstracting ability were in vain . . .

Occasionally one did get the idea of a certain amount of truculence and manipulativeness on his part. He seemed to relate on a fairly superficial level . . .

One got the idea of a sort of "scatter" of his concentration, and of relatively poor attention span . . .

Diagnosis impression:

We are unable to make a clear-cut diagnosis at this time. Since this boy has a long-standing history of impulsive acting out, and since he has never had a psychological test for organicity and has not had an electroencephalogram, these have been ordered and diagnosis is deferred until they are com-

plete. There is some suggestion of a possibility of a mild diffuse brain damage. Other than that, or on top of that, there is
certainly a tendency for sociopathic behavior and also there
are indications of possible marginal reality testing at times
. . . This leaves the range of diagnostic possibilities quite
open at this point. Brain damage would perhaps partially account for Roscoe's impulsivity, his short attention span, and
his aggressive acting out and school difficulties.

Recommendation:

This young man was placed on our waiting list for admission.
In spite of the fact that his parents report that his behavior
has been excellent since his return home from the residential
setting for disturbed boys, there is a long-standing history of
their denial of his problems and of their failing to pay heed to
professional advice. Their claims that he has been well behaved, therefore, must be regarded with caution. In spite of a
very firm stand by school and probate court people, Roscoe is
beginning to be truant from school and has been seen in the
company of known delinquent youngsters. As mentioned
above, psychological tests and an EEG have been ordered on
him. In the meantime, he and his parents were specifically
told that should he return to public school during the waiting
period and show exemplary behavior, he might possibly have
his admission postponed. He is placed on Librium 10 mg.
t.i.d.

Psychological test report:

Behavioral observations: Roscoe first appeared as sullen,
surly, distrustful, a youth hardened in the ways of adolescent
crime, and harboring rebellious disgust for adults. He maintained the tough, concealing front for about half of the testing
session—then he "opened up," and rather vehemently unbur-
dened himself of a host of fears and suspicions: that he would
be imprisoned at the hospital, that his friends would think he
was crazy because of this, that he would break out and run
away, that he "can't trust anybody no more," even his father.
He was only minimally cooperative, depreciated the tests (as
"silly" and "stupid"), and frequently refused to respond to the
less-structured projective items. Despite his rather emotional
outburst of personal material, Roscoe remained reticent and
withdrawn (i.e., nonrelating) until the completion of testing.

At this point (in the hall outside my office), he suddenly directed himself toward *me* in an apparently genuine effort at interpersonal communication: He talked at length about his interest in animals and the pets he used to keep, and related that he once had a dog that was run over by a speeding car. He also talked about a friend's racing motorcycle and described how his friend drove at high speeds and did dangerous feats. His description was clearly aimed at impressing me, but he was sincerely sharing important experiences nonetheless. This conversation lasted some fifteen minutes, until I had to stop it (because of another appointment), and I had the feeling it could have gone on longer. . . .

Test results: There is no evidence to suggest that Roscoe is suffering from an organic impairment. Motor control is occasionally poor due to impulsivity (carelessness, rapid execution) and expansiveness but his organization is good and he is capable of very fine and detailed "correct" productions when he is drawing something that holds his interest, like birds or animals or motorcycles. His performance improves with increased attention and concentration . . . Though only a partial intelligence test was administered, his subtest scores indicate that he is functioning in the "normal" range of intelligence.

Because of Roscoe's general nonproductiveness, it was really quite difficult to find out much about him . . . Roscoe's behavior reveals a conflict: despite his paranoid-like distrust and interpersonal distancing, he is still eager to reach out for people and attempt relationships . . . Assured of control and mastery, he doesn't have to be so distrustful and can move with some confidence *toward* people and relationships.

Roscoe does not appear to be presently psychotic. Rather, he seems to maintain well-sealed-off pockets of "craziness," especially in the area of social judgment. Here, empathy and humaneness are essentially, and startlingly, absent. He keeps this "pocket" (further described below) isolated and under strict intellectual control by clinging very tenaciously, even obsessively, to objective reality; he does not permit himself to fantasize or wander even briefly from what is literally "there" and safely real. This defensive style manifested itself in the testing by his extreme restriction on the projective tests; the "freer," more fantasy-inducing the stimulus, the more rigidly he preserves self-control, the harder he works to keep his threateningly bizarre thoughts hidden. Interestingly, the safer he feels, the more structured and unambiguously defined the task, the more looseness and productivity he allows himself. Apparently he takes his cues from the environment; if its safe and sound and structured, he can let out more of what is dangerous and uncertain within himself.

The "pocket of craziness" referred to above is a kind of judgmental deficit which involves a near-gleeful preoccupation with morbid aggression, with gore, with wrecked, crashed, and cut-up people—a nonchalant, cavalier lack of concern for what happens to others . . . Even though his psychopathic, almost bizarre, empathy-deficit is encapsulated within an obsessive-compulsive "reality-clinging," he is apparently quite comfortable with it; social judgment is grossly impaired. This may be a boy capable of cold cruelty to others.

In summary, then, Roscoe has made a very marginal, borderline adjustment. His obsessive controls work, insofar as they are successfully containing the psychotic-psychopathic core. Because of this defensive style, he is not now openly psychotic. Nor is there any sign of an organic deficiency. Individual uncovering psychotherapy with Roscoe would be difficult and inappropriate at best (because of his suspiciousness and manipulativeness) and dangerous at worst (because of the latent psychotic characteristics).

In fact, we should probably take our cue from him and encourage intellectual pursuits (e.g., chess, nature studies). A firm, reliable, interested, warm environment, in which he is permitted mastery and initiative, and supportive psychotherapy are recommended.

Status Quo

The evaluation just reported is at once pitiably believable and maddeningly incredible. It is pitiably believable because it is real, because it is, in its blind, unquestioning, unknowing stereotypy, crushingly accurate, and because it confronts us with a truth we already know, but do not like to recognize. Roscoe A., at thirteen years, four months, is a boy almost profoundly beyond rescue. He is a child who has never been. Born with all the potentialities of the species stamped in his genes, he has been sorely cheated in the most devastating of ways. He has been denied his birthright. He has been denied the discovery and use of his potential selves, and has been made into something he was not. Mortification must rank among the most profane, the most outrageous of human crimes. Roscoe has been a victim.

The evaluation is maddeningly incredible because it does not tell us of Roscoe's mortification—of the spectacle of his shriveling innocence, of his defenselessness, of his childish hope being choked off and annihilated. It does not even suspect or darkly hint at such things. It is maddeningly incredible because it is correct in its surface features, but wrong or mindless in its underpinnings. It fails to inform us of Roscoe, for it fails to touch him, to sense him, to palpate his existence or the bewilderment of his nonexistence. It fails to shape him, and it fails to understand from where his actions proceed. Moreover, it has neither used nor advanced our capacities for recognizing and apprehending the complexity and vulnerability of his circumstance. Its assessment of Roscoe, of his dynamics, of his capacities, of his diagnostic circumstance, is no different from that of six years earlier. Clinicians are perhaps prone to welcome reliabilities of this kind. It is a measure of scientism in their field. But it is not comforting to propose that this consistency may derive from dogma, from invariance in teaching, from unmodified belief systems, from unaltered method and undoubted technique; that we can be so transfixed by our own preconceptions that we fail to remember reliability may be totally unrelated to validity. Six years may seem to make no difference in evaluation outcomes, but the constancy in outcome may be a function of an unchanging method and nothing more. The same questions, the same methods, and the same answers are offered in both evaluations, despite the six years between them. The same six psychological tests are administered both times. The same people are interviewed. The same data are observed, the same data are ignored. The vantage point does not change. The boy is "morbid" and "borderline psychotic." The parents "deny," are "resistant," and "nonpathologic." The siblings are "well" and of incidental interest.

Death, death-terror, cardiac arrest, open heart surgery, are nowhere mentioned in either work-up, except obliquely as Roscoe's pathognomonic preoccupations. Family considerations
are beyond the conceptual pale. It is small wonder that the
same conclusions obtain. True, the later evaluation is prog-
nostically more pessimistic, diagnostically more dire, and clinically less thorough, less sophisticated. The change toward
bleakness is to be expected; hope dies with passing time. But
for this, the evaluations are virtually interchangeable. The second set of evaluators are no more informed than the first, and
no wiser.

And it is a maddeningly incredible thing, given the complexities of this world, and the variegated textures and richness of experience, that a developing human being, a growing,
expanding, apprehending, appreciating, intelligent organism,
can in six years virtually double the span of his lifetime and
quadruple the range of his experience, and *yet* be described
by his fellows as no more, indeed as perhaps a good deal less,
than what he was initially. This may say much about the tor-
por of his life and about the brutalizing qualities of our society, but it probably says a good deal as well about our means
of evaluating and appreciating that life and that society. It
suggests that there is something glaringly wrong with our belief systems, and our hypothetical constructs, and our methods
for assessing and confirming them. It suggests that we are the
all too easy victims of our own delusions. And there is something appallingly curious if not terrifying in it all.

VII

Conclusions and Further Thoughts

Chapter 13

Clinical Research and Death

Cultural Determinism

Cultural determinism has been a prepotent instrument guiding the selection and treatment of topics discussed in the preceding pages. It has provided an overriding vantage point for construing events. Cultural determinism is, of course, an explicitly dihedral orientation. It requires that when studying a given phenomenon, account must be taken of cultural inputs. Therefore, while it is legitimate to study the family as a closed social system for some limited purposes, it is misleading to conceive of the family as a corporate structure unto itself and to disregard its exchanges with the larger social order. But further, such an orientation suggests that one can not easily keep cultural factors or variables at "scientific" arm's length. Not only does the family have traffic with the enveloping culture, but the researcher does as well. He is not immune to its influences, and in some special ways he is an exponent of its most cherished values. Cultural inputs are not to be treated as variables impacting on subjects or patients alone. This recognition makes it necessary for the investigator to review his own penchants—to wonder about his own interests, preferred methods, and suppositions, and to view them as culturally influenced if not culturally dictated. Here is the greater challenge, for it suggests that scientific objectivity is a state of mind and an acknowledgment of bias; it portends a direct assault on the investigator-clinician's sensibilities. For precisely these reasons, an orientation of cultural determinism has heuristic import. It places one's "educated" observations and findings in a socio-historical context, and asks after their relevance. The research act is to be understood as a piece of culturally determined behavior, in its own way little different from the behaviors of persons researched. Both provide opportunities for enhancing human consciousness.

Given this framework, we may raise again certain questions about the ostensible topics of this book—death and the family. We may ask, for example, what is the American family about, what is it like, what are its major parameters? We may also inquire of ourselves, why choose to study the family at all? or, why study it in this particular way and to this particular end? We may pose a similar series of questions about the study of death and death fears. Why study them today? Why were they not subjects of earlier social scientific or clinical concern? The question of interest is not whether or not this book may enjoy a certain topicality, but why its subject is now so topical.

The Recent Popularity of Death Material

Is death indeed topical? The answer would seem to be yes. This book, for example, is part of a proliferating professional literature on psychological reactions to death—notwithstanding the fact that it is only inadvertently in the mainstream of that literature. The threat and fear of death were not themes consciously chosen for study. They emerged as significant in the course of home visits to the A.'s. That they did so, that they were previously missed, that they surfaced in the way that they did, that they were productive of paralyzing stress, and that they prompted a write-up of this kind underscores their significance as contemporary preoccupations in our society. They intrude themselves in clinical material, in everyday existence without solicitation; and, one suspects that they deliver a psycho-social wallop they did not in previous times possess. It is the character of their intrusion, as documented here, that places this book in the mainstream of a growing literature.

The problem of psychological reactions to death today remains one of recognition. Eyes have been averted in recent years. But while denial is still practiced in quantity, and while it affords some comforts, it incurs penalties as well. Only now are the severe psychic costs of death-denial being recognized, though, even today, the precise source of the pain remains obscured, or is often minimized. Still death has increasingly been getting its psychological due. While there is a long way to go, in recent years it has been receiving studied attention from some researchers in the mental health field.

A cursory check of titles listed in *Psychological Abstracts* substantiates this premise. A comparison of the years 1927, 1957, 1967, 1970, and 1971 yields the following: Three titles among 3,000 listed in 1927 deal with death or dying. In 1957, nine titles among 9,000 listed deal with death. In 1967, a total of 17,202 items are abstracted, and sixty relate to death and dying. In 1970, there were 147 papers and books on death and dying among the 21,719 publications reviewed. In 1971, of the 11,883 publications listed, ninety-one are concerned with topics relating to death. Over the course of forty-four years, death has become seventy-six times more popular as a topic of psychological study. It should be noted that the foregoing figures exclude publications on suicide, which show an even more phenomenal increment over the same span of time. Whether these figures reflect a reasonably proportionate concern over a phenomenon as ubiquitous as death, however, remains questionable. The publications in 1971 dealing with death still represent but 0.76 percent of the total production of mental health researchers during 1971. Certainly an obtrusive fact in a day when death itself is experienced as obtrusive.

Why Death Has Not Been Studied

Biology

One explanation for the lack of psychological research on death and death-fear is patently ethological in its premises. Like many ethological arguments, it so easily accounts for so much that it says everything and nothing. It recognizes the irrefutable fact that the researcher and the clinician share with all human beings a natural antipathy toward intimate experience of death and dying (Hebb, 1954; Hinton, 1967). An assumption is made that death-anxiety, distress about the prospect of death, or upset over the sight of a dead body have decided biological value; the fears assure survival of the species insofar as they serve to minimize unnecessary risk and premature death. Given the extended socialization period of human beings, and the adult's value to the species well beyond reproductive functions, one might even speculate that our fears of direct encounter with natural intraspecies death are, among all animals, most highly developed (Herzog, 1967).[1] In any event, many theorists seem to have little doubt about the existence of such fears in man, being committed to the position that genetic or constitutional determinants are decisive.

Psychology

It is to be expected, of course, that biologic factors find expression at psychological and cultural levels. Indeed, it is the manifestation of conflicts, defenses, and attitudes at these latter levels which dictates the inference that man has a biologically rooted aversion to death. It is generally agreed that the psychological and social development of man has succeeded in overlaying this fundamental fear with many elaborations and mechanisms so that death, dying, and the fear attendant on both, may be avoided or ritualized. To experience the fear is to acknowledge the reality of the threat, and the possibility that either might enjoy constant consciousness or ready access to awareness would, according to some theorists, serve to preclude normal functioning.

There is less agreement about how much of the fear is biologically rooted, and there exists a considerable range of opinion about how biological aversions toward death and dying translate into psychic phenomena and experience. The thesis developed in this book does not rest solely on the biological argument. For the present, at any rate, it is given less weight than others. This is not entirely a matter of taste, and is only partly an arbitrary decision. It is still too easy to reify cultural bias and excuse social premise through appeals to untested or untestable conceptions of biological determinism. Thus while we acknowledge a biological substratum to death-fears, our major interest is to elucidate that portion of the variance con-

---

1. War is no exception. Death in war has today, especially for Americans, become so remote and impersonalized as to fall outside the range of "intimate" experience. Nor does death in war represent "natural death."

tributed by psychological and cultural factors. Nonetheless, because they may shed light on motivations in the A. family, as well as explain why the topic of death has not been studied by clinical researchers, some usual conceptions of how biologic elements may be experienced at psychological levels are listed here.

1. *The psychological sense of immortality.* This belief, which is partly based on Freud's comments in his paper, "Thoughts for the Times on War and Death" (1915), holds that the unconscious can admit no concept of personal death. In the unconscious the infantile sense of omnipotence and immortality is maintained (Kubler-Ross, 1969; Weisman and Hackett, 1961). By definition, then, death should constitute a consciously perceived piece of threatening reality, a prosaic fact of the human circumstance, that is to be evaded, isolated, and denied. Then life can go on, and the unconscious premise of immortality can be preserved with minimum challenge. In concrete, day-to-day terms, this means that we avoid death each time we see it in others because to contemplate it fills us with a sense of dread, a sense of our own lack of omnipotence. This is, perhaps, one reason clinical researchers do not study death and the A.'s do not talk of its prospect.

2. *Death and esteem.* We avoid the contemplation of death because it reminds us that we are expendable and that the world can get along without us. It portends that others, our family and friends, can continue to function despite our departure and absence. There is no greater blow to self-esteem than the realization that one's existence is in some respect a matter of indifference. Personal surrender to this belief of expendability is probably tantamount to psychological death.[2] It is this notion, perhaps, that prompts Zilboorg (1943) to assert that behind "the sense of discouragement and depression, there always lurks the basic fear of death . . ." (p. 465). The relation between esteem and immortality, then, becomes clear. We have hinted at this repeatedly in our discussion of the A.'s. Mr. A. tries to ensure that he will be keenly missed or unforgotten by creating or extracting in advance both tangible and

2. See Freida Fromm-Reichmann (1955), for a discussion of the concept of "psychological death."

psychic postmortem obligations from his family. He seeks to cement object ties as the date of his surgery approaches. He provides his family little material or financial security, loads Roscoe with guilt, and Mrs. A. with increasing numbers of children. He has carefully prepared a legacy of crushing proportions. He has guaranteed that he will be missed.

3. *Death and separation.* The prospect of death fills us with dread, and dissuades the would-be researcher because it means irreversible and final separation and loss. Separation and loss connote suffering, loneliness, and a host of attached affects and experiences such as punishment and guilt. Death, therefore, can be said to merit avoidance on the grounds of psychic pains alone. The concept of unconscious immortality need hardly be invoked. To study death clinically is to invite grief.

Shifting to a more interpersonal level sheds additional light on the "inherent" need to shun death. First, it makes us realize to what extent attitudes toward death are influenced by the interpersonal competitiveness and jealousy of the living. Many of us would probably respond positively to Kaufmann's (1959) inquiry about how our feelings concerning our own death would change could we be assured that the world or all human life would end with our death. The fear that we might be denied those things that others enjoy comprises a good deal of the death-associated separation fear. Death becomes more palatable as it becomes less personally focused. Second, the interpersonal vantage point highlights the equally significant notion that it is correct to assume that people—clinical researchers and the A.'s alike—have a genuine desire to avoid cathexis of persons who are dying or who stand in close relation to imminent death. Except in highly specialized social roles, there would seem to be in our culture an inverse relation between a person's proximity to death and another's readiness to invest psychologically in him. This may place an exceptionally heavy burden on the dying person or on someone facing imminent death. Lindemann (1944) and Rosner (1962) have noted the phenomenon of "anticipatory grief reactions" and remarked on its disadvantages. Premature decathexis of a person on the threshold of death can make his struggle a lonely and private one, precisely at a time when he wishes otherwise. (Fulton, 1965). As Mr. A. seeks to engage his family, they pull away leaving him desperate and psychologically very much alone.

The family's parody of social exchange with Mr. A. extends to the professionals who would help him or study him. Doctors, therapists, and researchers are also placed in the unenviable position of having to cathect an individual who promises to separate in the immediate future. Not unsurprisingly, as we have endeavored to show, many professionals unwittingly turn from the task. Here then is another contributing factor to the nonstudy of the dying experience and its impact. If one were to dwell constantly on death and mortality, one would be loathe to make much emotional investment in others. By logical extension, if people are to be socialized they have to not think about death. The A.'s and their professional network have carried the questionable virtue of this logic to its incapacitating extreme. They are crippled by their *not* thinking about their major preoccupation.

4. *Death as unknowable.* Lilli Peller (1963) has said, "It is hard and almost impossible for a young child to understand sexuality. It is outright impossible for him to understand death." One need not limit the statement to children. Death, especially for the adult, places a formidable burden on one's intellectual comprehension and capacity for emotional honesty. People can experience sexuality, face and deal with it repeatedly, and even consensually validate the nature of their own experience through discussions with others. Sex can be taught, learned, and mastered, and cliché jokes suggest how quickly it can lose its "mystery." Hence, sex remains "unspeakable" only because it may be socially defined as such, or because certain of its aspects remain temporarily beyond the ken or experience of certain groups—e.g., children under age five. Personal death, however, remains "unspeakable" in a far more real, more incontestable way. Quite simply, we cannot subjectively experience death, know or tell about it. As Freud (1915) noted, "whenever we attempt to imagine [our own death] we perceive that we survive as spectators . . ." (p. 291). Death means unconsciousness. Hence, if we talk about death at all it is as an abstraction or as something that happens

to somebody else; we are seldom able to discuss private notions of personal death. This is, then, an embellished version of the earlier assumption that the unconscious cannot admit of personal death.

In its way, however, this version has a more compelling existential cast. It was Walter Kerr (1968), who once caught its essence. He suggested that it "may make one catch his breath, as from an invisible and sickening blow" to realize suddenly that one cannot remember when and how he first heard about death. Surely, someone must have told him during his childhood, and certainly information of such proportions should have lodged somewhere in his mind. But where? Can anyone retrieve the memory of that early, thunderous, recognition that it is our destiny to die? Most likely not. Was the insight ever truly assimilated? Probably not.

Death cannot be experienced. If one could experience it, one would not be dead (Bridgman, 1938; Weisman and Hackett, 1961). And if self-death is a state we cannot really know and cannot manipulate conceptually, then it is something that we cannot adequately master and, as we have attempted to emphasize throughout, mastery over natural forces is the American way. What the American ego cannot properly master renders that ego helpless and impotent. An experience of terror and of reactive protest, combat, and defense is the outcome. Belief in ultimate mastery we call "hope," and because we have "hope," death is never viewed in middle-American culture as opportune or appropriate. Our dedication is to fending it off, and not to accepting it. Thus we study ways to prevent death but not ways to accommodate it.

5. *Death and the problem of theoretical heritage.* Ready and armed with what is by now a rather elaborate theory of psychodynamic functioning constructed upon discoveries of "repressed sexuality," clinicians and researchers have badly neglected other possibilities. As Wahl (1958) so aptly put it, Freud described the child's curiosity about the nature of the universe as the "riddle of the Sphinx," and then proceeded to devote nearly all of his energies to the child's need for answers about the origin of things—the question, Whence came I? But the second half of the Sphinx's riddle remains unaddressed—

Whither go I? Too often, even today, anxiety about death or dying is interpreted as a derivative phenomenon, as a secondary or tertiary defensive manifestation of separation or castration anxiety, which is presumed to be more "primary." Rosenthal (1963) formulates this problem of theoretic legacies in explicit terms when she writes:

> If one can accept the belief that the fear of death stems from the castration fear, which in turn grows out of an inadequately resolved Oedipal conflict, why not then accept the converse—that the castration fear stems from the much more basic, original fear of death? (p. 623) [3]

and

> . . . in modern psychologic and psychoanalytic literature little if any mention has been made of the need to bring this all-encompassing inner agent of neurosis [the fear of death] into the open in psychotherapy. Unlimited attention, on the other hand, has been given to studying the psychotherapeutic treatment of all other instincts, impulses, thoughts, preoccupations, feelings and experiences, which in many cases are actually manifestations of the underlying fear of death . . . Examination of this fear is necessary in every analysis. It is the therapist's responsibility to be aware of this fear and to *help* the patient uncover it . . . without such consideration, treatment cannot fully plumb the depths of psychoneurotic or psychopathological manifestations. (pp. 620–22)

Similarly, Searles (1961) has maintained that at a theoretical level, affective recognition of the inescapability of death ranks in psychological import with such fundamental and traditionally accepted phenomena as weaning, oedipal situations, and anal training. In terms of clinical practice he feels it necessary that the therapist be more than intellectually aware of his own and "the patient's" death attitudes, and that the whole therapeutic approach be conducted in the light of this keenly experienced awareness.

---

3. This theoretical reformulation has, of course, been anticipated elsewhere (see, for example, Chadwick, 1929) in cultural analyses of the sequence of death and castration as punishments. Since castration is a diminished death punishment, castration anxiety may be viewed as a derivative of the more primary death fear.

While Rosenthal and Searles may not be considered as in the forefront of psychoanalytic thinking, their traditionalism is at least more measured and more reflective than that of many of their colleagues. They express a viewpoint which cannot be said to permeate the field. What prevails in its place is of course exemplified by the A. clinical history. In good part, the professional helping agents working with the family lacked the theoretical set and hypothetical constructs for receiving and dealing with the implicit communications regarding death-fears. Their handicap was not a personal antipathy toward death and death material alone—at least not in the fullest or most unobscured of senses. Their affective distaste for the material was buttressed by the relative lack of a theoretical frame for apprehending that which they disliked or feared. It is hard to do clinical research on topics outside one's purview or on topics for which there is no prescribed mode of conceptual approach. Death remains unresearched to the extent that researchers are impervious to its presence.

In the case of the A.'s, clinical apprehensiveness, theoretical bias, and forestalled insight are particularly compounded. When competing themes intrude they are seized upon by the A.'s helping agents. Death-fears are ignored or seen as derivative. Conceivably, alternative or complementary explanations might be advanced with more traditional premises. For example, castration could be seen to loom large as a theme. After all, Mr. A. undergoes surgery for a hernia, his wife avoids him sexually, he is preoccupied with repairing damage, with asserting his prowess, and with demonstrating his hypermasculinity. He and his sons relate incidents having to do with broken toys, damaged persons, injured fingers, inflamed legs. It is not the claim here that these elements are unconnected with "castration anxiety" as popularly conceived in psychoanalytic usage. Rather, we minimize their primacy. We submit that "castration anxiety" as an underlying force embraces less data and has less explanatory power than the death-fears which we have described.

b. *Death, mastery, and theory*. From the discussion in the preceding sections it is clear that the crux of death-fear involves explicit recognition of ego failure. Death is the obverse of ego mastery and control. In death the ego ceases to function; but even before death, the ego feels impotent in the face of its own demise. Fear, defense, and counteractive efforts are to be expected. In this regard Mr. A. is neither unusual nor aberrant in his reactivity. It is theory that is aberrant—theory fails to accommodate the expected and relegates the natural to the unnatural.

Perhaps nothing highlights the paradoxical attitude of psychologists and theorists better than awareness of the following: As previously noted, any number of personality theories (Festinger, 1957; Kelly, 1955; Lecky, 1951; McClelland, 1951) and systems of cognitive growth, socialization and child development (Erickson, 1950, 1956; Piaget, 1954) are predicated on notions of consistency, sameness, predictability, lack of discrepancy between expectation and event, or parts of self. At the same time, virtually all these theories ignore consideration of the single most obvious circumstance that threatens to erode and dissolve all the consistencies, the predictabilities, of the worlds and the selves we strive to integrate. Dying entails dissolution. All that the self has come to know, all that it has spent a lifetime in painstakingly constructing begins to ebb away. Apart from the fact of death itself, apart from anxiety regarding transfiguration, people have a highly active fear of the process of dying as well. Research and theory has, until recently, steered clear of the matter. Existential views have begun to supply a corrective. Thus, Heidegger's (1927) ontological concept of "being-toward-death" (*Sein zum Tode*) and Berdyaev's (1937) statement that the "fact that a person can think of death, that he knows his life is limited, continually directs the course of his living," are embellished by Sartre (1956). He suggests that it is not just the knowledge that one must ultimately die that engenders horror and discourages contemplation of death, but it is the relative lack of control over the circumstances of one's death that makes the difference. The need to minimize this "painful sense of ultimate powerlessness" (Fromm–Reichmann, 1959, p. 313), which results from unpredictability, prompts Shneidman (1963) to attempt a "psychologically oriented classification of death phenomena—an ordering based in large part on the role of the individual in his own demise" (p. 201). Mr. A. is but one example of how men deal with death and dying in notably personal ways.

Comments on Biological and Psychological Considerations

It may be argued that genetic or constitutional determinants and psychological factors provide substantial, if partial, reasons for the avoidance of death as a research topic. However, insofar as biological factors are inherent they ought to be fairly constant for the species. They certainly should be today what they were one hundred years ago. Thus, while biological factors can in part explain why clinicians have avoided the study of death in general, they cannot adequately account for why death and bereavement have of late been getting a good deal of social scientific attention.

Why the recent flurry of research on death has occurred is a question rarely considered by psychologically oriented thinkers. There is little present in psychological theories about death to suggest that man's relation to it had changed significantly over the years. Wahl (1958), for example, believes that in the area of death our reactions are hardly different from those of our most distant, primitive ancestors. If any reason can be forwarded to answer the question, why now? Wahl would likely argue that it resides in the historical origins and developmental narrowness of traditional psychoanalytic concerns. He sees these as retrospective and sexual rather than prospective and toward death. But even such a response begs the question. Indeed, one might legitimately ask why clinical knowledge and theory about sexuality were first. Psychodynamic theory about sexuality antedates similar considerations about death by some sixty years.

Borkenau (1955), a psychoanalytically influenced historian, argues differently than Wahl. He begins with the recognition that man's attitude toward death today is fundamentally different than it was in Freud's day. According to his thesis, man, convinced of his own immortality, is yet inwardly driven to pursue death. He lives in perpetual contradiction. Applying isomorphic enlargement, Borkenau asserts that the conflicting attitudes of the individual are also at work within the culture and that a shift of popular attitudes toward death from death-defying to death-denying are reflected in the undulating and cyclical nature of history. For Borkenau, our times are marked by a shift from death-defiance to death-denial, and thus we raise questions and study attitudes today that we would not in the past.

Despite the psychoanalytically inspired dualism, the over-simplified conception of one-way causality, the highly specu-lative and too easy isomorphism, and a view of society as a mere duplication of the individual's inner state, Borkenau is among the few psychologically minded theorists who recog-nize that our attitudes and relation toward death are perhaps not what they have always been. He endeavors to offer an ex-planation. His explanation suffers from a certain cultural short-sightedness. But, precisely because it does, it succeeds, in an odd way, in calling attention to the societal factors it im-plicitly defines by sheer neglect as being outside causal influ-ence.

Culture

The explicit criticisms of Borkenau's contentions are directed at his facile isomorphism and the conceptual narrowness of his view of causality in social affairs; they in no way minimize the conviction that cultural factors are often in the service, or for that matter, the disservice of individual man's psychological needs. Other psychologically oriented thinkers, however, do offer conceptions of society that are in some ways more useful and less ideologically confining than Borkenau's.

Hebb (1954) presents a view of society which is organized around man's inherent need to avoid emotional provocation. This is a view which he illustrates specifically with man's fear of death. According to Hebb, culture serves as man's protec-tive cocoon. Man is not by nature emotionally stable. Rather, his seeming stability rests upon his success in avoiding emo-tionally arousing situations:

> . . . the development of what is called "civilization" is the progressive elimination of sources of acute fear, disgust and anger . . . civilized man may not be less, but more, suscepti-ble to such disturbance because of his success in protecting

himself from disturbing situations so much of the time . . .
We read incredulously of the taboo rules of primitive society;
we laugh at the superstitious fear of the dead in primitive
people. What is there about a dead body to produce disturbance? Sensible, educated people are not so affected. One can
easily show that they are, however, and that we have developed an extraordinary complete taboo system—not just moral
prohibition, but full-fledged ambivalent taboo—to deal with
the dead body. (p. 830)

For Hebb, adjustment is a function of protected environ-
ments, predictability, lack of flux and surprise. Socialization,
moral education, rules of courtesy, dress, behavior, and speech,
all ensure that members of society will not act in ways that provoke others. Hence, while death occurs all about us, we strive
to erect ever more impenetrable barriers to its discussion
and to the fuller understanding of its meanings. On large scale
and small, our ingenuity for treating death lightly, for delegat-
ing it to remote places, and for causing it to appear trivial and
insignificant seems limitless. A review of psychological studies
of death concludes, "The material from empirical sources reveals that at a conscious, verbal level, people in [American]
culture do not seem to be seriously concerned with thoughts of
death" (Alexander and Alderstein, 1960, p. 91).

Examples abound. Death is rarely, if ever, considered an
open or polite topic of social conversation. The dead are concealed from view as rapidly as possible and removed to a funeral establishment as soon as funeral personnel can be sum-
moned. Children particularly are insulated from first-hand
contact with and observation of the dead. Humor, theatrics,
and drama become the easy handmaidens of the terrors we
live with. The popular arts are replete with events on stage
and in films that permit death to be outwitted or forestalled, or
that allow the very same individuals to die again and then
again, much as if death and its finality could be experientially
foresworn. Or when death is final, films and television characteristically refuse the audience any opportunity for building
emotional identification with the characters destined to die.

And then, too, when death occurs in the artifacts of popular culture it is seldom "natural death." Gorer (1956) remarks

that he "cannot recollect a novel or a play of the last twenty years or so which . . . describes in any detail the death from 'natural causes' of a major character . . ." (p. 58). Unnatural death, and especially violent death, is the death mainly represented in movies, plays, television, and novels. In moving pictures dealing with murder, the slain individual is never deeply mourned (Wolfenstein, 1950); rather, someone close to him takes on the mission of doggedly pursuing the killer, oblivious to the normal impact of the death. Wolfenstein concludes that death is not very real in American films, and that for the most part it functions as a convenient catalyst to other varieties of action. Almost never does it constitute an emotional reality in and of itself.

If such death-denying attitudes were confined to the rules of polite conversation and fantasy, there would be only some reason for concern. Unfortunately, the chances that such attitudes are so confined are small. When the denial and fantasy extend to or mirror real behaviors, and, in fact, become the unacknowledged bulwark for an economic, political, and social modus operandi, there is much reason for concern and chagrin. Ours is a social system that is little concerned with death. Indeed, death is made to seem irrelevant in an era of eternally manufactured delight (Agee, 1959).

Shifting Attitudes toward Death and Dying

It is true that every culture has its own values, ideas, beliefs, and practices regarding death, and one could argue effectively, as Hebb does, that these are institutionalized means of minimizing surprise and emotional provocation. It is also obvious that an individual learns the orientations of his culture toward death, and his conceptions of the meaning of death flow from these learnings. What is apparently less understood by psychologically oriented thinkers is that culture evolves and changes, and that such changes can have significant impact on individuals within that culture. This asocial view on the part of psychologists is in good measure a function of their disposition to study what goes on inside the individual's skin, and their propensity to either control all other variables or treat such variables as sources of uncontrolled variance.

The view of this study is somewhat different. It holds that the cultural context within which death is experienced in the United States, and the institutionally sanctioned responses to it have undergone dramatic change in the last decade. What is more, the extent if not the quality and direction, of this change is fundamentally greater in the United States than in most Western nations.

Having already taken Borkenau to task, we may now give him his due. There can be little quarrel with his broad observation: As a nation we have moved, if not from death-defying to death-denying attitudes, then certainly from death-accepting to death-rejecting postures. However, Borkenau, while making the right observation, seems to offer the wrong inference. The reversal in the American attitude seems more logically to be the consequence of shifts within society itself, and not merely the result of unconscious strivings and intrapsychic paradoxes.

Not a few writers have commented on this shift, particularly as it contrasts with modified attitudes toward sexuality (Bowers, Jackson, Knight, and LeShan, 1964; Gorer, 1965). Gorer, in fact, advances the highly interesting premise that the social taboos once attending sexuality have been superceded by taboos and suppressed anxieties about death and dying:

> Pornography would appear to be a concomitant of prudery, and certainly the periods of the greatest production of pornography have also been the periods of most rampant prudery. . . . Traditionally, and in the lexicographic meaning of the term, pornography has been concerned with sexuality. For the greater part of the last two hundred years copulation and (at least in the mid-Victorian decades) birth were the "unmentionables" of . . . basic human experience . . . around which so much private fantasy and semiclandestine pornography were erected. During most of this period death was no mystery, except in the sense that death is always a mystery. . . . In the twentieth century, however, there seems to have been an unremarked shift in prudery; whereas copulation has become more and more "mentionable," particularly in Anglo-Saxon societies, death has become more and more "unmentionable" *as a natural process.* . . . The natural process of corruption and decay has become disgusting, as disgusting as

the natural processes of copulation and birth were a century ago; preoccupation with such processes is (or was) morbid and unhealthy, to be discouraged in all and punished in the young. Our great-grandparents were told that babies were found under gooseberry bushes or cabbages; our children are likely to be told that those who have passed on . . . are changed into flowers or lie at rest in lovely gardens. The ugly facts are relentlessly hidden; the art of the embalmers is an art of complete denial. (pp. 58–59)

An intriguing idea emanating from Gorer's view is the implication that the study of sexuality emerged as the central topic of psychiatry for reasons having to do with prevailing cultural climates. While Western society was quite open about death in Victorian and Edwardian times, it was generally quite prudish about sex; thus it was in the sexual realm that psychological costs were likely to be incurred—particularly in the form of hysteria—and psychological insights needed to be achieved. It was no accident then, given the price of cultural suppression, that modern psychiatry and psychodynamic theory—the work of Havelock Ellis and Sigmund Freud—had their foundations in neuroses attributable to sexual conflict. By the same token, the ever-increasing scarcity of classical neuroses, especially *Grande Hysterie* and conversion reactions, and the concomitant increment in other categories of disturbance such as character disorders in modern clinical work is a much discussed and widely recognized phenomenon. Certainly, with shifting moralities, generational differences in socialization and formal education, rapid cultural flux, and the changing perspectives and expectations of people, one has every reason to anticipate that psychopathological manifestations and symptomotology will undergo change. Is it not also reasonable to expect that the actual content of the core conflicts underlying psychopathologies may also change with times and shifts in cultural climates? In brief, are sexual conflicts, even in our society, as predominant a source of pathology today as years ago? Is it too much to assume that today, as opposed to years ago, death attitudes play an increasingly important role in emotional disturbances—perhaps even, in some populations, vying with or superseding sexuality as the mainspring content of conflicts in psychopathology? If so, is it not also likely that on many occasions mental health professionals are still prone to look to old explanations for new clinical problems? The A.'s clinical history would certainly seem to indicate yes. As exemplified, the A.'s death material is repeatedly construed as sexual data, and then converted to "libidinized" meanings.

Shifting Attitudes toward Death and the Decline of Religion

The avoidance of death and dying and the de-ritualization of grief and mourning, both spreading rapidly in contemporary society, mirror still other important changes in Western culture. It seems possible, for example, to trace a relationship between shifting attitudes toward death and substantial changes in religious beliefs and practices.

A culture's attitudes toward death have traditionally been embedded in its religious emphasis, and, depending on the commitment of the society's members to theological doctrine, death may or may not constitute a daily challenge to the individual's self-conceptions. Since many religious concepts of death reside in a "prepared metaphysical system which serves to assuage the shock of death through the promise of a renewed and continued existence," it is presumed that the greater the individual's commitment to this religious doctrine, the more ready his acceptance of his demise as supremely natural and preordained (Fulton, 1965). When one recognizes that (a) subscription to the Christian faith in this country has waned considerably in the past seventy years, its influence eroded by rising secularism, until today less than 50 percent of the population is church affiliated; that (b) even among those who are church-going, deep-seated belief in future life is not the rule; that (c) cemeteries no longer stand in close proximity to churches as constant reminders that death is a requisite for life but are instead hidden from view or kept at some distance; and that (d) religious leaders play a limited, sometimes flagrantly pathetic role in today's funeral ceremonies, more often than not finding themselves with embarrassingly little or no direct knowledge of the person they eulogize;

then, one can begin to appreciate that natural death and the very processes of dying and decaying have become happenings of monstrous dimensions, too horrible to contemplate and too devastating to face directly without support or defense.

What, if anything, has replaced religion's promise of an afterlife? What does a more secular view offer man now in the face of death? Phrased in psychological terms, what is the cost incurred by the loss of a major defense, and what is the value of its replacement? These are crucial questions, and for the most part they remain unanswered. However, it does appear at present that the costs for the common man are considerable, and that a replacement is still wanting.

In the past, religion seemed to neatly obtund death's bite, at least as the common man endured it, by positing a fine, active postlife. Conceptions of this hereafter were sufficient to belie the very possibility that death was anything greater than a catnap followed by a trip into pastoral existence. We are today perhaps too ready to look upon the past with psuedo-sophisticated, mocking condescension. We tend to consider ourselves beyond or above the fetid little myths so willingly furnished in the past by organized religion. Indeed, there is ample justification for believing that some of these myths were as "cruel as cosmetics on a cadaver" (Agee, 1959). But, we must be wary of those tendentious attitudes which threaten oversight of the hard reality that outside of certain existential theories having limited appeal, no popular, meaningful alternative to religious myth has been substituted. The consequence has been a partial vacuum, and a need to further deny and distance death through the creation of ever more pervasive cultural taboos. The A.'s are representative of their time. They are not church-going people. They make no appeals to God, and they find no solace in religion.

Shifting Attitudes toward Death and Changes in the Family

Side by side with the decline of religion in America, and no doubt in some ways functionally related to it, some fundamental changes in the tempo, pattern, and style of American family life have occurred (Volkart and Michael, 1957). These have also, in their own way, prevented Americans from experiencing any real or direct confrontation with natural death and dying. The last seventy years or so has seen the virtual disappearance of rural America and the simultaneous rise and eventual dominance of what Eric Goldman (1968) has termed the "epoch of Metroamerica." The family unit has shrunk in size and shifted in type from a large, integrated, and extended group, under one or a few proximal roofs, to a small, individualized, and isolated group, lost in the impersonal uniformity of the American suburbs. A highly mobile society has emerged, given to frequent and often long-distance moves, with a style of family living that contrasts sharply with that of the geographically rather stable family in the past.

These changes have worked toward the dissolution of family traditions and heritages which in the past guaranteed a measure of individual identity, and, at the same time, assured some intimate and vivid experiences with death, dying, and their meanings. Experiences of this kind are now gone.

The high degree of mobility in our culture and the related disintegration of close-knit extended family units increase the probabilities that the old today will die away from family and among comparative strangers. In addition, the time family members will spend with the dying will be curtailed and fragmented since there are felt obligations to other family members and jobs some distance away. Indeed, distance often provides an expedient excuse for evasion of even minimal contact with a dying relative. The extended death-bed vigil by family seems a thing of the past. Its loss is particularly felt by children. In the past children were allowed to contemplate death, were allowed to remain at home when a fatal illness struck a member of the family, were included in the discussion and exchange of fears, and were allowed to feel that the grief was not theirs alone, but shared by others as well. Today they are deprived any occasion for participation (Kubler Ross, 1969). Gorer (1956) describes experiences as they were a century ago:

> It must have been a rare individual who, in the nineteenth century, with its high mortality, had not witnessed at least one actual dying, as well as paid his respects to "beautiful

corpses"; funerals were the occasion for the greatest display for working class, middle class and aristocrat. The cemetery was the center of every old established village and they were prominent in most towns. It was fairly late in the nineteenth century before the execution of criminals ceased to be a public holiday as well as a public warning. (p. 58)

Still other death-related functions have been defaulted today. For instance, knowledge of how to prepare a corpse for burial, which was very familiar to most nineteenth-century households, has almost totally vanished (Lydgate, 1961). It has been replaced by today's characteristic avoidance, specifically by the practice of relegating to trained and impersonal professionals the duties and rituals surrounding death and disposal of the dead (Fulton, 1965). To seem unmindful of death is today fast becoming an American trademark.

Shifting Attitudes toward Death and Medical-Technological Advances

In this country, receding consciousness of death has been enhanced immeasurably by the momentous technological and medical science discoveries of the last decades. As Fulton (1965) notes, the present generation of Americans is likely the first in the course of civilization to have never experienced death in its natural form. Preventive medicine and public health measures have so reduced natural death among the young that the average American family does not anticipate a death within its immediate ranks for twenty years or more. This is a far cry from the situation just fifty years ago. And there is still another facet of the picture to be considered, one which adds to the increasing odds that intimate association with death in its natural forms may successfully be kept outside the experience of most Americans, regardless of their age and excepting their own death. Glaser and Strauss (1965) report that in 1964 53 percent of *all* deaths in the United States occurred in hospitals. What additional percentage occurred away from home—in nursing homes, on highways, on battlegrounds—was not estimated. However, Glaser and Strauss make clear that dying away from home, away from familiar persons, and dying slowly from chronic illness, will prove even more common in the coming years. An estimated 80 percent of the persons who died in 1970, died away from home (Kubler-Ross, 1970). Hence, an ever easier avoidance of death and an even more available avenue for shunting concerns about death onto the shoulders of qualified but impersonal professionals make the human problem of awareness and of fear more salient than ever. Ironically, the greater the advancements of science, the more the denial of death's reality seems encouraged. Death may be forestalled today, but when it comes it promises to come with vengeance—and to be more lonely, more mechanical, and more dehumanized than it has ever been. For the unprepared and terrorized survivors of the dead, it holds forth the promise of increased psychic pain and functional disability.

Why Death Is Studied Today

Comments on Cultural Considerations

Where death and dying are concerned, the many complexities emanating from the religious and societal upheavals, and from the technologic-medical developments of the last half-century merge into one simple, sharp issue: death, despite or indeed because of its less frequent occurrence, is taking an ever increasing psychic toll. It has been the consistent experience of clinical workers that any defense or circumstance which enables people to persistently evade awareness of any basic aspect of reality—internal or external—is psychologically draining and costly. Energy is consumed and efficient role performance impeded or undermined. When death and dying are denied, dying persons suffer unduly, and the prospective or actual survivors writhe with self-pity, anger, fear, guilt, nightmares, and symptoms of unknown and unsuspected origins.

In the cultural and societal vicissitudes just discussed are some better answers to the two original questions: Why were death and dying not topics of earlier psychological study? And, why study them now? *Ludicrously simple as it might seem, these topics were not studied earlier because from a cul-*

tural and psychic standpoint they were not problematic. Death and dying were not evaded, but were more consciously tolerated as a piece of everyman's reality and experience. In turn, they are studied today because, as they have receded from consciousness with all the rapidity of present-day culture change and technological advance, they have become problematic and psychically expensive. People today retreat in awe before yesterday's routine event, and the range and locus of reasonable behavior and activity is sharply curtailed. Death and dying are studied today because we are given to studying professionally that which is dysfunctional, and worse yet, expensively dysfunctional.

The A. Death History and the Need for Research

Since it has been argued that death has only recently become a topic worthy of psychological study because modern cultural changes have caused it to be increasingly denied, and because this trend has begun to cost society palpable human pain and suffering then clearly some of the costs are increasingly self-evident. But some are not. We are probably not even aware of some costs as yet, and we may be aware of others only in ways unrelated to any concern about cultural taboos regarding death. We currently ascribe them to other factors and tally them on other ledgers. The A. history has exemplified all of these possibilities. The implications of false attribution deserve discussion.

That man, the animal erecting the greatest taboos against natural death, is also the animal most given to willful and even unprovoked killing of large numbers of his own as well as other species is a paradox worth noting. More specifically, it appears that as the cultural evasion of natural death and dying has increased in recent decades, violent, unnatural, and man-perpetuated death has simultaneously grown until it has, in the last thirty to forty years, reached levels unparalleled in history. Wars, concentration camps, rebellions, murders, and assassinations are among the more obvious forms of violent, unnatural death. Not only is violent death no longer an unexpected circumstance but, now that natural death is increasingly avoided and suppressed from consciousness, violent death has gained major prominence in the fantasy life of our culture as well. Violence on television, in spy novels, pulp magazines, war movies, horror comics, children's cartoons, all formats in which explicit visual or descriptive detail is given full play while little or no attention is awarded the affects that normally accompany death, offer without effort and without imagination a ready-made scapegoat for national ills.

Violence in national affairs is often seen as the result of violence in mass media, with the linkage presumably mediated by social imitation. This would not be the first time in the history of social science that the cause and effect model has been misapplied. The alternative possibility is that both outcomes (violence in natural affairs and violence in mass media) are effects of more complex, pervasive sets of underlying and interacting antecedent causes, one of which may be suppression of death as a natural phenomenon. In this view, violence in fantasy and violence in real life are both psychological substitutions or displacements, originating in culture-wide prudery toward natural death. As Lydgate (1961) has observed:

> The whole business of death is gradually being bowdlerized out of common experience, giving place to the Gothic fantasies of horror films which now seem more acceptable to the public than details of the real thing. (p. 14)

The behavior of the A. men is quite consistent with this premise. Mr. A. and Ricky hunt deer and pheasant. Roscoe has morbid preoccupations, a graveyard of his own, fantasies of violence, and away from home (the arena of the death taboo's strictest enforcement) is given to explosive attack and murderous rages. Yet, none of them can acknowledge directly Mr. A.'s proximity to natural death.

It has long been the position of mental health experts to look with compassionate condemnation upon substitute sexual gratifications. The general population has been less compassionate though its disapproval is at least as strong. When concerned with death, however, experts and society at large are far more permissive. Substitute gratifications in the forms of violence, killing, or horror are explicitly or implicitly sanctioned. One need only turn to the mass media to realize how much close detail and loving care are accorded the depiction of violent death. Even in this "liberated" age sexuality enjoys less explicit treatment. One could, in fact, argue on the basis of the foregoing and on the basis of the A. history that to limit or censor violence in fantasy media would serve to increase displacement to behavioral modes and acting out, thus creating results opposite to those desired and intended by censors.

However, far more reasonable than tampering with symptoms would be research and careful study into the linkages between violent death and the cultural taboos surrounding natural death. For if people cannot come to grips with death in any open and dignified way, then they will do so surreptitiously and in ways that will cost us dearly.

> If we dislike the modern pornography of death, then we must give back to death—natural death—its parade and publicity, readmit grief and mourning. If we make death unmentionable in polite society—"not before the children"—we almost insure the continuation of the "horror comic." (Gorer, 1956, p. 62)

And we might ask in addition of "real violence" as well? Roscoe A. may be an extreme case, but he is the extreme of a cultural configuration. He is most certainly not alone either in his behavior or his motives. Nor is he alone in his anguish.

The Mental Health Professional and Clinical Study of Death

Clearly, there is a great need for research and exploration in the area of attitudes toward death. Recognition that a problem exists is assuredly a first step toward phrasing questions, finding answers, and gaining control. But a cautionary note is in order. Exhortation to research the psychology and sociology of death comes easily, and this is surely not the first such plea. Implementation, however, is entirely another matter. We need only remember that in one of the most important research studies undertaken in World War II—the research on the American soldier (Merton and Lazarsfeld, 1950)—death was among the topics omitted. Although attitudes toward cowardice and fear were researched, they were considered independently of their likely connection to death attitudes. Research on the topic becomes in large part a matter of recognizing data in the natural setting and anxieties in the self.

But where in the clinical researcher's training does he have the opportunity to study death and dying? Being culturally emersed, he is protected and experientially distanced from death. How is he to recognize his defenses, his aversive conditioning, his counter-transference reactions in the face of death material and themes? He may seek to do so through psychotherapy, psychoanalysis, encounter experiences, or sensitivity training. It certainly seems reasonable to believe that if ambivalences toward salient figures in one's own life are worked out in treatment one will then be able to face the death of others or oneself more rationally and realistically. Nonetheless, as things stand now, the working through and analysis of death attitudes and material in treatment is left to chance. That is, impending death, actual death, or a past encounter with death must constitute part of a person's experience for it to be specifically addressed. Even in treatment, one is often disadvantaged by virtue of the fact that the therapist has had no experience or training of his own in the psychology of death. He also not only shares cultural biases, but given shifts in technology and medical innovations, he is not likely to have had personal or intimate encounters with death. Supervision of his work is also, and for the same reasons, likely to reflect negligence of death themes. Certainly, any systematized teaching on the topic is likely to be minimal—though prominent exceptions are beginning to be in evidence (Glaser and Strauss, 1965; Kubler-Ross, 1969). How different the situation is with sexual materials and themes, which are amenable to serving as the central focus of many therapeutic analyses. But the clinician is likely to first encounter death professionally and personally only when he is well into his adulthood—in today's world possibly age thirty or more. Before that, it is all too easily ignored as a piece of his training. As a piece of experience it is muted by defense. It can thus be readily appreciated that clinical practitioners and clinical researchers are ill-prepared to deal with death themes. While well-intentioned and even eager, they cannot help but be subject to gross error. The A.'s encounter with mental health professionals is representative. One can only wonder how many cases like theirs have not come to light, have been instead dismissed as failures due to resistances on other grounds. It is abundantly clear that researchers on death are still in the beginning stages.

Chapter 14

Clinical Research and the Family

The work on families that has taken place in the last fifteen years, as productive of new insights as it may have been, has nonetheless failed, in vital ways, to realize the fullness of its early promise. The family, ignored by psychoanalysis and psychology in general, has in recent years become a subject of popular study. The development of the field was often a matter of clinical expediency. When this was not the case, it was often the result of a mismarriage of ideas and methods for, unfortunately, the study of the family has been carried out with old and often inappropriate methods such as controlled experimentation, single variable to single variable research design, and clinic-based diagnosis, therapy, and research. This is hardly a new circumstance in the sciences, though the social sciences, by virtue of their newness, seem more predisposed to misapplications of this nature. In the past few years, psychology particularly has been witness in a number of its significant areas to the marriages—or more accurately the mismarriages— of time-honored and cherished yet often opposed traditional positions. The field of family interaction and dynamics provided the nexus for linking the clinical and the experimental. To be sure, strange partnerships likely exist in other realms of psychology as well. But in the field of family study the miscegenation has a uniqueness all its own.

Amalgams of this kind, always well intentioned, always seemingly an adventurous first step, are too frequently wrong headed. And more than occasionally they result in such disappointment and discouragement about a vital content area that it is prematurely abandoned as a research concern. Yet often the problem lies not in the content area itself, or in the researcher's tacit conviction regarding its worth, but in the application of traditional approaches and standards to new topics and ideas. One need only recall the problems of academic psychiatry. Some seventy-five years ago, the technique of psychoanalysis was especially developed to facilitate the study of specific problems and concepts. But, highly specialized and innovative methods, that have been honed and perfected on the specific class of problems for which they were first invented, are in time justifiably elevated to respectability; then, all too readily, they are promoted to the undeserved and unfair status of traditional methodology and dogma. It is here that one runs the considerable risk of confusing the end with the means, the product with the tool. Having become academically "legitimate" and "sanctioned," methodological forms then dictate the selection of problems and the approach to them. Obviously, the reverse circumstance should prevail. The content area, with its unique and inherent problems, ought to determine, in virtually every sense, the method and means employed.

There are only the faintest glimmerings that family researchers are aware of this issue today, or that the latter attitude is gaining some recognition. Still, the few glimmers are better than total dimness. Nonetheless, there is no denying that for the better part of fifteen years the situation in the field was in many ways dimly lit. In any event, having sounded this precautionary and rather polemical note, we turn to some considerations of family. This time we begin with some sociological observations.

The Family as a Subject of Clinical Study

Cultural Considerations

Risking oversimplification and a too facile explanation, we suggest that one major reason the family was not a topic of psychological study in the past is that it was not then in any serious trouble. Its internal patterns, customs, rules, and functions were consistent with the economic, educational, social, and political objectives and premises of society at large. The family has become a source of clinical concern and study in

post–World War II years because this no longer obtains. Social and technological changes have wrought such fundamental shifts in basic family patterns, that particular intrafamilial
arrangements no longer agree either with societal arrangements and goals or with the mythology of how things should
be. The more obvious changes that have occurred in the structure of the American family, and how they impinge on family
relationships and the development and "mental health" of family members are questions whose answers range well beyond
the intended scope of this chapter. They have been the bread
and butter topics of sociologists who have thoroughly explored
them. It should suffice to quote the following passage from
Max Lerner:

> ". . . the traditional family—large, three generations, patriar-
> chal, attached to the land, closely integrated in performing
> the collective economic functions of farm homestead or small
> shop or family business—has almost gone out of the picture.
> It is more likely to be small, two generation, mobile, whole
> family centered, equalitarian. The family no longer performs
> to the same degree the old functions of economic production,
> religious cohesion, kinship continuity and cultural transmis-
> sion." (Lerner, 1957, p. 551)

To this list of declining functions we may add the loss of a
combat function, which has been almost entirely transferred
from the family to the modern state; the loss of a *protective*
function, which has been transferred to government and to insurance companies; and also, perhaps, the loss of *recreational*
functions and *governmental-authority* functions, which have
been taken over by outside agencies such as the school and
municipality. A list such as this prompted Bertrand Russell
more than forty years ago to suggest that the family tottered
on the brink of extinction. Yet as an institution it is still with
us. The essence of the matter for our purposes is to determine
how and why it has survived, and the costs of that survival—
costs tallied in terms of anguish, guilt, pseudo-mutual object
relations, and intense inner anomie.

There is little evidence to contest the fact that the family
has lost many of its once vital functions. Even Ruth Benedict

was pressed into acknowledging "that changes are taking place
. . ." (Benedict, 1949, p. 159). But she and others of her persuasion are convinced that some functions have not been lost
—the individual-care function, the allowable sex function, the
procreation function—and that still other functions have risen
sharply in significance and replaced the lost functions. Most
prominent among these neo-functions are "the pursuit of happiness" (Lerner, 1957), a "companionship" function involving
the unity that "develops out of mutual affection and intimate
association of husband and wife and parents and children"
(Burgess and Locke, 1963), and a "personal relations" function
(Parsons and Bales, 1955; Rodman, 1965) or "collegial function" (Miller and Swanson, 1958).

The notion that the loss of basic functions, such as the
economic function, has permitted us to evolve a nuclear family
system that is centered on mutual affection, consensus, equali-
tarian self-actualizing opportunities, and interpersonal compe-
tence and accord is certainly one way to read history. But
from a clinical standpoint it simply does not agree with the
facts. Middle-class families are not "happy" or "interpersonally
competent." The waiting rooms of psychiatric clinics attest to
that, so does the divorce rate. Moreover, it does not make
sense conceptually since individualism and competitiveness
are still the cornerstone values of our culture. The family is obviously affected by the strong cultural affirmation of individualism, and thus the family exists not for the group but for the
benefit of its individual members (Sirjamaki, 1948). Individual
not familial values are to be sought in family living. And indeed, this strikes at the heart of the problem. To judge from
clinical data, not to mention from the vocal protests and efforts
of the counterculture, American middle-class values are as oriented to achievement, individualism, mastery, and future attainment as they ever were. Perhaps even more, since the
sense of family considerations has, in fact, waned severely
making the culture more pre-eminently individualistic than
ever before.

An alternative version of family history in the middle-
America of this century is possible: technological changes, ur-
banism, automation, and the factory system, did bring about

major changes in the family. There was a decided loss of functions as already noted. Other institutions such as corporate industry, the government, or the school took over these functions, thereby creating a vacuum and threatening the existence of the family as an institution. To the extent that this was so Bertram Russell was correct in his diagnosis of obsolescence. However, at least two factors have thus far mitigated the circumstances and delayed the demise of the family. One is cultural lag.

As defined by Ogburn (1964), a cultural lag exists "when one of two parts of culture which are correlated changes before or in greater degree than the other part does . . . The result is less adjustment between the two parts than existed previously" (p. 86). The two parts pertinent here are the family with its attendant values, and an industrial-technological society with its attendant demands. Fifty, eighty, or one-hundred years ago these two aspects of culture were in better adjustment than they are today. Over the years, changes in the social codes and ideologies governing the family were outdistanced by more rapidly occurring changes in the economic and technological spheres. The result was a growing disharmony. The family as an institution seemed to require a substitute or compensatory set of supports and justifications for the increasingly outdated valuations of it. As the family was threatened adherents rose to its support. In the 1950's, the virtues of "togetherness," "mutual support," "companionship," and other neo-functions of the family were propounded. But these values all too often lacked structural underpinning. Their application was like supplying mortar without bricks. To some the optimism was not only unfounded, but counterproductive. Barrington Moore has described what is perhaps the darkest side of this circumstance.

> One of the most obviously obsolete features of the family is the obligation to give affection as a duty to a particular set of persons on account of the accident of birth. This is a true relic of barbarism. It is a survival from human pre-history, when kinship was the basic form of social organization . . . Popular consciousness is at least dimly aware of the barbaric nature of the duty of family affection and the pain it produces, as

shown by the familiar remark, "You can choose your friends, but you can't choose your relatives." Even if partly concealed by ethical imperatives with the weight of age-old traditions, the strain is nevertheless real and visible. Children are often a burden to their parents . . . how many young couples, harassed by the problems of getting started in life, have not wished that their parents could be quietly and cheaply taken care of in some institution for the aged? . . .

> The exploitation of socially sanctioned demands for gratitude, when the existing social situation no longer generates any genuine feeling of warmth, is a subtle and heavily tabooed result of this barbaric heritage. It is also one of the most painful. Perhaps no feeling is more excruciating than the feeling that we ought to love a person whom we actually detest. (1960, pp. 393–94)

The second factor that has delayed the demise of the family is the fact that it has seemingly assumed a new if rather unenviable function. It is a function that darkly lurked beneath what the family theorists of the 1950's so optimistically advanced. This function, first noted in the 1960's by William Goode (1964), Clark Vincent (1966, 1967), and Otto Pollak (1967) pivots on the close ordered intimacy that is presumed to exist in the isolated nuclear family of middle America. Vincent has labeled it the "adaptive" function. It might also be called the "absorbent" or "reactive" function. Vincent (1967) states the thesis as follows:

> The rapid and pervasive social changes associated with industrialization necessitate a family system that, both structurally and functionally, is highly adaptive to the demands of other social institutions externally and to the needs of its own members internally . . . the family, to a greater degree and more frequently than any other major social institution, facilitates social change by adapting its structure and activities to the changing needs of society and of other social institutions. . . . (p. 25)

> . . . At least three crucial points may be hypothesized concerning the reciprocal adaptation among various social systems: (1) Social institutions or systems other than the family adapt only to the degree that such adaptation is in the inter-

est of their respective goals. (2) If there is a conflict of interests or goals, it is most frequently the family which "gives in" and adapts. (3) The family usually adapts for lack of an alternative and in so doing serves the goals of other social systems and facilitates the survival of a society based on social change. (p. 29)

There is a covert optimism in Vincent's view which, despite its unpropitious possibilities for the family, echoes the affiance of the theories of the 1950's. Goode's (1963) conception of the family's "mediating" function goes further in this direction. Pollak is somewhat less sanguine in his interpretation of the family's new role; for him, the new function derives from deprivation. It derives from the fact that in the course of losing its many former functions to outside agencies the family also lost great freedom in decision-making. He says:

The function which truly has been taken away from the family by other institutions is not education, health care, or homemaking, but the autonomy of setting its own standards . . . the twentieth-century model presents a loss of autonomy, a being put on the defensive. (1967, p. 194)

Thus, the family has become buffer between the individual and the larger society. The larger society is "geared to corporate organization, in which the individual is replaceable and, therefore, a conformist" (Pollak, 1967, p. 198). Deep emotional ties outside the family are discouraged. Social controls in the bureaucratic world are essential. The church, the school, the office, the market place, the university, the factory, the hospital, the corporation "cannot conceivably provide sufficient freedom for the amount of emotional release and input required by the individual" (Vincent, 1967, p. 31). One can hardly exist in such systems without "experiences of inadequacy," "anger," "demeaned self worth," and it is perhaps the greatest burden of this situation that these feelings cannot be "vented in the settings that generate them" (Pollak, 1967, p. 199). Herein lies the newly discovered absorbent function of the nuclear family. It has become the social unit wherein there is time and place and maybe tolerance for the expression and acting out of individual frustrations and needs. "Its numerical size, its isolation, and its lack of organizational tie-in make it appear ideally suited for this 'adaptive' function" (Vincent, 1967, p. 30). Perhaps defenseless is a better description. Indeed, the family may be a pawn in institutional struggles. This function of the family has kept it alive. Society has supported it with values of romantic love and filial love and, through mobility and isolated housing, with a shield of privacy that is sacrosanct. In the home one can regress, explode, or be childlike, and supported by the inviolate privacy taboo, no one outside the nuclear family need be the wiser. But it is a costly and corrosive process and, at this point in time, seems to be dysfunctional. There are reasons for this. The system promulgates overload. It places too many emotional eggs in the family basket, and then proceeds to crush them. The American family is today operating at such high levels of unspoken or unchecked emotional intensity as to leave no more margin for "shock absorption" (Parsons, 1955).

The very features that would seem to nominate the conjugal, nuclear family for this adaptive function—its privacy, small size, and binding love ethic—act to negate its value. The love ethic runs counter to the need to discharge rage and displaced hostilities. The small size means that a few persons must bear the overload of tensions and emotionality and antagonisms that they did not earn. Moreover, the fact that affects cannot be more widely distributed means that the same few persons must both carry the burden and be the objects of intense ambivalences that promise to make modulation of social intercourse virtually impossible. Our small, claustrophobic, nuclear family is explosively and exquisitely oedipal; it makes weekend neuroses the rule, and the creed of surrounding privacy ensures that which we have already stated—that each family resides with consuming guilt in the unshaken conviction that theirs is a special and lonely private hell.

It is no wonder that family study has recently come to the fore. Critical mass has been reached and become manifest in the fulmination of mental health and social scientific concern with family patterns, dynamics, interaction, and therapy. For the last fifteen years, these topics have comprised a frontier in psychiatry, clinical psychology, social psychology, and social work. The psychic and social costs of the family's plight have legitimized its study.

The A.'s as the Essence of the Cultural Configuration

The A.'s are best understood as a family residing within the mainstream of middle-American culture. They should not be construed as a family apart or outside of the range of accepted cultural norms. Rather they are best conceptualized as the substance of middle America—as the quintessential expression of the cultural configuration. As such, their efforts at resolution of conflict are fully consonant with the American ethos— including scapegoating as a favored mechanism.

The A. Home: Haven for Overload

This point needs no elaboration. From the outset, our attentions on the psycho-social interior of the A. family reveal how they epitomize the American style—cool on the outside, charged on the inside. Accumulated frustrations find expression only inside the family. Roscoe is the single exception, otherwise the family plays the bureaucratic game. It is in the interest of their economic survival to do so. Mr. A. is affable, sturdy in appearance, and reliable to persons outside the home. He never jeopardizes his job, working long hours to the final moments before surgery and returning early to work afterward. While we do not see him engage persons outside the family often, we do know of his attempts to impress others as assured and masculine. As Mrs. A. struggles to maintain her job, she subdues work-engendered anger, and protests any circumstance that might set her apart from her co-workers. Ricky and Sheila are models of social conformity in school. Ricky, like his father, plays over injuries in public. Mental health professionals see them all as healthy. Except for Roscoe, the family's public face is a cool facade. Their hell is in their home. Like other American families, they live there without a margin of safety. It is merely their misfortune that they must absorb a shock—a shock that thoroughly overtaxes the precariously balanced system. It is, however, also our conjecture that this happens as a matter of course in more families than the mental health research literature currently reflects. Family tolerance for stress is virtually nil. Casualties of the system are almost guaranteed.

The Acquisition of Privacy

We have described our social system as one which places such tremendous psychological burdens on families that it leaves them little margin for error and so overloads them with ambivalences and mutually exclusive affective meanings that they cannot tolerate crisis. An illness, a death, a move from one city to another, unemployment, separation of a teenager, the presence of an aged parent are all stresses which can potentially cause a family to founder. These are not unusual crises; some are to be expected in the course of development and others are unscheduled occurrences of fair, if intermittent, probability. This is precisely the point. Despite their commonness they are all too frequently devastating to American families. They are devastating because our social system insists they be absorbed within a family organization already pressed to the threshold of fragmentation. At the same time, the social system does not overtly recognize that such crises are highly likely to occur to each family in the society at one time or another. The problem is really not crisis per se, but denial of crisis. It is our commitment to a cheerful view of life; it is our American optimism. We fail to expect crises, and because we do, we fail to provide for them emotionally. And, we fail to care for the psychic casualties thereby created. Since no family can adhere to undeviating standards of normalcy all the time, casualties are continually created. Society then seeks to pretend they don't exist.

Our society cares little for its casualties—not only the disenfranchised, the poor, the families of minority groups and the deprived but also the middle-class casualties whom we create as well. The A.'s are but one example. We create them because, in the fullness of time, crisis is inevitable in anyone's existence.

We manifest our uncaringness in many ways. One is embodied in the American conception of rugged individualism and self-help, a concept that has the quality of a moral imperative for Mr. A. He cannot acknowledge deviancy, weakness, fear, or the need for help. He and his family will go it alone. Indeed, to admit the experience of anxiety during crisis, is in this culture tantamount to acknowledging that one is tainted by mental incompetence, mental illness, or irresponsibility. By extension, the reticence of mental health workers to move from the theoretical biases of the medical model—a model which often enough judges those in dire straits as "sick," resistant, unmotivated, or completely beyond reach—is another manifestation of our uncaringness.

These two sets of social definitions, self-reliance and mental illness, combine to ensure that those most in need of assistance are least likely to obtain it. If they are not successful in selecting themselves out, they are screened out. Only those persons or families willing to define themselves as "deviant" or "ill" are likely to be offered help.

Even though we tend not to care for the casualties we create, we must somehow deal with them, and this we do by ensuring that we don't see them. By keeping the family nuclear and isolated, by instituting an inviolate taboo against the invasion of family privacy, and by permitting "deviant" families social withdrawal behind impermeable barriers we guarantee that social casualties will be contained and hidden from view.

The isolated nuclear family. Basic to the sociologic persuasion that the family has become a dependent, reactive institution, whose main function is to evolve means for adjusting to changes in other social systems, is the notion that the nuclear family is fundamental to the continuance of industrial society because it is readily dissolved, tenuously constructed, and isolated. Isolation means independence from families of orientation, and this is excellently suited to the requirements of occupational and geographical mobility requirements presumed to be inherent in contemporary American culture. Sadly, isolation also means that most families suffer their crises without the direct emotional support of extended kin. This is supposed to be most especially true of the middle-class, white, urban segment of American society.

We recognize that the foregoing view is an oversimplified piece of sociology, subject to many legitimate constraints and refinements and that some students of modern society reported the passing of "industrial man" (Ferkiss, 1969). Others, in recent years, have challenged the validity of the very concept of the isolated, nuclear family unit and have produced research in support of their challenge (Litwak, 1960; Sussman, 1959; Sussman and Burchinal, 1962). These researchers have advanced the concept of "a modified extended family," and they have pointed particularly to the help patterns among kin during emergencies, at times of crisis, or on occasions of ceremony, as evidence for their claims. The isolated nuclear family is not as isolated nor as nuclear as sociologists of the 1950's would have it.

Without detailing here the arguments on each side of the issue, we would make the observation that both positions are valid because to a great extent they define different problems and discuss noncongruent phenomena. If help is defined by such items as giving assistance during illness, financial aid, gifts, and personal or business advice then those who espouse the notion of a "modified extended kinship pattern" are essentially correct. Extended families do frequently offer service. On the other hand, this argument takes little cognizance of the constancy or intensity of affective exchange and felt obligation between family members. It does not tally the emotional costs involved or register the conflicts created by the offer of occasional help from a distance. In other words, it doesn't deal with the conditional blackmail, enforced splits in allegiances, or crippling dependencies so often attached to the request for and acceptance of assistance from extended kin. To ask for help is to incur obligation, invite intrusion, curtail autonomies. Tensions between the nuclear family and the parents' families of orientation are often enough an inevitable outcome. We may have a "modified extended kinship pattern" in much of "post-industrial" America, but here, as elsewhere, the costs of the system have yet to be assessed. The rewards of the pattern are perhaps easily overestimated as well. When help is given it is frequently of a delimited, circumscribed kind. It does not represent wholistic or integral participation in the life of the nuclear family. The tensions that mount among family members on a day-to-day basis or in crisis still must find expression and distribution among their limited number. Extended kin seldom reside within the home of those they help and so are not feasible as "absorbent targets" for nuclear family stress. In our estimation, "the modified extended kinship pattern" is often more a liability than an asset, and it is probably not the solution to the problems caused by contemporary bureaucratization of the American family. Indeed, it may be an atavistic, stop-gap device which will complicate matters in the future.

Whatever the case may be, not all or even most of America is yet "postindustrial"; nor does the "modified extended kinship pattern" by any means characterize all middle-class urban society. Most certainly the latter cannot be said to describe the A. family. The A.'s appear irrevocably "isolated" and "nuclear." They are, in fact, almost prototypical in this regard. Mr. A.'s fierce Americanism, his pride in individualism, in self-reliance, in the "moral strength" of resolute striving, and his faith in the ultimate victory of the determined underdog, all make the prospect of appealing for help an admission of classical American failure. It does not matter if the prospective help agent is extended kin or community agency or child guidance center. To request assistance is demeaning and has the equivalence of besmirched loyalty to the national values. It is unpatriotic.

All of this is not to say that the temptations for requesting help are not there. They are, but they are indulged only in fantasy, or are denied outright, or are severely contained. The collective fantasy of kin support that grips the A.'s during visit eleven is an example of how they might wish for financial support from extended kin. It also suggests that extended kin are able and willing to assist family members. Nonetheless, for the A.'s it remains pretty much an unfulfilled wish. Aside from Roscoe's spending some time in the home of his maternal grandparents just prior to his entering the Day Treatment service of the child guidance center, there is no hint of any substantive support given by kin to the family either before or after Mr. A.'s surgery—despite the fact that Mrs. A.'s parents continued to reside but fifty miles from the A.'s home town of Revere.[1]

In sum, it seems safe to conclude that if not for Roscoe the A.'s would have succeeded in keeping their family's status as a cultural casualty from public view. Only Roscoe's displaced angers and his efforts at escaping the family home brought the A.'s plight to the attention of outsiders. Even then there was a reluctance to look. The A.'s adherence to the cultural norm, their existence as a small, nuclear, isolated family group practically sufficed to keep a situation of stress under wraps. The tragedy, of course, is that outside of particulars, the stress and the crisis were not unordinary. The family only treated them as such. That they did so is consistent with the ethos of privacy.

The cult of privacy and the need for barriers. We will have occasion later to deal with the matter of privacy in some detail. For the moment we wish to note it as a cultural phenomenon which ensures that our social casualties will be hidden from view.

There are many reasons for the progressive privatization of family life in American society. Some of them are peculiar to our social-industrial ecology, some are not. But, for the moment, we will consider only those that pertain most especially to this study. First, and perhaps most obviously, certain aspects of the urbanization and industrialization of modern American society have acted to enhance the demand for psychic and spatial privacy. Enforced face-to-face encounters with persons who are strangers and overcrowding are normal aspects of our lives. These circumstances have become so much a part of the American scene, that we take the longing for privacy for granted and accord it sacred status. We forget that the desire for aloneness is not fundamental among human

1. We cannot claim to know the details of the family's financial situation, nor the means whereby the surgeries were financed. Presumably, medical insurance provided coverage. It may also be presumed that the same code which prevented the A.'s from acknowledging that they needed or were receiving "psychiatric" help, also acted to dissuade them from accepting assistance from relatives.

motives, but that it is reactive to conditions of overcrowding and to repeated encounters with the unknown. We lose sight of the fact that families residing in unchanging pre-industrial societies enjoy less privacy and have less need of it than we. They can predict their daily circumstance with greater care. The likelihood of social surprise and interactional awkwardness presses us to cherish privacy.

Second, and relatedly, the American drive for mastery, accomplishment, achievement—in a word, the American striving to compete and overcome—in a social system erected on competition makes privacy a strategic necessity. Privacy not only creates a sense of possession, but constitutes a primary interpersonal defense. When a person withholds his intentions from another, when he conceals or obscures the inner state of his affairs and the extent of his knowledge he gains a competitive edge. We have noted that industrial society brings strangers into interaction. It creates unpredictability and makes mastery of the social encounter a significant issue in competition and achievement. To get ahead the American way, one has to become master while remaining unmastered. In this regard, privacy is power.

Third, it is necessary to consider the connection between social deviancy and the "adaptive" function of the nuclear family in bureaucratic society. Here we may simply assert that family life must be privatized to the extent that family members deem the norms of the society as antagonistic to the family's continuation of its style of life. Exposure of deviance invites criticism and portends loss of status and heightened vulnerability. The family with a "deviant" pattern finds it increasingly difficult to spend time with outsiders because outsiders do not blind themselves to aspects of the deviancy, but instead are likely to capitalize on it to the disadvantage of the family. Social isolation becomes a means of preventing the outside world from intruding, and since outsiders are seen as increasingly persecuting, the barrier between the family and the external world becomes progressively impermeable.

The A.'s are, of course, singularly dedicated to compliance with social norms. They seek in every way to minimize what they construe as their deviancy. As a consequence, they place a premium on their privacy, the home visits not withstanding. In all the visits to the A.'s home, there were just two occasions on which "outsiders" entered the house. Both were intensely awkward situations for the reasons outlined above. One occurred when Mr. A. brought his friend home from their ice fishing adventure in subzero weather; the other occurred late in the visits when a neighbor dropped by to obtain information for the yearly school census. Mrs. A. became totally flustered in this situation because she could neither explain my presence nor Roscoe's status with regard to school. She finally explained that he was "in a special school because he was handicapped." My presence went unaccounted for. The neighbor, though living but two houses away, knew virtually nothing of the family. Except for these two instances, there was no sign of friend, neighbor, or relative. The A.'s obviously ventured out and away from the home premises to work, school, or scout meetings, but seldom as a family group. Outsiders were rarely brought in. Even the children did not invite schoolmates or peers home. True, the home visitor's presence may have served to discourage invitations, but the nearly total lack of conversational reference to social contacts suggests that this was not the only or even the major factor in the absence of visitors. Outsiders are not comfortably admitted to the interior of the A.'s struggles, nor readily permitted glimpses of their self-presumed social deviance, their "unAmericanism." Like other families who sense they vary from propagandized social norms, the A.'s exclude relatives, friends, and outsiders who might remind them of their "differentness." Instead, they erect a boundary about themselves. The home visitor was virtually the sole exception, and, in this role, my presence was conditioned by my nonparticipation, my "professional" distance, and my potential for mitigating the felt accusations of resistance and deceit experienced by the family at the hands of the child guidance center.

The Triumph of Individualism

The A.'s are faithful to the cultural ethos. The primacy of individual needs holds sway through duress and crisis. Personal goals are rarely or minimally subverted to those of the group.

This is not to say that tensions which pull toward group cohesiveness do not occur. They do, but the A.'s ultimately coexist more than they coalesce. With but few exceptions, they never really unite and pull together as a team. In the throes of crisis they do not join forces or seek collectively to boost morale. There is only the illusion that they do so, and it is very much a matter of self-delusion. Mostly, they seek to be left alone. Thus, many of their mutually struck arrangements are in the interest of maintaining personal autonomy and privacy. The exceptions are the corrosive treatment of Roscoe and Sheila's rescue of Pamela. These exceptions permit the family to maintain a semblance of unified functioning. The notion that groups can "rise to the occasion" and put their collective "shoulder to the wheel" in crisis is not completely myth; but for the middle-American family it may require reformulation. It retains validity only if one can construe scapegoating as "rising to the occasion" and the murder of an identity as a collective cause. The middle-American family, in its capacity as "adapter-absorber" of change in expanding social institutions, may possibly have been victimized to the breaking point; its desperate efforts at internal adaptation and equilibration, and its adherence to a doctrine of individualism, may, in turn, have driven it to the point of routinely victimizing at least one of its weakest members—namely, a child. Roscoe A. is surely not alone in his plight.

Scapegoating the Child: Some Final Words

Lest the last sentence seem too extreme, it should be recalled that we have already identified scapegoating as the American way. There is no need to rescind the assertion now. In fact, in the light of our earlier analysis of structural and functional change in the middle-American family, there is every reason for reaffirming it at this point.

It is a popular conception that we are a child centered culture, and it is hard to dispute that the middle-class family of today is especially child-centered. Ostensibly, the phrase is taken to mean a preoccupation on the part of parents with child-rearing activities and with the emotional well-being, interpersonal satisfactions, and self-fulfillment of their developing child. "Happiness striving," "compassionate ethos," "affectional security," and a generally assumed deference on the part of parents to the needs of their offspring are frequently referred to. One even hears murmurs of a child-centered anarchy rampant in the American nuclear family, with the presumption that parents exist primarily for their children. This we challenge as a partial and misleading truth. Indeed, frequently the reverse prevails. Either way, there is no gainsaying the significance of children to the family. There is, however, some basis for questioning the common interpretation of this assertion and a clear need to examine the functional underpinnings for the family's child focus. We assert that the child is a prime candidate for scapegoating as well as exultation, and that his value to his family derives from the former function far more often than we are inclined to admit. Roscoe A. is enough to convince one of this. Like many a middle-American child, he has, despite disclaimers, fallen from his popularly postulated status.

Inherent in the conception of the child as scapegoat for his family is the notion that the child—like his family—has lost many of his functions. Once again, we may look to the impact of a growing urban industrial society. It has altered the meaning of children as children in the family. With increasing technological advance, and concomitant diminishing of agrarian enterprise, those values which favored high fertility and large families have given way to new ones favoring the small family. As noted, the factory, the public school, the private and civic corporation—places of employment outside the home—today subsume many of the functions that once belonged to the family; increasingly, the independence of the child from the family is emphasized. Children are no longer a valuable part of the work force. Increasingly, school programs which serve younger and younger children become available, and for many children today a school career begins at age two.

Children of today are in a very precarious position; their mere presence and their demands for socialization are sources of distress and duress for not a few parents. The child's place in the scheme of family life has been drastically compromised, and he need not be very old before he comes to know the full degree of his expendability. Admonitions to the contrary—that all is not as bleak as it seems, and that, in fact, precisely because the middle-class American family of today enjoys unprecedented quantities of free choice, privacy, leisure, and democratic decision-making, people will tend to marry and have children for reasons of love, intimacy, and emotional cohesiveness (Benedict, 1949)—are almost beside the point. First, they wrongly assume that any choice is rationally made. Second, the luxuries pointed out are purchased dearly, demanding heightened degrees of responsibility and felt obligation, which are not necessarily the hand maidens of rational, responsible action, but of guilt, conflict, and despair when those obligations are inwardly felt, but overtly unheeded. Third, the matter of free choice does not apply to children, but only to adults. Children must suffer the consequences. They often do endeavor to fight back, but such attempts are likely to land them in the courts or a setting for the emotionally disturbed child. While many parents feel socially and inwardly compelled to evince love for children whom they do not love, as many children are conversely duty-bound to simulate, to the point of self-delusion, affection for parents toward whom they scarcely feel nor owe tenderness. One cannot conceive of a better breeding ground for emotional and character disturbances. Indeed, recalling Lyman Wynn's (Wynn et al., 1958) vivid, palpable descriptions of pseudo-mutuality in schizogenic families, one cannot think of a more natural breeding place for schizophrenia or psychotic disorders of affect.

While parents in the past needed children to create a labor force and to perpetuate family lines, such traditional motivations for having children are seldom in evidence today. Today children are born not out of necessity but as a matter of ethological imperative, luxury, or ignorance. Moreover, today's urban life might be said to make the large family economically infeasible, and for parents who are competitive in the economic market children become a downright burden, a hindrance to opportunity and advancement. In the crowded isolation of the mobile urban community, where a person works at some distance from family, neighbors, and friends, his status among men, not to mention his identity, is likely to be less a function of his parents' status, or his home situation, or his children than a function of his own skills and attributes. Need for achievement and money predominates. The individualistic orientation is once again seen to run counter to—even to the point of undermining—those group principles implied by family life. Since children are no longer valued because they can fulfill the needs of one's own life, they become unwanted and are experienced as burdens. They are ready targets of resentment and are prime candidates for scapegoating in the face of parental failures. Parental frustrations and failures are many, for, in a society oriented toward economic attainment and advancement, the number of failures far exceeds the number of successes. It is surprising that this factor has not received greater emphasis in the analysis of current social movements. But the declining birth rate, contraception, legal abortion, child abuse laws, homosexual liberation, women's liberation, and the zero population growth movements are but some of the phenomena reactive to and reflective of the prevailing devaluative attitude toward children.

As we have seen, to be deprived of function is to be nominated for scapegoating. Expendability is perhaps the single most important determinant in the choice of a family scapegoat. But there are other related determinants, not the least of which is lack of status and minimal retaliatory power. One can afford to demoralize a child since he contributes little, and cannot counter his parents' strength; he is impotent in relation to them. Moreover, by ensuring parents a liberal amount of familial privacy, we practically provide them license to victimize one of their children.

All of this is to say that today's child is the logical, even ideal, repository for the accumulated frustrations, projections, and displacements of the parents. His crucial function has become that of freeing them psychically so that they might perform their key roles effectively and so that they need not confront each other with their displaced and mutual antagonisms. Once trained and molded in the scapegoat role, the child becomes indispensable to his family. He nucleates their grievances in a highly efficient and automatic fashion, and, as whipping boy, equilibrates the social system of the family. The economy imbedded in his playing his role well is so important as to constitute the single greatest impediment to his release from the role.

In human terms it is a horrible price to pay. Our society practices human sacrifice as a matter of course. I simply call attention to another seldom highlighted instance of our ingenuity in this regard. No one acts out in the A. family, except Roscoe, but then no one has to act out, except Roscoe. Roscoe has no recourse.

The Family Field as a Clinical Topic

Our view of the emergence of clinical interest in the family has, to this point, been decidedly sociological. We have advanced the thesis that clinicians ignored the family in the past because as a functional unit it was in harmony with external cultural institutions. It was not seriously overburdened and was not a scapegoat for societal ills. As this situation changed and times worsened for the family, sociologists and clinicians began reflexively and in the flush of cultural lag to come to its defense. They postulated neo-functions for it as an institution, initiated various means of therapy for it, and devised techniques for studying it. True, these methods were properly respectful of existent cultural taboos. The worshipful awe of privacy contributed mightily to problems of family investigation. This and other impediments to researching and treating the family will be explicitly addressed further on. For now we focus on other complicating factors that have compounded the problems of privacy, isolation, and taboo and have, as a consequence, substantially affected the ways in which family study emerged as a clinical topic. Basically, they have to do with the imposition of therapeutic and scientific traditions. In a way, these factors are also sociological, and they reflect a tradition boundedness all their own. Nonetheless, we begin with the clinical inside rather than the sociological outside.

The clinical study of the family has borrowed heavily from both psychoanalysis and classical psychology. It has taken the best and the worst of these traditions; in some instances it has borrowed the best and misapplied it. In all cases,

the history of family study has been a sorting process, a sepa-
rating of things to be kept and things to be discarded from
older systems. A peculiar hybrid seems to have emerged containing some startlingly original features, and other features
that are disappointingly naïve and pedestrian. One sometimes
wonders if the total complex is viable.

History: The Psychoanalytic Legacy

Any attempt to trace the evolution of interest in family dynamics and interaction from a clinical vantage point reveals
that family study had its roots in clinical psychiatric and psychological practice, or in abstract and deductive efforts to
make sense of such clinical phenomena as the communicative
behavior of schizophrenics. This is an important fact. For,
while the family is undoubtedly the most ubiquitous and natural human group (its present woes notwithstanding), research
on small group dynamics has, until very recently, left the family virtually untouched. Researchers have far preferred to use
ad hoc groups, whose existence is both more artificial and
more temporary and therefore easier to manipulate and control (Framo, 1965). Hence, the move to family work was decidedly clinical in thrust and not subject to rigorous investigations until recently.

The clinician works with the technical and theoretical
legacies of the psychoanalytic tradition. When one thinks of
psychoanalysis one thinks of the individual not the family. The
rights, the obligations, the self-knowledge, the integrity of the
individual are all aims of the psychoanalytic treatment process.
But as others have pointed out (Ackerman, 1958), psychoanalytic tradition has had definite but highly complicated and ambiguous impact on professional attitudes toward the families of
patients. Freud's writings continually provoke interest in the
family yet just as often turns interest away from an intrafamilial orientation (Spiegel and Bell, 1959). His "first theory of
neurosis," which called attention to the impact of intrafamilial
trauma and events, suggested that a family orientation to neurosis was possible. Similarly, the theory of psychosexual development seemed to hold forth implicitly the possibility that the
child's behavior at each phase of development could be influ-

enced by the actual behavior of family members, thereby affecting his ability to resolve conflicting internal forces. The formation of superego via incorporation of parental superego, and related concepts of identification, also seemed to point to the significance of the family.

Despite the foregoing, Freud managed to keep the family on the periphery of his theories. While it is true he conducted Little Han's treatment through the boy's father, at other times he issued warnings against the temptation to involve parents and relatives of patients. Instead, his focus turned increasingly toward investigation of the vicissitudes of internal drives and structures, toward the impact of unconscious forces on memory, and the ubiquitous nature of childhood fantasies and conflicts. This focus stemmed in good part from his recognition that adult patients were presenting reconstructions of childhood memories rather than real events. This insight left its indelible mark on the history of psychoanalysis. It was not until later neo-Freudian reconceptions that the costs of this insight were recognized. It had obscured yet another insight for while childhood memories of trauma may refer not to actual events, they can reflect elaborations of real fantasy-provoking situations.

The consequences of the traditional Freudian stance are obvious. As Anna Freud has observed (1965), the distortions presented by an adult patient in transference account for the analyst's readiness to believe that similar forces were at work in the patient's childhood, and that internal, not external, factors are responsible for his illness. In early work with children the same referential frame was adopted. One looked at the child as an individual. To be sure, the child was perceived as immature, but, nonetheless, one attended to his inner life, his unfolding ego development, his fantasy, and the ubiquitous nature of the conflicts he experienced. The reality of family influences were given only secondary consideration. The child, despite his evident dependency on his family, continued to be treated as a self-contained system.

History: The Advent of Ego Psychology

The late 1940's and early 1950's brought a shift in both theory and clinical practice. At the theoretic level, the analytic ego psychologists (Erikson, 1950; Hartmann, 1939), began to call attention to the enculturating tasks of the family as a social system. Freud's view of social and familial factors as inhibiting, repressive, and punitive were reevaluated. Erikson began to emphasize what the family could grant rather than deny the child, and he called attention to the way in which the social system seduced the child into its particular style of life, thereby influencing considerably the formation of the child's identity.

Concomitantly, by the middle 1950's, clinical workers, both within and without the analytic tradition, were noting that linkages existed between parental and child disturbances, and moreover that the child's progress in treatment was directly related to parental attitudes (Burlingham, 1955; Buxbaum, 1954; Hellman, 1954; Johnson, 1953). Such clinical explorations inevitably led to a desire to see such forces operating in the flesh, and the study of interaction between parent and child led directly to many of the current modes and concerns in family work. The shift in orientation, however, was for the most part confined to the mother–child relation. The father was missing, and his influence went unaccounted for.

History: The Preparedness to Study Family Systems

There followed the insistence (Ackerman, 1958) that while Freudian concepts need not be rejected, their limitations had to be recognized and further supplemented by consideration of the total family. Ackerman, for example, stated that the study of partial relationships, of mother–child and father–child, was no longer tenable. The social casework model which for some time had involved both parents in the treatment of the child did not go far enough, for the tendency was to treat the parents in their parental roles vis-a-vis the child, and not to attend to the interconnections of such relationships with those of the marital pair. The notion of the family as an interlocking social system and as a network of interdependent relationships came to the fore, and with it the notion that treating the individual, or even a set of subrelationships, produced an artificial and misleading view of the problems involved. This involved recognition, not only of the fact that five hours a week of individual treatment could not counteract the influences of the remaining one-hundred and sixty-three hours with the family, but that even if one were successful in producing change in the child or in the mother–child relation, it might have dire repercussions on other aspects of family relations and interactions—perhaps the selection of another child as scapegoat, the disintegration of a father, or the demise of the family unit. This recognition seemed to imply that the real costs of therapeutic "successes" in the past could not be properly assessed since they had seldom been calculated in terms of their impact on the total family.

History: The Need for a Language

The move to a consideration of the family system and its relationship to mental health was inevitable from an evolutionary standpoint. Yet despite the implicit recognition of family dynamics, this recognition has not yet fed back effectively into actual clinical diagnostic practice.

By the 1960's, a growing number of investigators were ready to study the family, but they faced a set of common problems. From the psychological view, the concept of the family as a subject of study was virtually without a history. There existed no core of shared concepts, no tangible guidelines, and certainly few established facts. While aspects of family phenomena had been well explored and subrelationships had increasingly come into focus, the family as a unified social system existed primarily as an idea. The problem was compounded by the limitations that would-be investigators experienced in themselves, the limitations imposed by their training in the monadic framework which viewed psychopathology as resident within the individual patient. Shedding some sixty years of a tradition which they themselves recognized as richly steeped in well-explored concepts and insights proved difficult. In most cases it was conscientiously done, and in some cases (Jackson, 1965) contentiously insisted upon.

Pioneers in this area—Ackerman (1958), Bateson (1960), Bell (1962), Haley (1959), Jackson (1965), Lidz (1964), Satir

(1965), Wynne (1961)—have spent the better part of a decade or more immersing themselves in intensive clinical observation of disturbed families. Concomitantly, they have amassed long lists of valuable descriptions and concepts. Inevitably, while each investigator has to a greater or lesser degree departed from traditional analytic concepts, each has, at the same time, found it necessary to organize his preceptions around concepts derived from different traditions and disciplines. Hence, they have looked less to Freudian theory, and increasingly to the work of men such as Cooley (1929), Dewey and Bentley (1949), Kluckhohn (1949), Mead (1935), Parsons and Bales (1955), and to developments in social psychology, sociology, anthropology, general systems theory, and communication theory (Lidz, 1962). The individual predilections exhibited by the investigators in choosing non-Freudian vantage points meant that they entered the study of families at disparate levels and with different sets of "new eyes." This has resulted in a plethora of new insights and terminology which, though potentially interrelated, has not yet been integrated. It has also resulted in a premature and false sense of satisfaction.

An adequate history of clinical interest in the study of the family has yet to be written. When it is written, the history will show that as an avant-garde movement in mental health, the study of the family manifested a tendency to unconsciously reify much of what it proclaimed to have changed for the better. This is not to imply that its advances are insignificant; they have simply been well short of their advertised spectacularity. There is no doubt that self-congratulatory attention to pockets of success have succeeded in obscuring areas of unquestioned traditionalism.

It is, of course, one of our major contentions that the clinical study of the family grew for sociological reasons of which its pioneers were but dimly aware. As a result, the field has developed unevenly and emerged as an oddly shaped domain of study. Sectors of remarkable achievement exist side by side with features of embarrassing naïveté. There have been substantive and highly sophisticated advances in communications theory, in conceptualization of role allocation, in the laboratory study of family interaction patterns and decision-making processes, and in the analysis of power distribution and task assignment. At the same time, there have been appalling over-sights and misapplications, and numerous examples of poor timing in choice of variables selected for study. There has also been a steadfast adherence to traditional methods, tried and true codes for choosing samples and for conceiving of and con-ducting research. We turn to a consideration of some of them now.

Resulting Lacunae and Unaddressed Problems in Family Study

Insufficient Attention to Ecological Factors

Hartmann (1939) some years ago proposed the "adaptive point of view." It is a proposal full of unrealized promise, and, over the years, it even seems to have assumed the status of environ-mental tokenism. For the psychoanalytic field and its family-oriented successors, Ackerman (1958), Boszormenyi-Nagy (1965), Ehrenwald (1963), seem to retain a static conception of environmental forces that pales beside the dynamic concep-tualizations of the psyche offered by psychoanalytic meta-theory. Reference to the impact of environment is still all too de-void of an appreciation of environmental patterning of stimuli and their differential social and situational salience. Also ig-nored are accountings of adaptive tasks that are required, evaded, or interfered with by environmental circumstances. Reference to "situational potency" (French and Zajonc, 1957), group defensive operations, family discharge opportunities, and mutual coping arrangements are similarly seldom encoun-tered in the literature. These are not minor residual omissions from the analytic tradition; they are of the utmost significance at theoretical and practical levels. If indeed human behavior is to a large extent generated by the social context in which it occurs, rather than being the result of a portable reality cre-ated by individuals, then the locus and mode of attempted in-tervention ought to shift drastically (Lennard and Bernstein, 1969).

The history of the A. family would seem to make this

abundantly clear. The ramifications of their adaptation to prolonged illness, to death-fears, and to surgical crisis are manifold and far reaching, permeating in profound ways role assignments, defenses, discharge of tensions, interpersonal alignments, and core configurations of identities. Yet none of this was clear until the family was observed in their home, in their natural surroundings. In retrospect, one might argue that their home should have been the locus of mental health intervention.

That psychotherapists and most family therapists are still limited to seeing partial relationships or subsystems—the official patient, his father and mother—that they still expect the family to come to an office, that they still adhere to fifty-minute hours (*GAP Report*, 1970), and most startingly, that they still operate without benefit of observation of natural family interaction suggest the tentativeness and limited quality of some of the revisionistic zeal that has characterized the family field.

Adherence to Obsolete Conceptions of "Symptom"
Meaning and Origination

This feature of residual Freudianism has been succinctly described by Finch and Cain (1968):

> The family interaction/family dynamics approach has suffered at the service of becoming widely associated with its most dramatic case material as ideologic contributions to child psychopathology. We hear and read much clinical case discussion which represents a return in new context of the older, substantially discredited psychoanalytic "meaning of the symptom" approach. Thus, children's symptoms are seen simply as direct transmissions of an unconscious parental demand, or the direct embodiment, representation, or acting out of a parental wish; or the family is seen as wanting, needing, and producing a particular symptom or disturbed mode of behavior; or the family is pictured as ferociously resisting therapeutic efforts to dissolve or "take away" a symptom. Although the relationship between family dynamics and children's symptoms is sometimes almost as clear, simple and "one-to-one" as the above suggests, for the most part such an approach utterly neglects the question of the relationship be-

tween character structure and symptomotology. It loses the distinction between elements contributing to the formation of symptom versus later accretions and contributions to the symptom's maintenance; and the developmental distinctions between what a family "needed" at an earlier point in its history and what its much changed family dynamics "require" at a later point are frequently neglected. . . .

This dramatic symptom orientation overshadows the basic richness of the family interaction approach's unique contribution: the demonstration that each parent and child is reciprocally related to all other members of the family system, that major aspects of the relationships often are in insufficiently delicate balance that changes in the psychic state of one family member or in the relationship of two of them will immediately reverberate through all other members of the family and their relationships, that each family member plays for every other a multiplicity of roles and functions, conscious and unconscious, and that these interdependent roles and functions consist of interlocking aims, perceptions, modes of behavior, identities, impulse gratifications, superego counterpoints, and that once these patterns have consolidated, shared defense organizations and homeostatic-like mechanisms are evolved to maintain them unchanged. (p. 434)

Finch and Cain are directly addressing the atavistic conception of symptom inherent in much family work and theorizing. The issues of symptom origin, choice, and maintenance, as well as the proper articulation of relations between them are central to their concerns. Finch and Cain raise these questions but offer no answers. Others have not even bothered with the questions, much less the articulation of epigenetic phenomena.

Again the A. history is both pertinent and useful. It underscores the point so cogently made by Finch and Cain, for in it one may delineate components of behavior that have representational meaning in the classical psychoanalytic sense from those that do not. For example, it is possible to construe Roscoe's preoccupation with graveyards for dead animals both as a direct attempt to mourn in advance for his father, and as a piece of empathic identification and self-mourning. After all, Mr. A. hunts animals, and Roscoe fantasizes himself a "bird" and collects feathers. However, it would be another matter to suggest that Roscoe's antisocial acting out was the result of "superego lacunae" or that it had the subtle sanction of parental encouragement. His behavior is far too complex and situation specific for so simple an explanation, though this was, to be sure, an explanation forwarded by the psychologist during Roscoe's first evaluation at the child guidance center. Similarly, Roscoe's "masochism," or his interest in nature and the arts cannot be attributed solely to a feminine identification with his mother's orientation. To do so would ignore his relationship to his brother, and his brother's relationship to his parents. Moreover, it would totally bypass the matter of developmental phase-specific readiness for taking on certain attitudes and beliefs about self. In short, Roscoe's behaviors or "symptoms" make sense only in the context of his interconnectedness with other family members and other times and events. They cannot be summarily dismissed as the reflection of a contemporaneous facet of mother.

To some extent, this may sound as if we are arguing the obvious—that symptoms are multidetermined and highly complicated phenomena. In good measure we are; but, we are also urging a more epigenetic view and a more ecological-interpersonal-developmental view. We are de-emphasizing the role of direct transmission of intrapsychic events, either from one person to another or from mental representation to overt behavior and physical expression, and we are pressing for something more.

Much of the clinical study of families, like the bulk of psychiatric and abnormal psychology literature over the years, has focused on "symptom" or "syndrome." Investigations have typically begun at the phenotypic end. Clusterings of "pathogenic" outcomes, such as "schizophrenia" or "learning disability," have been cast as independent variables. The medical model and classic experimental research design have been wedded in a fashion that still holds sway. It continues to lead us into conceptual cul-de-sacs. We are still too reliant on a symptom orientation and on notions of pathogenesis and hypothesis validation. But stress, social change, adaptation, and psychic cost seem more compelling variables at this point in

time. Naturalistic method and grounded theory are the preferred approaches in our frame of reference.

Insufficient Attention to Behavioral Variation and Interpersonal Settings

Because the environment is often so predictable and consistent
it is often ignored. The lack of environmental variation in combination with the observer's immersion in it tends to blind him
to the ecology and leads him to attribute behavioral variation
to internal states. Discarding this piece of egocentrism has
been hard for family researchers, and even more difficult for
those with heavy psychoanalytic persuasions. Data which fail
to fit the theory that conceives of personality as a set of enduring, invariant dispositions to behave in given ways, are prone
to be dismissed as the result of error variance. That the same
person can be understood as having entirely different meanings and attributes depending upon who is doing the perceiving is something rarely considered in clinical descriptions.
Roscoe is to his teachers an explosive, hyperaggressive,
unmanageable boy of unpredictable proclivities. He is to his
parents a well-behaved child, not at all given to hostile expression. While peers at school are intimidated by his rage, his siblings do not hesitate to abuse him. They shower him with disapproval and ridicule without the slightest fear of retribution.

In a similar vein, scant attention has been given in the
research literature to the most obvious of possibilities, namely,
that a parent can be an importantly different individual to
each of his children. Mr. A. is a very different person to Ricky
than to Roscoe, and his meanings for each of his daughters
show imperfect overlap. Nor has a corollary proposition received proper recognition in the literature—that the same parent will have a different identity at varying points in his own
development, and will therefore have different meanings to
the same child at varying points, or to two children of disparate age. Yet a third underrated factor was cited by Finch and
Cain (1968), who state that a parent can be significantly different to each offspring at different points in *his* development.

> . . . due not only to his own maturation and development
> and many other internal and external forces, but also to what

is differently evoked within him from his own past as each of his children moves through the accented psychic drives, strains and conflicts of each phase of development. (p. 431)

The power of parental identification with progeny has too long been underestimated. Yet its meanings to family interaction are obviously profound. For example, as earlier noted, Mrs. A. seeks to simplify and make more tolerable the experience of long-standing stress by employing the mechanism of "splitting." She identifies Sheila with ego-syntonic aspects of herself as a child and treats her accordingly. She abjures Deedee as the dystonic underside of her childhood virtuosity and then proceeds to live vicariously through her. She reduces complexities around the boys in like fashion. Roscoe is accorded the resentment once harbored toward her younger brother, while Ricky receives the positive affects transferred from the brother. The children are thus altercast on the basis of parental proclivities, with their fate in the family hardly a matter of their own attributes and contributions.

The Apparent Nonexistence of Significant Others and Behavioral Specialization

It is remarkable that research literature on the family should, relatively speaking, be so devoid of reference to persons outside the "primary triad." This triad, usually consisting of mother, father, and patient offspring, so dominates the literature that one cannot help but conclude that most clinical researchers consider other family persons peripheral, if not insignificant. Some investigators have, in fact, given this view explicit statement (Bowen, 1960; Lennard and Bernstein, 1969). Finch and Cain (1968) are among those who have pointed up short-comings inherent in such a view. The neglect of significant others and of behavioral specialization has also been cited by Jackson (1965) as an impediment to progress in family work.

Jackson asserts that regardless of personal histories, intrapsychic conflicts, or personality traits, as members of a family live with each other and work together toward common goals, an inevitable trend toward behavioral specialization among group members takes place. It does so as a natural function of the group process; it is the way family work gets done. This notion, of course, is explicitly sociological, and decidedly Parsonian in its functionalism. One ramification of this view is a "balance" theory, or a "deficit" theory of family operations. For our purposes the two are synonomous. Both theories imply that no two persons can or will occupy the same psychological or sociological space, and that the total gestalt will therefore tend toward reasonable balance, even if balance may not always be "healthy" or "uncosting" for individual family members.

The more concrete implications of such theory are only now beginning to be explored (Kent, 1970; Warren, 1971), but clearly one aspect of the model sorely in need of investigation is the role of the long neglected "peripheral" other in the family setting—the sibling or the grandparent in the home. The grievous oversight of siblings has been noted frequently enough. A goodly percentage of interactional studies of families have ended with the refrain that the research needs replication with a sibling in the place of the identified patient as the third member in the standard triad assembled for such studies. But even this request misses much of the potential significance of the sibling. A control is being sought for a comparison group rather than other social determinants or interactive factors. The researcher is posing the question, "Do the parents treat a well sibling as they do an offspring who is the labeled patient?" The researcher is not asking about the impact of one child upon his brother or sister. The elaborate research design employed by Mishler and Waxler (1968) exemplifies this variety of attempt to rectify the neglect of well siblings. It addresses one crucial issue, while it totally bypasses another.

Based upon our observations of the A. family, the interaction between and among children in the home cannot be unheeded. We need not belabor the point: Roscoe's relation to Ricky, Sheila's to Pamela, and Deedee's lack of contact with each speak for themselves. They are as essential to the construction of the family's dynamics as the interaction between Mr. and Mrs. A., or that between either parent and any given child. What needs explanation is not the import of sibling exchange, although it certainly deserves elaborated investigation, but its relative neglect by family researchers. As Finch and Cain (1968) have observed:

> For a long period the study of siblings was lost to oversimpli-
> fied speculations in research about ordinal position, derived
> from Adlerian psychology, or retarded by valid but stereo-
> typed and limited conceptions of siblings as primarily repre-
> senting rivals and vehicles for Oedipal displacements by chil-
> dren. (p. 432)

Donald Irish (1964) in a ten-page review of sibling interaction studies spends 15 percent of his time lamenting the inattention to research in the area, and 30 percent of his energies account-ing for impediments to its study. The entire literature extant on the topic is covered in three and a half pages. Irish con-cludes his slim review by citing eight hinderances to the in-vestigation of sibling interaction. These include (1) parental re-sponsibility and an adult-directed orientation; (2) occupational pressures among family researchers to focus on parental perspectives; (3) the primacy and greater universality of mar-riage, which leads to concentration on adult relationships; (4) the greater methodological ease of studying grown-ups; (5) the attenuation, within our mobile society, of sibling relationships during adulthood; (6) adultopomorphic attitudes that mislead the adult researcher into thinking he knows what is significant for the child; and (7) the sex of researchers—predominantly male—which ensures that those having least first-hand experi-ence with children are those most prone to study it. The eighth item Irish cites as an impediment is the one we have been emphasizing throughout—the legacy of Freudian thought. Irish notes the Freudian emphasis upon the develop-mental regimes of infancy, at the expense of later socializing influences such as sibling interaction.

The continuing tendency to overlook siblings seems inher-ent in Freudian dominated thinking on yet other counts. As Philip Reiff noted some years ago (1961), Freud's propensity for choosing the oedipal theme and father–son relation as the profoundest of human conflicts was a matter of selective sleight of hand by which the myths of "Joseph and his brothers, Cain and Abel, Arthur and his knights, the Trojan peers, the

Nibelungs, the daughters of Lear" (p. 214), were left uncon-
sidered. Moreover, understanding sibling rivalry solely as competition for parental attentions is gross oversimplification. Interference with transitional play phenomena and invasions of
arenas of privacy are, for example, early and major sources of
acrimonious sibling relations that have little direct connection
with parental favor. Relatedly, much sibling rivalry may be
seen as a jockeying for psychological space, distinct ego
boundaries, and unique identity, and, as such, siblings ought to
be brought into focus as crucial agents in a child's development. Their significance ranges beyond serving as models for
identification or as objects offering opportunities for learning
interpersonal skills, though these too are features often neglected by practitioners of family research. Their impact is
great by virtue of their particular set of interlocking roles in
complicated family structures, where they may take on vital
functions as parent surrogate, external superego, provocateur,
or scapegoat. The import of Friedman's (1964) efforts and
those of Lidz et al. (1963) notwithstanding sibling interaction
remains relatively neglected.

Insensitivity to Socio-Cultural Phenomena: Family Therapy,
Family Research, and Family Theory

To step outside of one's setting while living in it, and to simultaneously bring off a reasoned criticism or objective view of it,
is no easy matter. Although therapists routinely ask their
clients to step outside the self in order to evaluate it, they are,
as a group, notoriously unable to remove themselves from
their milieu and theoretical context to attain similar ends.
Family clinicians are, on the whole, hardly exceptions to this.
The crossing of discipline boundaries seldom occurs with ease.
For family clinicians to press beyond the bounds of psychoanalytic practice, method, and tenet is in itself no small achievement. To expect that in addition to conceptions of group pro
cess and communications theory, they should simultaneously
have embraced sociological perspectives is perhaps unfair.

   Although understandable, the absence of the family clinicians' cultural relativism is blatant and decidedly limiting. It
distorts or nullifies potential contributions. In any study on

family therapy or any report of family interaction research, other than the work of Parsons, Bales, or Norman Bell, one will be hard-pressed to locate a single sociologist among the authors listed in the references. Any of the numerous sociologists who have spent a career in the study of how the American family is being restructured—Burgess and Locke (1963), Farber (1964), Goode (1964), Hill (1949), Ogburn and Nimkoff (1958), Pollak (1967), Sussman (1959), Vincent (1967)—will be glaringly absent. It is as if the family existed in a social vacuum.[2]

To the extent that one believes the problems family clinicians study are the result of stresses created by the press of social change, then one must assume in like degree partial insight and handicapped intervention on the part of the clinician. This kind of deficiency is, of course, not newly encountered among family workers. It is perhaps only a little more surprising there. A lack of cultural vision is shared with many traditional Freudians, and its presence among family clinicians may be deemed a vestige of psychoanalytic orthodoxy. But for rare persons such as John Spiegel, clinical students of the family remain starkly asociological.

Spiegel, of course, has attended to socio-cultural influences on the family with his energies most effectively given to the analysis of the cultural strains and conflicts evoked by the process of acculturation (Spiegel, 1964). In so doing, he has borrowed heavily from anthropological sources as well as sociological concepts. He has also delineated a comparatively useful profile of the dominating, middle-American ethic. We have conscientiously tried to relate to facets of this image in our description of the A. family. We have explicitly employed Spiegel's schema in our analysis of the A. predicament, and we have endeavored to understand their responses to their predicament in the light of their cultural origins and commitments. We feel to have not done so would have lessened our dynamic conceptualization of the family in significant ways. Indeed, as-

2. The lament is little different from that sounded by family theorists about traditionalists in psychiatry and psychology. They complain that traditionalists too frequently deal with the individual as if he existed in an interpersonal vacuum.

pects of the family's history and behavior would have escaped comprehension and we would have had to chalk them up in tautological fashion to "irrationality" or a "group unconscious." If we had not also attempted the contextual location of the A. family in the dominant culture, we would have been deprived of some substantial insights into their significance as a societal representative. We should not underestimate the meaning of this last consideration. If family study and family therapy are responsive to the last shudderings and gaspings of a declining, already obsolete, social institution—as not a few have said of the family (Russell, 1929; Moore, 1960; Cooper, 1970)—then it certainly behooves family clinicians to be aware of those facts. Otherwise, family clinicians are likely on the basis of cultural lag and moral imperatives to act as advocates for traditional conceptions of what the family should be. They are likely, blindly and blithely, to continue their conservative swim upstream against the current of social change, ever expectant of reversing the irreversible, and always hopeful of reifying values and institutions that have lost their function.

The Neglect or Negation of the Natural

All of the inadequacies of family study which we have discussed to this point impede progress in family therapy and in research on family patterns and shape the clinician's continuing experience with families. In combination, these inadequacies suggest that clinical researchers are likely to seek variables that are consistent with conceptions of the family as a closed system, i.e., internal to the family's corporate structure. In addition, they suggest that researchers are inclined to select samples on the basis of "symptom," and to link pathogenic syndrome with family pattern. These factors also suggest that "family" is primarily conceived as a "three-person group," and that family structure is unchanging (statically defined by some ideal that may be used as a reference point for "health"), and is, by extension, universal in its organization. Finally, they promise that family research will take place in the researcher's domain, on his premises, and under his control. The typical research design that results is a study of two groups of "families" with one group consisting of a "deviant" child and his parents and the other of a "normal" child and his parents. Both groups are set to work on a "task" in the researcher's office or laboratory. Outcome variables such as efficiency in decision-making, verbal exchange, and social influence are tapped via the "task," and their association with "pathology" or "health" in the family are determined by their relative strength and patterning in each set of families.

Research of this type has dominated the field of family study for nearly fifteen years. It epitomizes the miscegenation of clinical and experimental traditions because it misapplies the best features of each. It could also be argued that its timing was premature; nonetheless, such research had to take place before its limitations could be discovered. Assessment is now possible, and, in our opinion, its outstanding limitation is the apparent abhorrence it creates in researchers for naturalistic methods of family study.

Abhorrence of naturalistic study of families seems born, in large part, of an ultra-respect for privacy. Above and beyond the matter of privacy, however, it seems to be a consequence of the ubiquitous rush for scientific respectability that haunts most of the social sciences. Here as elsewhere, scientism is often purchased at a cost, most especially when researchers prematurely pay homage to the trappings of science, to its rigor, objectivity, operationalized methods, and large sample design, rather than to its essence. The resulting studies are likely to be less informative and heuristic than personal or case history accounts.

The death knell of premature "scientific" research on family interaction may have been sounded by the elaborate, carefully designed and admirably well-intentioned study of Mishler and Waxler (1968) which produced results of sophisticated equivocalness and unorderable complexity. Little matter that the researchers' presentation was both elegant and dignified, or that their conception was the ultimate in experimental rigor applied to family. To judge from the journals in succeeding years, the experimental study of family interaction has not enjoyed extended life. Nor has its demise been long lamented.

Indeed, even before the publication of the Mishler and Waxler work there were some solid hints that the leap from the clinical, impressionistic studies of Bateson et al. (1956), Lidz et al. (1956), and Wynne et al. (1958), which were intensive and purposively clinical and thus often lacked controls and formal hypothesis testing intent, to laboratory studies conducted under highly controlled conditions, was premature. The reasons were all interrelated.

First, crucial information gaps existed. Families had not been observed behaving "naturally" in their usual habitat, the home. This was true even of the highly clinical efforts of the Palo Alto group (Bateson et al., 1956), the Yale group (Lidz et al., 1966), and the National Institute of Mental Health group (Wynne et al., 1958). In fact, as recently as 1967, Freeman (1967) could locate just twenty-eight references in the clinical literature in which home observations had been employed or suggested. The majority of these involved a single visit per family, and some frankly devalued the method as intrusive or unworthwhile, while others used home visits for purposes other than observation of family interaction such as keeping a therapy hour with an ill patient.[3] Yet, as early as 1956, Behrens and Ackerman (1956) had called for the home visit as an aid in family diagnosis and therapy. The call went largely unheeded until the 1960's (Friedman, 1962; Friedman et al., 1965; Speck, 1964; 1971), and even then family clinicians were relatively slow to the scene. Those making most frequent use of home visits were, embarrassingly enough, *not* family clinicians, but behavior modification therapists. But behavior modifiers were not interested in observation of total family interaction or in mapping family patterns, they were interested in establishing baselines for the occurrence of specific symptomatic behaviors and the antecedents and consequences of problem episodes. They have contributed considerably to the development of observational methods, however (Hawkins et al., 1966; O'Leary et al., 1967; Risley and Wolf, 1967; Zeilberger et al., 1968), and more importantly, they have contributed to the breakdown of social reticence regarding researchers in the home.

3. Freeman's review, of course, does not cover nonclinical material, and so omits earlier excursions into home observation by sociologists and developmental psychologists. See, for example, Buhler (1939), Blood (1958).

One suspects that respect for the sanctity of the home, compounded by the comfort and upperhandedness that accrue from seeing patients on one's own ground rather than theirs, has had much to do with the delay in home observation and home treatment of families. In fact, clinical research in the home is still a rarity. It is our feeling that until naturalistic observation of the family succeeds in mapping the territory of family interaction, more rigorous, experimental methods of study will remain premature by virtue of their lack of context.

A second reason they have been so stems directly from the first. Because families had not been observed interacting in situ, it was difficult to know what variables of family life were worth studying in the laboratory, how best to get at them, what hypotheses should be tested, and what, if anything, could be made of experimental results. Thus, variables chosen for study in experimental research on families were often suspected of irrelevance or of having only minimal relevance; methods used were artificial, of questionable significance to the family, and inconsistent from study to study; hypotheses chosen for testing were mundane; and experimental data and results were usually interpreted in the light of prevailing social values of what family structure ought or ought not to be.

A third factor also has bearing on the situation. Family researchers very often graduated to research from clinical beginnings. Ingenious designs for studying potentially interesting problems of family patterns were sometimes suddenly rendered useless by a glaring oversight in control—the kind of control an experienced researcher would have instituted at the outset. For example, much of Haley's otherwise commendable work (1964, 1967) must be invalidated for want of social class or statistical controls. As remarked earlier, among the controls glaringly omitted from laboratory research on family interaction is the "well" sibling or, for that matter, any sibling. If clinical students of family work have neglected the "significant other" in their focus on the primary triad of father, mother, and disturbed child, then experimental researchers on family have officially relegated him to the obscurity of nonexistence. Bowen (1960) states that the favored persons for study in the family are the father, mother, and "sick" offspring, and that others are peripheral, while Lennard and Bernstein (1969) declare:

> We are inclined [to the] . . . view that the primary family
> members involved in the family conflict are the father, the
> mother, and the patient, and that, in effect, father, mother,
> and the identified patient form the family group of most inter-
> est for study. (p. 96)

Future Prospects

At this point there can be no mistaking our position. Correc-
tives in family study will come with the researcher's attempts
to create for himself and others an awareness of the unrecognized consequences of living in our time and place. This has
not and will not be an easy task, for it implies that the researcher must simultaneously maintain distance from and intimacy with the object of his study. In effect, he should for a
time depart from the posture of simulated objectivity with
which he is prone, by training, to regard his material. He must
step outside his own frame of reference not only to investigate
the phenomenon under study, but also to research his own institutions, and his own frame of reference. He must question
tradition, reassess legitimized modes, and challenge en-
trenched taboos. By extension, he must risk trespassing cherished prohibitions and must hazard the disruption of accepted,
established means and goals. He must rethink his own proclivities.

The process has been cogently described by Gutmann
(1969):

> . . . we are most likely to stimulate new attention and to gen-
> erate new kinds of data by stepping out of accustomed action
> frameworks, and by waiting for unexpected regularities to an-
> nounce themselves. Then the agents implicated in these in-
> ferred regularities, and the events that summate to them be-
> come, more and more explicitly, our data. We have not
> declared in advance what the data should be; rather, in our
> experience, it has *forced* itself on our attention. (p. 163)

> In effect, we create data by stepping out of our accustomed
> ecologies, and by changing our relation to them. We cannot

usually objectify as new data that which is reciprocal or *eco-logical* to us in a close-knit, umbilical way. We truly *experi-ence* the fact that we are air breathers, and "air" becomes an objectified datum, only when we first fall into the water. (p. 164)

The Use of Naturalistic Observation and Small Sample Research

Given all that has just been described, methodological advance in the realm of family study seems to require, at this point in time, a departure from traditional clinical psychiatric and experimental psychologic modes. They are too limiting and too skewed. The need to give greater attention to the way behaviors distribute in the real world and the press for a more ecologic framework suggest that the family clinician may best achieve his goals by adopting anthropologic and sociologic attitudes. Most immediately we advocate the use of naturalistic observation and intensive, small sample research aimed at the generation of data, social principle, and hypothesis, and the delineation of family terrain. The sheer demand for description is reason enough to pursue this course. A comprehensive, grounded scheme for unfolding the shifts and stresses attending family development has as yet to be devised, although some abstract efforts (Hill and Rodgers, 1964; Rodgers, 1964) are available. The careful accretion of in-depth, observational data on families of different race, ethnicity, social class, geography, size, and age would go a long way toward filling out such a scheme. Moreover, such description would simultaneously provide some backdrop for the study of social "deviance," and for the impact of those highly probable crises that give rise to what we boldly called "cultural casualties."

Oscar Lewis was an exemplar of this approach. Lewis (1950) proposed an anthropologic orientation to family study that would obtain a more "reliable and objective statement of the cultural patterns of a given society" (p. 468), and allow a better understanding of the relationship between culture and the individual. He suggests:

Intensive family case studies might help us to bridge the gap between the conceptual extremes of the culture at one pole and the individual at the other. The family would thus become the middle term in the culture-individual equation. It would provide us with another level of description. And because the family unit is small and manageable, it can be described without resort to the abstraction and generalization which one must inevitably use for the culture as a whole. Likewise, in the description of the various family members we see real individuals as they live and work together in their primary group rather than as averages or stereotypes out of context . . . Family case studies can therefore enable us to better distinguish between and give proper weight to those factors which are cultural and those which are situational or the result of individual idiosyncracies . . . One of the advantages of studying a culture through the medium of specific families is that it enables one to get at the meaning of institutions to individuals. It helps us to get beyond form and structure, or, to use Malinowski's term, it puts flesh and blood on the skeleton (pp. 472–73). There is a need for intensive individual family case studies in cultures all over the world. The publication of such studies would give us a literature on comparative family life not now available and would be used by many social scientists. . . . (p. 475)

Lewis followed through on his own recommendations, and led the way in developing and perfecting an ethnological reporting system that rests on the close detailing of observed family life (1959, 1966). He confined his attentions, by and large, to the poor and to single family households. On occasion he highlighted the kind of family crises that we have described in the report on the A. family.[4]

During the time that Lewis was developing his ethnological data collection method, others were exploring similar strategies. Gans (1962), for instance, became a participant-observer in the Italian West End of Boston, living in the slum area for the seven months preceding an urban redevelopment. Rainwater employed similar techniques in a study of black families in a federal slum (Rainwater, 1970) and Henry (1963, 1967, 1971) took up residence in the homes of families having a psychotic child in a residential treatment institution. Henry states:

4. See Lewis, *A Death in the Sanchez Family*, (New York: Random House, 1969), and "The Death of Dolores" in *Transaction*, vol. 6, no. 7, May 1969, pp. 10–19.

Direct observation of families functioning in their native habitats should be the microscope that reveals new phenomena of family existence and so provides the possibilities of new theory. (1967, p. 31)

It is hoped that the report on the A. family accomplishes something in this regard.

The Intensive Study of Family Crisis and Adaptation

A working premise in all that has been said in this book is that the A. family is not singular in its troubled state. The A.'s problem and their pattern of reactivity may be special to them, but this is only to say that the particulars of their stress differ from those of their neighbors'. It does not imply that their neighbors are unstressed. Quite the contrary, periodic crisis and stress are inevitable for all families. To the degree this is so, it is not enough to study families demographically and ethnologically, even if intensive naturalistic methods are employed. One must in addition begin to calculate the prevalence and varieties of stress encountered by families of different types, and closely observe their respective modes of adaptation. This means attention to both developmental crises and to "unanticipated" but "not improbable" crises. Only in this way can some of the mythologies about "mental illness" be adequately dispelled.

The study of family crisis or stress has not been a preoccupation of clinicians, and, perhaps because it has not, there has been a tendency to extend notions of pathogenesis from the individual to the family. If the clinical study of the family is to reach beyond this model, it must embrace sociologic and anthropologic outlooks. Unfortunately, however, while sociologists have spent some energy studying family crisis (Clausen and Yarrow, 1955; Hill, 1949; Komarovsky, 1940), they have attended more to the classification of precipitants and less to the examination of the adaptational process (Farber, 1964). Thus, Burgess et al. (1963) list types of crisis-provoking situations, as does Hill (1958). Hill is, in addition, preoccupied with ascertaining whether a given class of critical events is more disruptive of family stability than another set. Implied in his thinking, however, is a conception of an adaptive re-equilibration of the family system, a conception he does not elaborate.

He makes no attempt, for example, to classify adaptive modes employed by families; as a consequence, there is no possibility of linking a type of crisis with a type of adaptive reorganization. As Farber (1964) notes, "the ways in which families *meet* critical events are not generally as well conceptualized as are the stimuli [producing them]" (p. 392). Farber goes on to say:

> It would be equally plausible to suggest that the crisis situation is one which induces a process in family life which is counter to the ordinary organization of the norms and values of the family members . . . [and] . . . if crisis is regarded as inducing a certain type of distorting process to the initial organization, then this new process can eventually be identified . . . the importance of the study of crisis lies in the insights it provides for advancing knowledge about processes of family interaction and organization. (Farber, 1964, pp. 392, 393, 394)

It is precisely these processes that we have endeavored to detail in the descriptions of the A. family. How they compare with reactive and adaptive processes in other families facing similar or dissimilar stresses remains a significant empirical issue. The territory of family stress is almost uncharted with regard to interactional processes in the face of disruptive forces. Observational data are badly needed. Here once again, we find compelling reason for advocating naturalistic field study as the research method. In fact, with respect to the stresses to which we refer, it may be the *only* method possible (Willems, 1969) because ethical constraints and the inherent character of the phenomena make the impact of natural catastrophes, deaths, accidents, illnesses, and unemployment unresearchable by artificial, experimental means.

Some Problems in the Naturalistic Observation of Families

It is easy enough to point the direction for future research. It is somewhat more difficult to illustrate, as we have done with the A.'s, a circumstance or proposed method. And it is entirely another matter to realize, in full form, prospects for the future. A series of highly complex and as yet unresolved problems will be encountered along the way. We cannot possibly itemize and discuss them all here. We can, however, touch upon the more salient issues that presented themselves in the course of observations and analysis of the A. family.

The Reticence to Infringe Privacy: Ethical Factors

The move to naturalistic observation as a research method results in some trade-offs in the realm of ethical considerations. One set of problems is exchanged for another. As McGuire (1967) and others (Willems, 1969) have observed, there exist three "ethically sensitive" areas in social psychological research. The first has to do with the use of noxious or potentially harmful psychological manipulation in experimentation. The second pertains to deception as a manipulative method destructive of interpersonal trust. The third concerns the invasion of privacy. McGuire acknowledges that the last problem is likely to be aggravated by naturalistic observation. However, he argues that "the first two problems can be largely circumvented when the social psychology theorist develops the will and the skill to test his hypothesis in a real world that he never made, and takes experimental advantage of natural manipulations that he can neither produce nor control" (p. 131). There is every reason to suspect that McGuire is correct in principle although there is some question whether the trade-off is as favorable as McGuire's analysis would imply. In fact, our experience with observation suggests that at times it may not be devoid of manipulation, intended or not, and our analysis of family function in a bureaucratic society portends greater rather than lesser ethical concern in the wake of naturalistic method. Neither point, however, dissuades us from advancing it as the method of choice for family investigation. Rather, they lead us to a closer examination of the effects of the observer and a re-evaluation of the role of privacy in our society. The matter of ethics with respect to privacy seems to hinge on its changed meanings in contemporary America.

Traditionally, privacy in our culture seems to have been a special matter for moral, legal, and political reasons. To suggest that it be delimited in any way is to court social outrage. As a privilege, it is highly congruent with democratic institutions like the secret ballot, private ownership, and personal property. But like much else we have discussed, the form of the social phenomenon has altered over the years. Decades ago, privacy was assured by geographical distance, but compromised by the presence of extended family in the home. Today, the extended family system no longer exists, but privacy is threatened by physical proximity in urban areas. One consequence of urban crowding, therefore, has been the creation of psychological distance between families in an effort to preserve some semblance of privacy. This circumstance, remarked upon by many social commentators, is very much evident in our cities, where each family is a stranger to its neighbors. In metro-America, the "isolated nuclear family" is isolated not only from relatives, but from other neighboring families.

Interestingly enough, as the population has increased, as people have left the rural for the urban, and as the mass media have intruded themselves more and more upon the family, the social isolation of the family seems to have grown apace. And it has become a qualitatively different kind of privacy than was previously known. In the past, privacy had two facets, being both inwardly and outwardly directed. It meant limited receptiveness to outside events and influences, and therefore a minimum of threat to family stability and authority. It also meant minimal exposure of the family to outside scrutiny and social judgment. The family, with its tradition of authority and the presence of elderly members, had to provide and did provide its own internal system of checks and balances.

By contrast, the family today suffers from overreceptivity to external influence through reference and membership groups and through the mass media. Concomitantly, it experiences underexposure or diminished visibility to outsiders with regard to its internal workings; it has minimal self-disclosure. Then too, and this is the major point, nobody is looking anyway.

On the surface, and no doubt originally, in the face of increasing urbanization, the insurance of privacy served the interest of democratic tradition, and the preservation of individual liberty and personal identity. Private ownership extended not only to chattel and goods, but to thought as well.

After all, one existed as a separate individual to the extent that one's thoughts were one's own and unshared by others. It was and is a matter of psychological integrity. But at what point does the privilege of privacy, so exalted by most Americans, shade into irresponsibility and abuse? Barrington Moore (1960) has suggested an answer: when it becomes defensive and serves the interest of psychological pain and misery; when, in his view, it becomes an excuse for cloaking an outmoded taboo.

In effect, this forces us to discuss freedom and the individual's rights and obligations in a "free, democratic society." It is not our purpose to advocate abridgment of privacy. We have not lost sight of the fact that most taboos have healthy and positive elements, and that they have ethical significance or connote moral imperatives with respect to an individual's behavior toward others and his community. On the other hand, what *is* recognized is that a culture also protects its taboos via defensive activities such as denial. More specifically, it is implied that the insistence on privacy for the family—privacy in the sense of freedom from self-disclosure—has come to conceal the taboo which surrounds any acknowledgment of feelings of disaffection between family members, and most especially negative feelings between parent and child. While these are forbidden feelings, they are despite the taboo almost inevitable given today's social system and the contemporary structure of the family.

Sumner (1940), as cited by Farberow (1963), has remarked that the purpose of some taboos is to protect and secure, while the purpose of others is to repress and obliterate. Most taboos serve both functions, and the crucial matter is the balance of value judgments. When taboos are shielded and perpetuated without "useful society-enriching functions," or when they promote self-defeating or asocial, and destructive activities and occurrences, then they are in need of re-evaluation (Farberow, 1963). Such, it would appear, are the circumstances that have come to prevail with respect to privacy, intrafamilial disharmony, and family deviation from popularly accepted, if imagined or mythological, norms. In brief, we assert that too often privacy no longer ensures integrity, or protects individuality per se; rather, it shields anger, fear, conflict, hate, and "deviancy" in the family home.

Not a few social psychologists and family therapists have called attention to this fact (Ackerman, 1956; Farber, 1964; Miller and Westman, 1964, 1966). The greater the discrepancy between cultural norms and family behavior, the greater the fear of public exposure, the greater the risk of losing public esteem, and ultimately, the more impermeable the barriers to social contact with the outside world that surrounds the family. In this manner, privacy has become a legitimized but cultish means of perpetuating the myth of family solidarity, stability, and devotion. Yet much of the theory and data at our disposal contradicts the myth. On the one hand, are the increased rates of divorce, suicide, child abuse, child neglect, child rejection, and adolescent runaway; on the other, reduced birth rates and fewer internal checks and balances within the family.

As social scientists, psychiatrists and psychologists have played a major role in perpetuating the myth. Often in the name of ethics they have endorsed the cultural denial. As with death, they have not been immune to social mores. The taboos surrounding privacy have proved sufficiently powerful to resist change; they have also shaped the nature of scientific exploration. Even after the family became a legitimate topic of study, researchers have ignored the ecology created by privacy. Least observed has been the psycho-social interior of the "normal" middle-class American family. More freely observed have been the insides of schizophrenogenic families, deprived families, and minority group families. Privacy is a right that family clinicians moralistically and culturally respect in selective fashion. They seek to preserve privacy for families empowered to refuse them entrance. The costs of the general denial and the special selectivity now exceed the gains accruing from their perpetuation.

In our estimation, the problem of invasion is primarily that of the researcher. His reticence reflects his allegiance to social mores and constraints that are outdated and in dire need of change. One need but recall that psychoanalysis, a technique constructed around intense and deep exploration of "private" and unconscious personal terrain, achieved success by means of self-selection—that is, by the patient's voluntary agreement to the psychoanalytic process and contract and by the guarantee of confidentiality. With similar guarantees, the psychotherapeutic process has been increasingly studied in recent years via videotapes, audio-recordings and observation through one-way screens. Admittedly, this has occurred with a good deal of resistance on the part of clinicians, but nonetheless it has occurred.

The function of the family at this juncture in American society suggests some formidable problems. There is no denying that the question of invasion of privacy is a real one. Yet the time to redress imbalances has come. There is little reason to believe that once the researcher's trepidation is overcome, agreements and protections could not be worked out for the observation of families in situ. Education regarding the common occurrence of crisis and upset will be necessary, but, the primary concern may prove to be that of free choice. Some families may simply object to being observed. Others may welcome the opportunity if they are asked. Moreover, it is highly plausible that the more apparent social relevance accompanying naturalistic methods will provide enhanced justification for the transgression of privacy. After all, a number of families in clinic settings have volunteered, or at times even insisted upon home visits by the clinician (Anthony, 1970; Freeman, 1967; Henry, 1971) so he could see "how things really are." One could conclude that much of the reluctance has been on the part of the clinician.

Obtrusiveness and Observer Effects

The reactive effects of naturalistic observation are among the more perplexing aspects of the method. Since the situation observed is by definition arranged by persons other than the researcher, the investigator is, in every sense of the word, an interloper. As an intruder he is bound to change the field of study itself, and this is the paradox of naturalistic method. One seeks to achieve a vantage point on behavior that is not artificial, but in the process the behavior may be altered.

There are a number of ways of dealing with these effects.

One is to argue that they are minimal, and in so doing to underscore the potency of the observational method. This is what Henry has done in reference to his presence in the homes of families having a schizophrenic child. He lists seven factors which mitigate obtrusiveness (Henry, 1971). We paraphrase them briefly because we believe they are all in good measure valid for our experience with the A.'s.

1. *Family as culture.* Henry reasons that every family is unique, and that it maintains its uniqueness even in the face of determined efforts by therapists to change it. The resistance to change is the result of long-practiced team work; an observer is not likely to disrupt it. Henry concludes that "since all biological systems tend to low entropy, and since an interactional constellation in a family is a biological system, the biosocially determined tendency is not easily disturbed" (1971, pp. 457–58).

2. *The factors of custom and strain.* Henry argues that families become accustomed to the presence of the observer. They must go on about the business of living their collective life and cannot remain ever vigilant; therefore, fixed patterns of behavior are bound to emerge.

3. *Impulses and fixed behavior patterns.* Many behavior patterns are simply "unconscious" and are displayed in the presence of the observer because the family is unaware of them. Impulsive behavior will emerge merely because it is uncontrollable.

4. *The position of the observer and the situation of the subject.* To some measure this is akin to the prior point. There is a tendency to overweigh the impact of the observer. Henry feels this is due to the observer's projection of his own learning, understanding, and insight into the observee's mind. The observee, however, lacks the observer's sophistication, and thus often does not realize what one should inhibit or conceal in the presence of an observer.

5. *Participation of the subject in the research.* The tendency to distort or conceal is reduced by the healthful motives of the family to assist the investigator in achieving understanding. For the A.'s there was added impetus to cooperate as they sought vindication in the eyes of mental health professionals, school, and community.

6. *The pressures toward habitual behavior exerted by children in the home.* This is virtually self-explanatory. Children are both more impulsive and less knowing of what should be concealed. They exert a press on their parents to behave in habitual ways and are likely to embarrass them by revealing "family secrets." Their tolerance for delay and their socialization regarding circumspection are both less than the adults'.

7. *Inflexibility of personality structure.* Henry asserts that personality is not subject to ready change, and that this "fact makes a massive contribution to the validity of naturalistic studies in the home" (p. 458).

While not disputing the sagacity of Henry's observations, it must be recognized that he portrays but one side of the matter. Observer effects do occur, and they can create problems for naturalistic observation as a preferred method. The question is how much impact do they have, and how fundamental is it on those particular aspects of the observed phenomenon which the researcher wishes to study. These considerations suggest alternative strategies for handling the problems of intrusiveness.

Recognizing the legitimacy of Henry's claims, the researcher can try to demonstrate that his impact as observer has been minimal with respect to those variables crucial to his premises. This, in fact, is an issue we have considered. As reported elsewhere (Bermann, 1973), statistical analyses of some segments of the A. data show that the A.'s did not behave remarkably differently in later visits than during the first few. In other words, as a family, they were not more guarded in earlier visits. Patterns remained essentially the same through twelve visits. However, this is not to say that there were no observer effects. Rather, it is to suggest that with regard to given variables and given concerns—in this instance, the acuteness of family response to observer entree and accommodation to observer presence—observer effects were minimal.

There were other effects which the observer felt, sometimes quite keenly. It is not always clear how they related to the behavioral interactions recorded, although one may assume they were not without their influence on variables of interest. Two effects deserve particular mention. The first is the family's efforts to embrace (incorporate) or extrude the observer. This involves the attempt to "freeze him out," or, failing this, the attempt to cast him in a familiar or complementary role with which the family can deal. The second is related to the long-term impact of the observation process itself; the effect of the constant presence of an external public, an audience whose smallest responses raise to the level of family awareness interactional patterns which otherwise might not have critical dimension for the family. In short, this last effect has relevance to the unintended and even serendipitous therapeutic effects of observation.

A family will usually respond in one or both of two ways toward a home visitor. If they have misgivings about accepting an observer they will generally make some initial effort to exclude him to block his purposes. The mother in one family hung her laundered sheets up to dry in the archway between the living and dining room directly after the family had seated itself for dinner in the dining area and the observer had settled on the living room couch to watch what transpired. The A.'s attempts along this line were less extreme, and were readily neutralized. They included playing the stereo extra loud to drown out the sound of conversation, and situating the observer near a blaring television set. Simple requests and reminders about the purposes of the visits sufficed to remedy the situation and reduced their extrusive efforts.

Following the failure of these kinds of attempts, families will adopt a second-line strategy which has a similar purpose, namely, dislocating the observer from his observing position. This strategy is buttressed by the wish to cast the observer in a "familiar" or "complementary" role. It is as if the family, begrudgingly accepting the "intruder's" presence, now seeks to relate to him in practiced and predictable ways. In the second visit, for example, Mr. and Mrs. A. made an attempt to altercast the observer as a diagnostician-therapist. They did this knowing that it was a breach of contract, and only had to be reminded of this fact to relent their press. In similar fashion, other families endeavored to pull observers into the social system by treating them as friends or guests. They tried serving cocktails and asking the visitor to dine with them.

This awkwardness of not knowing how to respond to an

observer, and the unease created by his "neutral" and "ambiguous" presence lead to still other outcomes that smack of altercasting. These are perhaps best conceptualized in Bowen's terms as "triangling" (Bowen, 1970).

> As tension mounts in a two person system, it is usual for one to be more uncomfortable than the other, and for the uncomfortable one to "triangle in" a third person. . . . This relieves the tension between the second and third. (p. 12)

During my visits to the A. family I was constantly "triangled in" in blatant or subtle ways. I had to maintain conscious attitudes in the face of these attempts. For example, when Mr. and Mrs. A. approached me as "therapist" in the second visit they were "triangling" me in an effort to relieve the tensions between themselves and their caseworker. They were in one corner, the caseworker in another, and I in the third. In making me an ally they potentiated tension between myself and the social worker at the center. By declining their press, I forced them to maintain the tensions where I thought they belonged—between parents and social agency. Similarly, when Roscoe showed me how well he could draw or play music he was endeavoring to pull me into the sibling system or the parent-sibling system. Roscoe, Ricky, and I described three angles of the triangle on a number of occasions during the visits. By successfully "triangling" me, Roscoe succeeded in reducing tensions between himself and Ricky, while increasing them between Ricky and me. As must be obvious to readers, I was far less successful in evading Roscoe's efforts at deneutralizing me than in evading the efforts of others. Still other instances of "triangling" occurred when Mr. A. juxtaposed me as "friendly audience" in his counterphobic struggle to hold Mrs. A. at bay. Conversely, Mrs. A.'s talking "freely" with me about her past sometimes acted to place Mr. A. on the outside or at least at the far apex of the triangle.

Whether one prefers the term "triangling" to those of "splitting" and "aligning" is less significant than the realization that the complexities of interpersonal dynamics are innumerable and threaten to overwhelm the observer at times. As Bowen notes:

> A three person system is one triangle, a four person system is four primary triangles, a five person system is nine primary triangles, etc. This progression multiplies rapidly as systems get larger. In addition there are a variety of secondary triangles when two or more may band together for one corner of a triangle for one emotional issue, while the configuration shifts on another issue. (1970, p. 13)

Despite the best of intentions and the utmost diligence, the observer in a family cannot be without some effect. As a person on the scene he is attractive to others in interpersonal vying. It therefore becomes axiomatic that the observer record rather than whitewash what he perceives to be his reactive effect on the family.

Therapeutic benefits of naturalistic observation were inconsistently but decidedly experienced in the visits with the A. family. An observer of family life inevitably brings with him the aura of the larger society, with all its values and norms. He also brings a reputation, deserved or not, for special insight. As family members watch him watch them they are forced outside their own frame of reference, or, phrased another way, they find observing egos that adopt the outsider's stance awakened within themselves. They begin to wonder how they appear to persons outside the family, and they are increasingly intrigued by self-scrutiny. Behaviors and interactions within the family are focused on, and the standards of society at large applied. There were numerous occasions when I found one or more of the A.'s observing me as I watched still others in the family interact. I could sense that they were wondering about my evaluation of what I saw transpiring, and that accordingly they were prompted to reconstrue the behavior—behavior that might previously have been routine and frequent and automatic and unquestioned.

Insofar as the observer must attend selectively, he is bound to give off cues to the family. Here again he cannot be without effect. Every nuance of his responsivity is an indication to the family of his interests, his attitudes, and his judgments regarding significant and insignificant behavior. And the family is eager to have these cues and to utilize them, especially when the observer makes claim to neutral, nonparticipant stance, and when as a consequence his evaluations are unimposed and unsolicited. For the A. family in particular, it seemed far easier to make therapeutic use of the observer than of sanctioned therapeutic agents. Their need to maintain a facade of rugged individualism and self-reliance negated ready acceptance of assistance offered through the usual channels. When help was not proffered, however, the family, and most particularly Mrs. A. who was most desirous of support, could utilize cues to helpful ends without overtly acknowledging them, and so they were somewhat capable of modifying their patterns. Within limits, the observer's presence permitted them to do so without public embarrassment. It is not happenstance that when I shifted roles and moved from observer to therapist, I was no longer acceptable to Mr. A. As a "neutral," "nonhelping," "nonparticipant" observer I was tolerated, even welcomed. As a "help-agent" I was of necessity rejected out of hand.

Coincidentally, it is also my impression that the A.'s made greatest use of me as an observer during the second half-dozen visits. During this period they were most attendant to what I was watching, and the scapegoating of Roscoe was at a minimum. With the approach of Mr. A.'s surgery in the third half-dozen visits they had less time to devote to me, and it was during those weeks that I was most truly incidental and unintrusive; the family was otherwise preoccupied.

Ethical Considerations: The Role Conflict of the "Clinician-Observer-Researcher"

Role conflict is at once the most real and the most painful problem for the clinical researcher who aspires to doing naturalistic observation in the family. If nothing else, the report on the A. family is a documentation of this dilemma. In its extreme it may be posed in the following questions: At what point does a witness to inhumanity implicate himself as inhumane by virtue of his inaction? At what point does he in all conscience *have* to intervene and drop the role of observing researcher? Unfortunately, there are no ready or simple answers to these questions. As a matter of fact, in the final analysis there may be no answers at all, but only sound or at least calculated judgment.

These questions throw into bold relief the antagonistic

tensions inherent in the role of "clinical researcher." By training the clinician is an interventionist; he seeks in some immediate sense to exchange bad for good. By the same token, the
researcher is a noninterventionist; his dedication to a research
undertaking predominates and obligates him not to contami-
nate the subject matter he has under study. At first blush, it
may appear that the problem devolves to personalities. In re-
searcher-clinicians for whom the research component dominates, one may expect conservatism, adherence to observation,
and nonintervention. In clinical researchers for whom the clinical commitment outweighs the research dedication, one may
expect a more ready move to intervention.

In the absence of absolute answers there are some guidelines that would suggest that nonintervention is the wiser and
more preferred mode except in the most extreme cases. We are
inclined to this view on the basis of the following:

1. *The need to evade "triangling."* It has already been
pointed out that the press to be engaged in familial alignments and splits is great. It takes effort and skill to resist it.
From a research standpoint, the reasons for resisting are obvious and have already been enumerated. From a clinical standpoint, there are also sound reasons for resisting, though they
are perhaps less clear. In brief they are these: As soon as the
clinical researcher permits himself to be "triangled" he loses
not only his research objectivity, but a good deal of his potential
clinical potency as well. His clinical potency is predicated on
his accurate reading of events and his nonjudgmental attitudes.
Once "triangled" he is implicated, and, like it or not, he is taking sides. Moreover, he will be seduced into partisanship without full vision. His vision will be distorted once he is aligned,
and his capacity for helpful intervention will be decidedly
limited. Thus for the observer to participate defeats his intent
as researcher *and* as clinician.

2. *The questionable success of any intervention.* Even if I
had deemed it desirable to intervene in the scapegoating of
Roscoe or in the A.'s denial of death-fear, there is considerable
doubt in my mind that they would have tolerated such interference. Their needs for denial in these regards were too great.
We have already mentioned that they could not accept me in

a "helper" role. In other words, clinically inspired intervention, even when seemingly desirable, may prove less than effective and even deleterious. The decision for intervention must be weighed against the probabilities of its dismissal or acceptance. In most instances, it is our guess intervention attempts by researchers would be rejected or only worsen matters. This is not to say that family therapy cannot be done in the home. It can and in many cases that may be the best place for it, but it should be contracted for as such and not done under the guise of research. This leads to a third and important point. Research requires intellectual honesty and tough-mindedness. Those not possessed of it will not, by virtue of attrition alone, do the kind of research proposed in these pages.

3. *The need to accomplish the research task: tough-mindedness.* Here we need only quote Henry (1971):

> It would therefore have been preposterous to have hurled myself upon the parents every time I felt they were doing something pathogenic; and it would have been absurd also if I had become so overwhelmed by the pathogenic behavior I witnessed that I had to run screaming from the house. . . . This being the case, I maintained calm. Living in the homes of these families, one constantly encounters situations that might be unsettling to an untrained observer. Experience and training, however, impose automatic restraints. I imagine it must be remotely akin to the experience of an officer watching his men die on the battlefields. (p. 459)

In the final analysis then, our judgment dictates nonintervention. There are conscientiously imposed limits, or, if you will, exceptions to this judgment. The exceptions are those situations calling for legal or physical intervention: child scapegoating, neglect, or abuse that insists the child be removed from the home; familial disorganization or "deviance" that the courts would recognize as justification for interference; or the threat of physical accident or injury that the observer by his own action could and should prevent.

Methodological Problems

Besides the ethically related issues we have discussed, there exist some fundamental but partially soluble technical problems. These must be addressed by clinical researchers who would seek to advance the cause of naturalistic observation.

1. *The need to sample more situations.* The study of the A.'s reported here is limited by its focus on a given period of time within the day—the dinner hour—and suffers from almost exclusive sampling of a total family behavior—that is, of behaviors manifest when all family members are present. The potential value of studying family subsystems and the interrelations between subconstellations is something we could only hint at. Henry's live-in method has the advantage of providing access to these subunits (Henry, 1971), but lacks the longitudinal advantages afforded by periodic visits. In order to take full advantage of naturalistic methods of observation in the home, researchers will have to achieve some combination of the two approaches, or phrase their research questions in accord with each.

2. *The need for reliable home observation.* There is no guarantee that what one observes and reports would be observed and reported by another. This is a phenomenally tacky and nearly insurmountable problem. If live observers are to be used, it suggests that two persons observe simultaneously and then compare their protocols. This, of course, hazards simplification of recording in order to ensure agreement, and raises the possibility that categories of interaction will be defined in such broad terms as to render them insensitive or meaningless. It also raises the specter of two intruders in the natural setting, a prospect that seems certain to quickly denaturalize circumstances. The ideal solution might be approximated by the utilization of refined and unobtrusive audio-visual recording devices. This portends a whole new set of ethical and legal questions around the privacy issue, but it would permit observers to review family interaction at leisure. Researchers could work out and establish coding agreements in careful and unhurried fashion. The problem of selective attention, of course, would then reside in the location of camera or in the decisions of the cameraman.

3. *The need for a reliable set of coding categories.* Assuming that reliable observation can be achieved, the need for demonstrating reliable encoding of described behaviors per-

sists. Because it involves interpersonal interactions, this task takes on an entirely different aura than that which psychologists usually face in coding procedures. One must not only demonstrate that coders can agree on discrete categories of initiation and response, but one must show agreement as well in the segmenting of units of interaction. Moreover, since interaction implies a stimulus-response framework, it is often not sufficient that coders agree on the simple coding of stimulus or response. They must agree that a given stimulus is linked with a given response. It is conceivable that high reliabilities can obtain for given categories in the marginals of an interactional matrix, but not for the relevant cells within. In other words, coders may be in 75 percent agreement about what constitutes a "cooperative" act of initiation, and they may agree on what a "negative" response is 75 percent of the time, and yet seldom agree that a given "cooperative" act by a person *A* receives a "negative" response from person *B*. Methods for establishing reliabilities in contingency analyses of this kind are only now in the earliest stages of development (Kalter, 1971).

4. *The need for establishing observer and coder reliability over time.* This concern is related to the problem of "researcher drift" in both observation and in coding. Researcher drift is the possibility that coder, observer, or both may do their jobs differently at the close of their work than at its outset. Drift of this kind is a commonplace in social science. A coder will modify his rules as he proceeds. An observer will look for and search out different behaviors, and become more acutely discerning—or more careless—as he spends more time at his task. Ideally, in order to facilitate confidence in one's interpretations, each of these possibilities should be ruled out by a reliability check accomplished by checking the old work against the new, or by having the coder or observer reaffirm his skills against some established standard.

Psychological Problems

The research problems just outlined are formidable. They represent challenges that must be met if naturalistic observation of families is to be practiced as a method of choice, and if clinical researchers are ever to successfully accumulate and pre-

serve for general use archives of primary data on family interaction. We have tried to articulate the reasons for amassing
archives on families of different origin, background, class, race,
ethnicity; if nothing else, such collections of observational data
would permit placement of families like the A.'s in the general
scheme of things. One could calculate the extent of their typi-
cality, of their cultural representativeness. One would know if
their plight were common in degree, if not kind, and if their
mode of adaptation to stress resembled that of other families.
This, of course, is crucial. Until such archives are made available this report on the A. family stands as a set of hypotheses
—a set of hypotheses about the A.'s specifically, about clinical practice and clinical research, about middle-American culture. Ultimately, it is a set of hypotheses about each of us and
our families.

There is, naturally, a world of psychological difference between grounded propositions of the variety offered here and
their consensual acceptance and interpretation as pieces of established, prevalent fact. This hardly need be acknowledged.
It is given that the sheer amount of comprehensive, reliable
data that can be brought to bear on such propositions will
make all the difference. The situation is, however, sometimes
complicated by the difficulties encountered when one attempts
to move from having less to having more comprehensive and
reliable data. Exhortations to research of new and special
kinds, while common enough, are frequently insufficient to en-
gender needed change. Follow-through and implementation
are other matters entirely—matters often befouled by the tendency to do the familiar, the easy, and the minimally problematic. Moreover, this problem sometimes shades perceptibly
into issues of public and social scientific tastes—tastes that are
readily infused by the latent fear that some cherished and traditional institutions might crumble if subjected to the research
method and scrutiny most demanded by, and tailored to, the
propositions put forward. At this point, the psychological difference between grounded proposition and consensual acceptance takes on another aspect, better likened to the difference
between "worry" and "disappointment," or "anticipatory concern" and "disillusionment."

Since "N of 1" research remains primarily suggestive, since it is a first approximation of the way things are or might be, there is always the danger that it will be kept at arms length, or dismissed out of hand. It may be treated lightly precisely because it is taken seriously. This is most especially so when its implications herald social consternation of a general kind. After all, it is easier and safer to countenance worry than to suffer disillusionment. One can always dismiss "worry" as "needless worry"—i.e., as untested and therefore senseless pessimism. "Disappointment," on the other hand, is based on the exhaustion of alternative ways for construing unhappy facts. "Disillusionment" means the safety of speculative margin is gone. The tension of doubt between "worry" and "disappointment" marks the social challenge and tests the researcher's resolve. Certainly, it would seem more desirable to confront some unhappy facts than to continue to turn away from them and remain the unknowing or dimly perceiving victims of their debilitating effects.

This book has been full of cruel and unhappy events. The array of propositions put forth to explain these events has also had an unhappy cast. Some of them can be described as embarrassing to a few of our cultural traditions, others as harsh and even unseemly conjectures about the "American way." These propositions are likely to invite the reticence of those who hold conventional assumptions, be they popular or professional views about life in this country. Indeed, for a nation that prides itself on its future orientation, it cannot be entirely pleasant to contemplate how awareness of shifts in our social evolution might follow, rather than precede, the eruption of socio-technological change. Nor can it be especially pleasant to consider that the traditions we automatically maintain and endorse might have the character of oppressive taboos for many of us, or that they might, via cultural lag, force painful social maladjustments—a process which involves repeated exercises in human brinksmanship. It can perhaps prove repelling for us to entertain the possibility that we play a stumbling, halting game of catch-up in the psychological realm; that when the going gets rough, that when survival is at issue, that when psychic costs become prohibitive, that then, and only then, do we react with change. It may be additionally embarrassing for most of us to envision that even when we do attempt to change, it is a modification in surface terms that we engineer—a modification predicated on the principles of compensatory measures. That there is a new vogue in social science research surely means that something different is occurring, but it does not explain itself or reveal what underlies the change. It cannot be pleasing to conjecture on the possibility that the nature of cultural lag often remains invisible to those of us caught up in it, and that hence we are likely as not to display our ignorance by dealing with social change by reinforcing premises and taboos that have already gone past their time.

It may be disheartening as well to recognize that psychic adaptation does not occur synchronistically with technological change, and that we nonetheless continue to deal with prevalent deviancies from outdated social norms as if they were statistically unusual events—as if they were numerical anomalies and embarrassments in need of social cosmetics. That substantial numbers of Americans live in private hells is a potential finding that many of us would rather leave undiscovered. Even if we should be forced to recognize the large numbers of cultural casualties, we are likely as not to shy from the implied indictment of our social system and its values that such a discovery might justify. Instead, we would probably find it more expedient and less offensive to cling to the old "disease" model of mental illness, to the concept of the individual's pathogenesis, and, in so doing, convince the victim of his incompetence. In that way he will renounce his self-sufficiency and autonomy and make himself available to us for experimental study as a diseased entity.

Concomitantly, it is a distressing thing to entertain the real probability that in our culture it is infinitely more dehumanizing to be removed from responsibility for one's own actions than it is to maintain a semblance of self-regulation through the nonconscious but systematic destruction of another human psyche less privileged and more defenseless than one's own.

These are, all of them, unpretty hypotheses. One can well

understand the general societal reluctance and the particular disinclination of clinical researchers to confront such hypotheses head on. They are unpleasant to behold even in the relative safety of abstraction. To scrutinize them seriously, to verify them in the concrete, in the specific, in the aggregate, promises to make one heartsick. But until we do precisely these things we will remain in a position of fundamental impotence. We will continue to live amidst cruelties of epidemic proportions. We will continue to humiliate and dehumanize our children in the name of love. We will continue to drive millions into the "sanctity" of their own homes, where, in the private confines of family, they can sweat in shame and guilt about their self-presumed deviance from the American ideal, sacrifice their children, and abuse each other's psyches. Until we put these unpretty hypotheses to the test, until we reorder our priorities, alter our perceptions, restructure our methods, and until we make social criticism proper game for clinical research, hardship and human tragedy will continue to be commonplace and inevitable outcomes. Families like the A.'s will go untouched, left in crisis and stress to their own devices; or, even more terrifyingly, they will be driven underground, their plights abetted by professional misefforts. These are consequences we can ill afford, for it is not unlikely that we are, all of us, the A.'s.

Appendix

Coding System for Family Interactions

The following code system is adapted from one devised and employed by Charlotte Buhler in a study of Viennese children and their families. Her study, conducted in the mid-1930's, was probably the first effort at studying interaction *within* the family circle. Buhler's coding system is highly elaborate, involving numerous decisions around each bit of information. It is presented in outline form—i.e., categories for coding are labeled, but not defined or clarified by criteria for coding; on the other hand, some examples of coding are provided in the text. Since her categories seemed basically well suited to the coding of family interaction, we have modified the system by reducing the number of decisions to be made, and, at the same time, developed a coding scheme with definitions, criteria and examples. This coding scheme is directly applicable to the data obtained from retrospective accounts of home visits.

A given interaction as described in the process material is coded in its *approach* aspect and in its *reactive* aspect—i.e., as a one-step interaction sequence.

General Conventions for Coding

1. Do not code any interactions involving the observer as a participant.
2. Number sections of interview coded to correspond to numbering of codings listed for the interview.
3. Number each response to the same initiation with the same arabic numeral; distinguish the different responses by following the arabic numeral with an alphabet letter, e.g., *a, b, c,* etc.
4. When an interaction is first described in general terms by the observer and then a few specifics are mentioned as well,

code the general description of the interaction first and then each of the specifically mentioned interactions separately. Give all the interactions the same arabic numeral but different alphabet letters. For example:

> This was followed by a brief discussion concerning the TV program, a who-did-what-to-whom type of discussion since they had tuned in on the middle of the show. The participants in this were Jeff, Scott, and Mr. B. Mr. B. admitted that he didn't know, and Scott came up with the suggestion that one character was a traitor. Mr. B. changed the subject and explained to Scott why they were using a certain kind of plane (it was a war picture).

This could be coded as follows:

Participants	Initiation	Response
6a. Jeff, Scott, Mr. B.	Conversation	Positive-direct
6b. Jeff, Scott→Mr. B.	Conversational; objective (coder infers they asked him if he knew)	Positive-direct
6c. Scott→Jeff	Conversation	Prevented (Mr. B. replies)
6d. Scott→Mr. B.	Conversation	Avoidant; changes subject
6e. Mr. B.→Scott	Objective; conversation	Passive-objective (coder infers Scott accepts role as interested listener)

I. APPROACH, or INITIATING ACTIONS

A. *Cooperative-Affectional*

These include initiations of interactions in which the initiator uses a friendly, warm, helpful, cooperative approach to another person—embracing, kissing, hugging, snuggling, caressing, smiling, cooperation in mutual endeavor, facilitation of others' goals, nurturant behaviors, giving help, being charitable, giving praise or compliments. As explicit examples:

The boys and the girls were setting the table and were busy putting the groceries away.

The older girls helped Mrs. R. in the kitchen. . . .

Mrs. A. was now playing the organ with Ricky and Roscoe singing as she played. . . .

Pamela approached Mr. A. flirtatiously and attempted to sit on his lap.

As he left, Mr. R. patted his wife on her bottom. . . .

Sheila put her arm around Pamela and coaxed her gently into eating. She praised her each time Pamela took a bite. . . .

Pamela hurt herself and Mr. A. picked her up and held her in an effort to comfort her. . . .

B. *Conversational*

Conversational initiations involve the making of personal statements, the telling of stories, the expression of opinions, the use of subjective attitudes in talking to or about others; most generally it ought to include phenomena like gossip, discussion that has entertainment value, or "human interest;" also reflective statements prefaced or introduced with a phrase like "I think . . ." or "let's hope . . ." or "it would be nice if . . ." as well as guesses or speculations; for the most part, conversational statements are about persons or situations outside the immediate family presence— e.g., about work, school, movies, or past experiences of family. Examples:

Mr. A. said, "Isn't it silly that people do not know enough to grease their motorcycle."

Deedee talked about the dance at school, and described how cleverly the teacher had recruited a volunteer to chaperon.

Mrs. A. went on at great length about her uncle who was a retired sea captain and devoted to nautical things and matters. . . .

C. *Objective*

Objective statements initiating interaction include questions, explanations, informing communications, etc. They

are in pure form, usually neutral in tone, devoid of personalized valence or attitude.

> The phone rang and was answered by Mr. R., who returned
> to the table some minutes later and said to his wife, "You'll
> never in a million years guess who that was."

> Ricky asked his mother which was bigger, Red China or the
> United States.

> Mr. A. wanted to know who had won the baseball game.
> Ricky replied that his team had, though they had been losing
> most of the game. (NOTE–The answer given by Ricky begins
> to shade into *conversation;* but it, as well as the father's ques-
> tion, are also coded *objective.*)

> Deedee turned to her mother and said she felt ill.

> Pamela announced the milk tasted funny, and she didn't want
> to finish it. (NOTE–To the extent this last statement is seen
> by the observer-coder as having manipulative overtones it
> should also be coded as *mildly influencing*—i.e., Pamela is
> trying to con her way out of not finishing her milk. To the ex-
> tent the statement conveys no truth about the milk—i.e.,
> everyone else drank it without noticing or commenting on its
> funny taste—it is exclusively manipulative and should be
> coded *mildly influencing* and not at all as *objective.*)

D. *Influencing: Mild*

Mildly influencing initiations are those in which the initiator tries to get another to do something by way of convincing, proposing, advising, urging, suggesting, directing, asking permission, requesting forgiveness, giving unsolicited
apologies, etc. If there is doubt about whether an initiation
should be coded *weak* or *strong* influence, code it *weak*.

> Mrs. A. reminded Roscoe as she had Ricky, "I think it would
> be nice if you washed your hands before sitting down at the
> table."

> Mrs. R. insisted Mr. R. try a piece of the fruitcake. She ex-
> tolled its virtues to him. He simply refused. (NOTE–Mrs. R.
> has attempted to *mildly influence* Mr. R. He has responded
> *negatively.*)

> Sheila asked her sister to please move her feet.

Mr. R. said he felt it would be good if all of them attended church in the morning. Peter and Jimmy sighed. (Note—Mr. R.'s effort at *mild influence* has met with *negative* response.)

Roscoe grabbed a glove and shouted suddenly, "Let's play some ball."

Stuart opened the conversation by bring up a hunting trip he was going on this weekend. Mrs. P. cautioned him not to take more than two other boys with him since they might lose track of each other. (Note—Mrs. P.'s comment is coded as both an *avoidant—citing obstacles* response, and as a *mild influencing* initiation.)

Ricky was obstinate. He refused to budge. Finally Roscoe had to go around him. (Note—Perhaps also coded for *antagonism*.)

E. *Influencing: Strong*

Strongly influencing initiations are those in which the initiator attempts to get the other to comply or to do something via cajoling, pleading, insisting, demanding, ordering, threatening, warning, forcing, physical forcing, raising of the voice; in other words, via any effort at coercion.

Mrs. A. fumed and claimed she would not repeat herself again. Either Roscoe did it immediately or else.

When Pamela didn't stop, Mr. A. raised his hand. She stopped. (Note—The extent to which the initiation includes elements of anger would determine whether *antagonism* ought to be coded here in addition to *strong influence*.)

Roscoe poked the dog. Ricky pounced, "If I see you do that again, I'll wring your neck."

F. *Disapproving (Emotional-Evaluative)*

Disapproving initiations include critical, negative, devaluing kinds of communications which do not necessarily carry the burden of blame and/or personalized anger or contempt. In pure form, disapproving initiations may be devoid of affect or emotion, and convey primarily negative judgment of another person's habits, styles, actions, behaviors or situation.

She said, "Why don't we turn the TV off," and looked at Mr. R. who, with hardly any gesturing at all, shook his head, and the TV set was still on. Mrs. R. said it was too loud, and she went over and lowered the sound. (NOTE–The coding of this sequence is as follows: Mrs. R. is *disapproving* of having the TV set on and of Mr. R. for wanting it on—this is not as clear here as it might be if it were not ripped from the context of the visit; Mr. R. responds to Mrs. R. *negatively;* Mrs. R. initiates a second *disapproving* interaction by saying the TV is too loud and turning it down.)

Ricky talked about the swimming meet at school to which he would be going. Roscoe wanted to know if he could go too. Ricky assured him he could indeed not attend since he was not a student in the public school. (NOTE–Here the devaluation is explicit if one knows the context—i.e., Roscoe is a patient in the Day Treatment program of a psychiatric facility for children, as a result of exclusion from the public school system. The haughty venom on Ricky's part implied by the observer's use of the words "assured" and "indeed" also legitimizes coding the response as *antagonistic;* i.e., inflammatory— see below.)

Mr. R. spoke very little to the family and most of what he said was in terms of directing them in their manners and telling them to behave themselves better at the table. (NOTE– *Mild influence* and *disapproval* toward the family on Mr. R.'s part is self-explanatory in this example.)

Roscoe tried to measure the distance from Michigan to New York on the map and announced that it was 2,000 miles. Mr. A. laughed and Roscoe became embarrassed.

G. *Blaming-Accusing* (*Emotional-Evaluative*)

Blaming-accusing initiations are those in which there is not merely disapproval, but disapproval with volitional, responsible attribution attached to the individual who enacts the disapproved behavior—i.e., the other is held responsible for his "objectionable" behavior.

At this point Ricky could no longer contain himself and he blurted out, "What are you doing, Roscoe?" Roscoe tried to explain . . . but Ricky grabbed the plane from him . . . saying that he did not want it broken. (NOTE–Ricky's behavior is coded as *blaming-accusing* toward Roscoe because the message is clear: Roscoe is blamed in advance by Ricky as endangering the model plane.)

Mrs. A. then chastised Roscoe for having taken not only the guitar but the music as well. She said it was particularly unnecessary for him to have taken the music for obviously he had no intention of playing.

Ricky announced that Roscoe had the crab in a bucket with sand and that Roscoe knew full well that the sand would cause the crab to suffocate.

"He (Ricky) spilled that milk purposely," Deedee said to her mother. (NOTE—This initiation is coded two ways. Since Ricky is present to overhear his sister's remark, her initiation toward him is coded *blaming-accusing*. Her initiation toward the mother, however, cannot be similarly coded as *accusing*—Deedee is not accusing the mother—but should be coded as *conversational* if Deedee is really expressing an opinion to her mother, or *objective* if Deedee is not distorting the situation. If Deedee is trying to get Ricky in trouble with Mrs. A., then it might also be appropriate to code Deedee's initiation toward Mrs. A. as *mildly influencing*, and that toward Ricky as *antagonistic* as well—see below.

H. *Joyful* (*Emotional-Evaluative*)
Joyful initiations are those in which the initiator expresses overt pleasure, enthusiasm, glee, strong approval, excitement of a positive nature. Behavior here would include grinning, laughing, jumping up and down, etc.

Pamela giggled aloud as she watched cartoons on TV. (NOTE—The initiation here is joy, though not necessarily directed at any person in the family—i.e., no target.)

The children got more and more wound up as they discussed the coming vacation trip to Florida.

Roscoe was enthused about the prospect of a trip to the museum, and let his mother know it. . . .

I. *Antagonistic Initiations*
Antagonistic initiations are those in which the initiator betrays contempt, disaffection, disgust, hate, ill will for the

person toward whom he is behaving. The attempt to belittle, intimidate, and/or injure or provoke the other person simply because he is the other person is crucial here. *Antagonism* thus differs from *disapproval* insofar as it is directed at the personality rather than the act or situation—as is the case with *disapproval*. Blameworthiness may or may not be at issue. This category includes most teasing and all taunting remarks.

Virtually everything that Roscoe did and said Ricky countered. He acted in a superior manner and demonstrated his superior ability so that when Roscoe was unable to pull the bow back past his nose, Ricky grabbed the bow away from him and demonstrated to me that he could pull it back all the way to his ear. (NOTE–The effort at embarrassing Roscoe is clear. Ricky seeks to belittle his brother.)

Roscoe attempted to wind up, throw and follow through in major league fashion. It came off awkwardly. Mr. A. laughed out loud and with derision. Roscoe looked at his father questioningly and with some red-faced embarrassment and hurt.

Mrs. R. looked piercingly at her husband. It was a withering look, full of bridled contempt and rage, which Mr. R. chose to ignore.

Pamela came over and sat down in front of Roscoe and the TV set and began to push at Roscoe in order to move him away. Mrs. A. told Pamela it was all right, that Roscoe was not bothering her and that she should leave him alone. Roscoe did not respond except to back up. (NOTE–This sequence may be coded as follows: Pamela to Roscoe, *antagonistic*—she pushes him away; Roscoe's reaction to Pamela, *passive-objective* and *withdrawing* (see below). Mrs. A.'s initiation to Pamela *mildly influencing*—recommended or suggested action—as well as *disapproving;* Pamela's response is coded as *ignores* [see below] since she effectively does nothing to acknowledge her mother's remark.)

Pamela jumped off her father's lap saying "yecch," she did not want to be near him or touch him. Mr. A. looked stunned and abashed. He said nothing. (NOTE–Here Pamela's behavior is coded *antagonistic* because of her disgust reaction to father, and her making it public enough to hurt him.)

II. REACTIONS

A. *Positive-Direct*

Direct, positive responses are those which return directly and without any negativism the social initiation of another. Included are returning a greeting, answering a question, supplementing or augmenting the other's approach, often to the extent of exceeding the other's expectation or intended purpose.

> Mrs. A. commented to Pamela that she looked tired, and should stay in bed real late in the morning. Pamela replied, "Sure I will; I won't get up until lunch time." (NOTE—Mrs. A.'s initiation toward Pamela is coded for *mild influence* and *cooperative affection*—nurturance being involved. Pamela's response is seen as *directly positive* as she wholeheartedly endorses, even elaborates, the mother's suggestion. Her response may also be coded as *cooperative* [see below].

> Mrs. A. is serving dinner and says to Sheila, "Hang on a second . . . I'll get around to you in just a minute." Sheila answers, "No problem. I had a late snack and can wait."

> Ricky is playing baseball with Sheila and Roscoe. Mr. A. comes from the house with Pamela. Pamela insists on having a turn at bat. Ricky says to the others, who initially object, "Pamela can play ball real well. You haven't seen her bat recently."

The last sequence may be coded as follows:

Participants	Initiation	Response
1. Ricky, Sheila, Roscoe	Cooperative (playing ball)	Cooperative (playing ball)
2a. Pamela→Sheila, Roscoe	Mildly influencing (insists on turn)	Negative (by Sheila, Roscoe)
2b. Pamela→Ricky	Mildly influencing (insists on turn)	Positive-direct; cooperative (support)

B. *Passive-Objective*

Passive-objective responses are those of passive-compliance or submission. The response is not directly positive, but is one of going along, obeying, absorbing, incorporating, or accepting the role assigned by the initiator. There may be some hesitancy or resistance involved, in which case *avoidance* or *negativism* would be coded in conjunction with the *objective* response. The response is labeled *objective* because of its apparent indirection—one complies with a direction or carries out an activity without directly responding to the initiator, i.e., the action is focused on an object or situation outside the initiator. It is at the same time a *positive* response insofar as it entails the approval, albeit passive, of another person's wishes, attitudes, or behaviors.

> Mr. A. cautioned Ricky against playing hardball in a street lined with parked cars. Ricky, without a word, picked up his bat and ball, waved for Roscoe and Sheila to come in. The three of them departed for the school yard. (NOTE–Mr. A.'s *mildly influencing* response is silently complied with by Ricky, and subsequently by Roscoe and Sheila.)

> Mrs. X. urged Ronald to practice his music lesson. With some unhappiness Ronald disappeared to the back of the house. A few minutes later the sounds of a French horn could be heard between lulls in the conversation.

> Ricky motioned Roscoe away. Hands thrust in pockets, Roscoe silently retreated.

C. *Cooperative*

Cooperative responses are the counterparts—usually—of cooperative-affectional initiations. Mutual or joint activities or enterprises in which there is smooth flow of role interaction, for example, would be coded for cooperative initiation and cooperative response.

> Deedee and Sheila set the table while Mrs. A. was busy in the kitchen cooking and placing food in serving dishes.

D. *Negative Responses*

Negative reactions are those in which there is refusal, resistance, marked hesitation, or unwillingness to respond to an initiation which the responder recognizes and acknowledges, but does not want to react positively toward.

Included are outright refusals and negations, displays of stubbornness, obstinacy, and opposition. Reactions coded in this category are usually unmistakable as behaviors of direct or overt opposition.

> Mrs. R. urges Mr. R. to wear a jacket outside since it is chilly. Mr. R. says no, he'll be active and stay warm by moving.

> Roscoe claims he has found a dead squirrel. Ricky says, "No you didn't . . . it's dead now but it wasn't when you found it. (NOTE–It should be clear that Ricky's response should be coded *antagonistic* as well as *negative*.)

> Mr. A. asked Roscoe to return the crab to the creek. Roscoe did not respond but was obviously unhappy. He kicked at the floor briefly, then shook his head slowly. Mr. A. repeated his request. Roscoe slowly left the room for the basement where he had the crab in a bucket. (NOTE–This sequence is coded: Mr. A. *mildly influencing;* Roscoe *avoidant* [see below] and *negative;* Mr. A. again initiates with *mild influence;* Roscoe complies—a *passive-objective* reaction.)

E. *Avoidant Reactions*

Avoidant reactions occur in those cases where the target of an initiation seeks to divert direct response while simultaneously trying not to be positive or overtly negative. They may be seen as oblique responses of noncompliance, hesitation, defensiveness, evasion, etc. As such, they may be thought of as the negative side of passive-objective responses. The principle forms avoidant reactions take are: *waiting for further information* (e.g., "I don't understand what you want me to do. Tell me more," or "It's hard to know what to think until we see what happens"); and *citing obstacles* (e.g., making excuses of one kind or another like, "I can't now because both my hands are full already," or, "Mrs. A. says to Pamela, 'Don't you remember we agreed no more playing with your doll today?' To which Pamela replies, 'But I just wanted to see if her hair and clothes were dry yet'). *Self-defense* is a related avoidant reaction (e.g., Mr. A. to Roscoe, who is pulling out his chair preparatory to sitting at the dinner table: 'Don't you know you're supposed to wash your hands first?' Roscoe answers defensively, 'I was just getting my chair ready before going to wash my hands'); both *citing obstacles* and *self-defense* often have the avoidance and/or denial of guilt as their basis; *doubting* and *hesitation* are still other forms of avoidant reactions (e.g., "I'm not so sure it's a good idea," or "Let's wait a few minutes and see what happens"); *stating counter-wishes, bargaining, bringing up nonessentials,* and *changing the subject* are still other defensive modes employed as avoidant reactions (e.g., "Mrs. A. to Ricky: 'Look at the way you've thrown your school clothes around. An absolute mess.' Ricky: 'Mom, my tooth hurts something fierce')."

F. *Prevented Reactions*

Prevented reactions are those which are rendered impossible by external circumstances. They tend to be rarely coded, though some families are likely to evidence them more than others. Typically they occur because someone else has responded for the target person, because the initiator himself has continued his initiation without leaving time for the target person to respond, or because the target person is out of earshot or absent without the initiator being aware of this fact. If an initiation is made to more than one person but only one responds, then the others' response should be coded as *prevented* with a note in parentheses as to who prevents a response.

G. *Ignoring Reactions*

Ignoring reactions are those in which no visible social reaction can be observed to the initiation. On the surface, the target person seems not to notice the other's approach. In some instances he may have been genuinely preoccupied and not noticed the approach. More often the ignoring response is likely to be an extreme form of *avoidance*—a deliberate refusal to respond by pretending not to hear or know.

H. *Embarrassed-Withdrawal (Fear Reactions)*

Fear reactions include embarrassed-withdrawal reactions such as blushing, shyness, awkward laughter, staring at the floor, and similar characteristic behavior forms, which lead to sufficient loss of esteem that the favored response becomes that of leaving the field either physically or psychologically. Also includes anxious crying.

Roscoe estimated the distance from Chicago to New York to be 2,000 miles. Mr. A. laughed out loud. Roscoe turned red and became silent.

After Ricky's criticism, Roscoe stood in the middle of the room, his hands thrust in his pockets, looking intently at nothing except perhaps the living room floor.

Mrs. A. asked her husband what the temperature had been outside during the four hours he had been ice fishing. Obviously she, as well as all in the room, knew it had been subzero. Mr. A. did not reply and awkward silence ensued, everyone staring at the food on their plates.

Mrs. B. hit Scott on the hand, telling him to be more careful. He cried briefly.

I. *Antagonistic Reactions*

Antagonistic reactions betray contempt, disaffection, disgust, hate, ill will for the person being responded to. It is an evaluation of the person (initiator) rather than the given act or initiation.

Deedee offered belatedly to assist her mother in looking for Pamela, who disappeared while Deedee was presumably watching her. Mrs. A. swept past Deedee with a flat, "Drop dead!"

Ricky shoved Sheila aside in his haste. She followed his movement out of the room with contemptuous eyes.

J. *Overt Pleasure*

Overt pleasure reactions are those in which the target person expresses overt pleasure, enthusiasm, glee, strong approval, excitement of a positive nature. Behavior here would include grinning, laughing, jumping up and down, etc.

K. *Reference to Absent Member*

An initiation made toward an absent family member is listed like any other interaction; however, the response column should include "reference to absent member."

Denise remarked that now she knew why Steve had closed his door (while he practiced clarinet). . . . Implication was that he needed to close it because he wasn't playing very well.

This remark was made to three other family members besides Steve, who was still practicing in his room. Hence, it should be coded as follows:

Participants	Initiation	Response
12a. Denise→Mr. B., Mrs. B., Scott	Conversational	?
12b. Denise→Steve	Emotional-evaluative: disapproving	Reference to absent member

L. *No response noted by observer*

When there is no response noted by the observer and one cannot be inferred from the context, a question mark should be placed in the response column as in the above example.

Selected Bibliography

Ackerman, N. W. 1956. Interlocking pathology in family relationships. In *Changing concepts of psychoanalytic medicine,* ed. S. Rado and G. E. Daniels. New York: Grune and Stratton.

——1958. *The psychodynamics of family life.* New York: Basic Books.

——1961. Emergence of family psychotherapy on the present scene. In *Contemporary psychotherapies,* ed. M. I. Stein. New York: Free Press.

——1971. Prejudicial scapegoating and neutralizing forces in the family group. In *Theory and practice of family psychiatry,* ed. J. G. Howells. New York: Brunner/Mazel.

——1967. The future of family psychotherapy. In *Expanding theory and practice in family therapy,* ed. N. W. Ackerman, F. L. Beatman, and S. N. Sherman. New York: Family Service Association of America.

Ackerman, N. W., and Behrens, L. 1956. A study of family diagnosis. *American Journal of Orthopsychiatry* 26:66–78.

Agee, J. 1959. *Agee on film.* Vol. I. New York: McDowell, Oblensky.

Agee, J., and Evans, W. 1966. *Let us now praise famous men.* New York: Ballantine Books.

Alexander, I., and Alderstein, A. 1958. Affective responses to the concept of death in a population of children and early adolescents. *Journal of Genetic Psychology* 93:167–77.

——1959. Death and religion. In *The meaning of death,* ed. H. Feifel. New York: McGraw-Hill.

——1960. Studies in the psychology of death. In *Perspectives in personality research,* ed. H. P. David and J. C. Brengelmann. New York: Springer.

Anthony, E. J. 1970. The mutative impact of serious mental and physical illness in a parent on family life. In *The child in his family,* ed. J. Anthony and C. Koupernik. New York: Wiley-Interscience.

Arthur, B., and Kemme, M. 1964. Bereavement in childhood. *Journal of Child Psychology and Psychiatry* 5:37–49.

342 *Scapegoat*

Baleś, R. F., and Slater, P. E. 1955. Role differentiation in small decision-making groups. In *Family, socialization and interaction process,* ed. T. Parsons and R. F. Bales. New York: Free Press.

Bateson, G. 1960. Minimal requirements for a theory of schizophrenia.
Archives of General Psychiatry 2:477–91.

Bateson, G.; Jackson, D.; Haley, J.; and Weakland, J. 1956. Toward a
theory of schizophrenia. *Behavioral Science* 1:251–64.

Behrens, M., and Ackerman, N. W. 1956. The home visit as an aid in
family diagnosis and therapy. *Social Casework* 37:11–19.

Bell, N. 1962. Extended family relations of disturbed and well families.
Family Process 1:175–92.

Benedict, R. 1949. The family: genus Americanum. In *The family: its
function and destiny,* ed. R. N. Anshen. New York: Harper.

Berdyaev, N. 1962. *The destiny of man* (1937). New York: Harper.

Bermann, E. 1967. Family diagnosis: an experimental approach to family
interaction and decision making. Paper presented at Mental
Health Research Institute Colloquium, January, 1967, Ann Arbor,
Michigan.

———1972. Family problem solving and family patterns. Unpublished
manuscript, University of Michigan.

———(in press). Regrouping for survival: approaching dread and three
phases of family interaction. *Journal of Comparative Family Studies.*

Bermann, E., and Lebby, S. 1971. Verbal exchange in three kinds of
families. Unpublished manuscript, University of Michigan.

Blood, R. O. 1958. The use of observational methods in family research.
Marriage and Family Living 20:47–52.

Borkenau, F. 1965. The concept of death. In *Death and identity,* ed.
R. Fulton. New York: Wiley and Sons.

Boszormenyi-Nagy, I. 1965. The concept of change in conjoint family
therapy. In *Psychotherapy for the whole family,* by A. S. Friedman, I. Boszormenyi-Nagy, J. E. Jungris, G. Lincoln, H. E.
Mitchell, J. C. Sonne, R. V. Speck, and G. Spivack. New York:
Springer.

Boszormenyi-Nagy, I., and Framo, J. L. 1965. *Intensive family therapy:
theoretical and practical aspects.* New York: Harper.

Bottome, P. 1939. *Alfred Adler: a biography.* New York: Putnam.

Bowen, M. 1960. A family concept of schizophrenia. In *The etiology of schizophrenia*, ed. D. D. Jackson. New York: Basic Books.

———1970. Toward the differentiation of a self in one's own family. Unpublished manuscript, Washington, D.C.

Bowers, M.; Jackson, E.; Knight, J.; and LeShan, L. 1964. *Counseling the dying*. New York: Thomas Nelson.

Bridgman, P. W. 1938. *The intelligent individual and society*. New York: Macmillan.

Brown, N. 1959. *Life against death*. Middletown, Conn.: Wesleyan University Press.

Buhler, C. 1939. *The child and his family*. New York: Harper.

Burgess, E. W.; Locke, H. J.; and Thomes, M. M. 1963. *The family from institution to companionship*. New York: American Book.

Burlingham, D. 1955. Simultaneous analysis of mother and child. In *Psychoanalytic Study of the Child*, vol. 9, pp. 165–86. New York: International Universities Press.

Buxbaum, E. 1954. Technique of child therapy: a critical evaluation. In *Psychoanalytic Study of the Child*, vol. 9, pp. 297–333. New York: International Universities Press.

Cain, A. C.; Fast, I.; and Erickson, M. 1964. Children's disturbed reactions to the death of a sibling. *American Journal of Orthopsychiatry* 34(4):741–52.

Carey, F. 1972. Doctor says few families escape mental illness. Associated Press dispatch, *Ann Arbor News*, April 24, 1972.

Chadwick, M. 1929. Notes upon fear of death. *International Journal of Psychoanalysis* 10:321–34.

Clausen, J. A., and Yarrow, M. R. 1955. The impact of mental illness on the family. *Journal of Social Issues* 11:3–5.

Cleveland, E. J., and Longaker, W. D. 1957. Neurotic patterns in the family. In *Explorations in social psychiatry*, ed. A. Leighton, J. A. Clausen, and R. N. Wilson. New York: Basic Books.

Cooley, C. H. 1929. *Social organization*. New York: Scribner.

Cooper, D. 1970. *The death of the family*. New York: Pantheon.

Dewey, J., and Bentley, A. F. 1949. *Knowing and the known*. Boston: Beacon Press.

Ehrenwald, J. 1963. *Neurosis in the family and patterns of psychosocial defense*. New York: Harper.

Elles, G. W. 1961. The closed circuit: the study of a delinquent family. *British Journal of Criminology* 2:23–29.

Erikson, E. H. 1946. Ego development and historical change. In *Psychoanalytic Study of the Child,* vol. 2, pp. 359–96. New York: International Universities Press.

——1950. *Childhood and society.* New York: Norton.

——1956. Growth and crisis of the "healthy personality." In *Personality in nature, society and culture,* ed. C. Kluckhohn, H. A. Murray, and D. Schneider. New York: Knopf.

——1956. The problem of ego identity. *Journal of American Psychoanalytic Association* 4:56–121.

Farber, B. 1964. *Family: organization and interaction.* San Francisco: Chandling.

Farberow, N. L. 1963. *Taboo topics.* New York: Atherton.

Feifel, H. 1961. Death-relevant variable in psychology. In *Existential psychology,* ed. R. May. New York: Random House.

——1963. Death. In *Taboo topics,* ed. N. Farberow. New York: Atherton Press.

Ferkiss, V. C. 1969. *Technological man: the myth and the reality.* New York: Mentor.

Ferreira, A. J. 1963. Family myth and homeostasis. *Archives of General Psychiatry* 9:457–63.

Festinger, L. 1957. *A theory of cognitive dissonance.* Evanston, Ill.: Row, Peterson.

Finch, S., and Cain, A. 1968. Psychoanalysis of children. In *Modern psychoanalysis,* ed. J. Marmor. New York: Basic Books.

Framo, J. 1965. Systematic research on family dynamics. In *Intensive family therapy,* ed. I. Boszormenyi-Nagy and J. Framo. New York: Harper.

Freeman, R. D. 1967. The home visit in child psychiatry: its usefulness in diagnosis and training. *Journal of the American Academy of Child Psychiatry* 6(2):276–94.

French, J. R. P., and Zajonc, R. B. 1957. An experimental study of cross-cultural norm conflict. *Journal of Abnormal and Social Psychology* 54:218–24.

Freud, A. 1965. *Normality and pathology in childhood.* New York: International Universities Press.

Freud, S. 1955. Totem and taboo (1913). In *The complete psychological works of Sigmund Freud*, ed. J. Strachey, vol. XIII. London: Hogarth Press.

———1961. Thoughts for the times on war and death (1915). In *The complete psychological works of Sigmund Freud*, ed. J. Strachey, vol. XIV. London: Hogarth Press.

———1949. *Moses and monotheism* (1939). New York: Knopf.

Friedman, A. 1962. Family therapy as conducted in the home. *Family Process* 1:132–40.

———1964. The "well" sibling in the "sick" family: a contradiction. *International Journal of Social Psychiatry*, Special Edition 2:47–53.

Friedman, A.; Boszormenyi-Nagy, I.; Jungris, J. E.; Lincoln, G.; Mitchell, H. E.; Sonne, J. C.; Speck, R. V.; and Spivack, G. 1965. *Psychotherapy for the whole family*. New York: Springer.

Fromm-Reichmann, F. 1959. *Psychoanalysis and psychotherapy*. Chicago: University of Chicago Press.

———1955. *An outline of psychoanalysis*. New York: Random House.

Fulton, R. 1965. *Death and identity*. New York: Wiley.

Furman, R. A. 1964. Death and the young child. *Psychoanalytic Study of the Child* 19:321–33. New York: International Universities Press.

Gans, H. J. 1962. *The urban villagers*. New York: Free Press.

Glaser, B. G., and Strauss, A. L. 1965. *Awareness of dying*. Chicago: Aldine.

Goffman, E. 1959. *The presentation of self in everyday life*. New York: Doubleday.

Goldman, E. 1968. *The tragedy of Lyndon Johnson*. New York: Dell.

Goode, W. J. 1963. *World revolution and family patterns*. Glencoe, Ill.: Free Press.

———1964. *The family*. Englewood Cliffs: Prentice-Hall.

Gorer, G. 1965. The pornography of death. In *Encounters*, ed. S. Spender, I. Kristol, M. Lasky. New York: Simon and Schuster.

Group for the Advancement of Psychiatry. 1970. *Treatment of families in conflict*. New York: Science House.

Gutmann, D. 1969. Psychological naturalism in cross-cultural studies. In

Naturalistic viewpoints in psychological research, ed. E. P. Willems and H. L. Raush. New York: Holt, Rinehart, and Winston.

Haley, J. 1959. The family of the schizophrenic: a model system. *American Journal of Nervous and Mental Diseases* 129:357–74.

———1964. Research on family patterns: an instrumental measurement. *Family Process* 3:41–65.

———1967. Speech sequences of normal and abnormal families with two children present. *Family Process* 6:81–97.

Handel, G. 1967. *The psychosocial interior of the family.* Chicago: Aldine.

Hartmann, H. 1939. Psychoanalysis and the concept of health. *International Journal of Psychoanalysis* 20:308–18.

Hawkins, R. P.; Peterson, R. F.; Schweid, E.; and Bijou, S. W. 1966. Behavior therapy in the home. *Journal of Experimental Child Psychology* 4:99–107.

Hebb, D. O. 1949. *The organization of behavior.* New York: Wiley.

———1954. The mammal and his environment. *American Journal of Psychiatry* 3(1):826–31.

Heidegger, M. 1927. *Sein und zeit.* Halle: Max Niemeyer. (*Being and time.* Translated by J. Macquarrie and E. Robinson. New York: Harper, 1962.)

Hellman, I. 1954. Some observations on mothers of children with intellectual inhibitions. In *Psychoanalytic Study of the Child,* vol. 9, pp. 259–73. New York: International Universities Press.

Henry, J. 1951. Family structure and the transmission of neurotic behavior. *American Journal of Orthopsychiatry* 21:800–818.

———1963. *Culture against man.* New York: Random House.

———1967. My life with the families of psychotic children. In *The psychosocial interior of the family,* ed. G. Handel. Chicago: Aldine.

———1971. *Pathways to madness.* New York: Random House.

Henry, J., and Warson, S. 1951. Family structure and psychic development. *American Journal of Orthopsychiatry* 21:59–73.

Herzog, E. 1967. *Psyche and death.* New York: Putnam.

Hess, R. D., and Handel, G. 1959. *Family worlds.* Chicago: University of Chicago Press.

Hill, R. 1949. *Families under stress.* New York: Harper.

———1958. Social stresses on the family. *Social Casework* 39:139–50.

Hill, R., and Rodgers, R. H. 1964. The developmental approach. In *Handbook of marriage and the family*, ed. H. T. Christensen. Chicago: Rand McNally.

Hinton, J. M. 1967. *Dying*. Baltimore: Penguin Books.

Horkeimer, M. 1949. Authoritarianism and the family today. In *The family: its function and destiny*, ed. R. N. Anshen. New York: Harper.

Irish, D. P. 1964. Sibling interaction: a neglected aspect in family life research. *Social Forces* 42:279–88.

Jackson, D. D. 1965. The study of the family. *Family Process* 4(1):1–20.

———1967. The individual and the larger contexts. *Family Process* 6(2):139–47.

Jahoda, M. 1958. *Current concepts of mental health*. New York: Basic Books.

Johnson, A. 1949. Sanctions for superego lacunae of adolescents. In *Searchlights on delinquency*, ed. K. R. Eissler. New York: International Universities Press.

Johnson, A., and Szurek, S. A. 1952. The genesis of anti-social acting out in children and adults. *Psychoanalytic Quarterly* 21:323–43.

Johnson, A. M. 1953. Collaborative psychotherapy: team setting. In *Psychoanalysis and social work*, ed. M. Heiman. New York: International Universities Press.

Kalter, N. 1971. The comparison of sequential and non-sequential data analysis of classroom interaction: a methodological study. Ph.D. dissertation, University of Michigan.

Kaufmann, W. 1959. Existentialism and death. In *The meaning of death*, ed. H. Feigel. New York: McGraw-Hill.

Kelly, G. A. 1955. The psychology of personal constructs. New York: Norton.

Kent, J. 1970. Behavioral style and adjustment; a study of sibling differences. Ph.D. dissertation, University of Michigan.

Kerr, W. 1968. *Thirty plays hath November*. New York: Simon and Schuster.

Kierkegaard, S. 1944. *The concept of dread*. Princeton: Princeton University Press.

———1944. *Either/or, a fragment of life*. Princeton: Princeton University Press.

348 *Scapegoat*

Kluckhohn, C. 1949. The family in a democratic society. New York: Columbia University Press.

———1951. Values and value orientations. In *Toward a general theory of action*, ed. T. Parsons and E. A. Shils. Cambridge: Harvard University Press.

Kluckhohn, F. 1950. Dominant and substitute profiles of cultural orientations: their significance for the analysis of social stratification. *Social Forces* 28:276–93.

———1956. Dominant and variant value orientations. In *Personality in nature, society and culture*, 2nd ed., ed. C. Kluckhohn and H. Murray. New York: Knopf.

———1958. Variations in the basic values of family systems. *Social Casework* 39:63–72.

Kluckhohn, F., and Spiegel, J. 1954. *Integration and conflict in family behavior*. Report no. 27. New York: Group for the Advancement of Psychiatry.

Komarovsky, M. 1940. *The unemployed man and his family*. New York: Dryden Press.

Kubler-Ross, E. 1969. *On death and dying*. New York: Macmillan.

———1971. The dying patient. Papers presented at the University of Michigan Medical Center, May, 1971. Ann Arbor, Michigan.

Lebby, S. 1971. A comparison of reading problem, behavior problem and control families, utilizing objective techniques of data collection. Unpublished manuscript, University of Michigan.

Lecky, P. 1951. *Self-consistency: a theory of personality*. New York: Island Press Cooperative.

Lennard, H. and Bernstein, A. 1969. *Patterns in human interaction*. San Francisco: Jossey-Bass.

Lerner, M. 1957. *America as a civilization. Volume II: Culture and personality*. New York: Simon and Schuster.

Lewis, O. 1950. An anthropological approach to family studies. *American Journal of Sociology* 55:468–75.

———1959. *Five families: Mexican case studies in the culture of poverty* New York: Basic Books.

———1966. *La Vida: a Puerto Rican family in the culture of poverty— San Juan and New York*. New York: Random House.

———1969. *A death in the Sanchez family*. New York: Random House.

———1969. The death of Dolores. *Transaction* 6(7):10–19.

Lidz, T. 1962. The relevance of family studies to psychoanalytic theory. *Journal of Nervous and Mental Diseases* 135:105–12.

——1964. *The family and human adaptation.* London: Hogarth Press.

——1968. *The person.* New York: Basic Books.

Lidz, T.; and Fleck, S. 1965. *Family studies and a theory of schizophrenia: the American family in crisis.* Des Plaines, Ill.: Forest Hospital Publications.

Lidz, T.; Fleck, S.; Alanen, Y.; and Cornelison, A. 1963. Schizophrenic patients and their siblings. *Psychiatry* 26:1–18.

Lidz, T.; Fleck S.; and Cornelison, A. R. 1966. *Schizophrenia and the family.* New York: International Universities Press.

Lindemann, E. 1944. Symptomatology and management of acute grief. *American Journal of Psychiatry* 101:141–48.

Litwak, E. 1960. The use of extended family groups in the achievement of social goals: some policy implications. *Social Problems* 7:177–87.

Lydgate, J. 1961. Where is thy sting? *Spectator* 206:308.

Malreaux, A. 1970. *Memoirs.* New York: Harper and Row.

Martin, B. 1967. Family interaction associated with child disturbance: assessment and modification. *Psychotherapy: Theory, Research and Practice* 4(1):30–35.

McClelland, D. C. 1951. *Personality.* New York: Dryden.

McGuire, W. J. 1967. Some impending reorientations in social psychology: some thoughts provoked by Kenneth Ring. *Journal of Experimental Psychology* 3:124–39.

Mead, G. H. 1934. *Mind, self and society.* Chicago: University of Chicago Press.

Mead, M. 1935. *Sex and temperament in three primitive societies.* New York: Morrow.

Merton, R. K., and Lazarsfeld, P. F., eds. 1950. *Studies in the American soldier.* New York: Free Press.

Miller, D. R. 1962. The study of social relationships: situation, identity and social interaction. In *Psychology: a study of a science,* ed. S. Koch, vol. 5, pp. 639–737. New York: McGraw-Hill.

Miller, D. R., and Hutt, M. L. 1949. Value interiorization and personality development. *Journal of Social Issues* 5:2–30.

Miller, D. R., and Swanson, G. 1958. *The changing American parent.* New York: Wiley.

Miller, D. R., and Westman, J. 1964. Reading disability as a condition of family stability. *Family Process* 3:66–76.

———1966. Family teamwork and psychotherapy. *Family Process* 5:49–59.

Mills, T. M. 1953. Power relations in three-person groups. *American Sociological Review* 18:351–57. Reprinted in *Group dynamics: research and theory,* ed. D. Cartwright and A. Zander. Evanston, Ill.: Row, Peterson, 1960.

Mishler, E. G., and Waxler, N. 1968. *Interaction in families.* New York: Wiley.

Mitscherlich, A. 1970. *Society without the father.* New York: Harcourt, Brace and World.

Moore, B. 1960. Thoughts on the future of the family. In *Identity and anxiety,* ed. M. Stein, A. Vidich, and D. White. New York: Free Press.

Murrell, S., and Stachowiak, J. G. 1967. Consistency, rigidity, power in the interaction of clinic and non-clinic families. *Journal of Abnormal Psychology* 72:265–72.

Naegle, K. 1960. Some problems in the study of hostility and aggression in middle-class American families. In *A modern introduction to the family,* ed. N. Bell and E. Vogel. New York: Free Press.

Ogburn, W. F. 1964. *On culture and social change.* Chicago: University of Chicago Press.

Ogburn, W. F., and Nimkoff, M. F. 1955. *Technology and the changing family.* Boston: Houghton Mifflin.

———1958. *Sociology.* Boston: Houghton Mifflin.

O'Leary, K. D.; O'Leary, S.; and Becker, W. C. 1967. Modification of a deviant sibling interaction pattern in the home. *Behavior Research and Therapy* 5:113–20.

Opler, M. K. 1967. *Culture and social psychiatry.* New York: Atherton.

Parad, H. J., and Caplan, G. 1960. A framework for studying family in crisis. *Social Work* 5(3):3–15.

Parsons, T. 1955. Family structure and the socialization of the child. In *Family: socialization and interaction process,* ed. T. Parsons and R. F. Bales. New York: Free Press.

Parsons, T., and Bales, R. F. 1955. *Family: socialization and interaction process.* New York: Free Press.

Peller, L. 1963. Further comments on adoption. *Bulletin of Philadelphia Association of Psychoanalysis* 13:1–14.

Piaget, J. 1951. *Play, dreams and imitation in childhood.* New York: Norton.

———1952. *The origins of intelligence in children.* New York: International Universities Press.

———1954. *The construction of reality in the child.* New York: Basic Books.

Pollak, O. 1967. The outlook for the American family. *Journal of Marriage and the Family* 29:193–205.

Rainwater, L. 1970. *Behind ghetto walls.* Chicago: Aldine.

Rapoport, L. 1962. The state of crisis: some theoretical considerations. *Social Service Review* 36(2):211–17.

Rapoport, R. 1963. Normal crises, family structure and mental health. *Family Process* 2(1):68–80.

Reiff, P. 1961. *Freud: the mind of the moralist.* Garden City, N.Y.: Doubleday.

Risley, T. R., and Wolf, M. M. 1967. Experimental manipulation of autistic behaviors and generalization into the home. In *Child development: readings in experimental analysis,* ed. S. W. Bijou and D. M. Baer. New York: Appleton-Century-Crofts.

Rodgers, R. H. 1964. Towards a theory of family development. *Journal of Marriage and the Family* 26:262–70.

Rodman, H. 1965. Talcott Parsons' view of the changing American family. In *Marriage, family and society: a reader,* ed. H. Rodman. New York: Random House.

Rosenthal, H. 1963. The fear of death as an indispensable factor in psychotherapy. *American Journal of Psychotherapy* 17:619–30.

Rosner, A. 1962. Mourning before the fact. *Journal of American Psychoanalytic Association* 10:564–70.

Ruesch, J., and Bateson, G. 1951. *Communication: the matrix of psychiatry.* New York: Norton.

Russell, B. 1929. *Marriage and morals.* London: Liverwright.

Sartre, J. 1953. *Existential psychoanalysis.* New York: Philosophical Library.

———1956. *Existentialism and human emotions.* New York: Philosophical Library.

———1956. Self-deception. In *Existentialism from Dostoevsky to Sartre,* ed. W. Kaufmann. New York: World.

Satir, V. M. 1964. *Conjoint family therapy.* Palo Alto, Calif.: Science and Behavior Books.

———1965. The family as a treatment unit. *Confinia Psychiatrica* 8:37–42.

Schmidt, V. S. 1971. A comparison of children's aspirations and of parental expectations as a function of underachievement in children. Ph.D. dissertation, University of Michigan.

Searles, H. 1961. Schizophrenia and the inevitability of death. *Psychiatric Quarterly* 35:631–65.

Shneidman, E. 1963. Orientations toward death: a vital aspect of the study of lives. In *The study of lives,* ed. R. W. White. New York: Atherton.

Sirjamaki, J. 1948. Culture configurations in the American family. *The American Journal of Sociology* 53:464–70.

Speck, R. 1964. Family therapy in the home. *Journal of Marriage and the Family* 26(1):72–76.

Spiegel, J. 1957. The resolution of role conflict within the family. In *The patient and the mental hospital,* ed. M. Greenblatt, D. J. Levinson, and R. H. Williams. Glencoe, Ill.: Free Press.

Spiegel, J., and Bell, N. 1959. The family of the psychiatric patient. In *American handbook of psychiatry,* ed. S. Aristi. New York: Basic Books.

Spiegel, J. P. 1959. Some cultural aspects of transference and countertransference. In *Individual and family dynamics,* ed. J. H. Masserman. New York: Grune and Stratton.

———1964. Conflicting formal and informal roles in newly acculturated families. In *Disorders of communication,* ed. D. M. Rioch, vol. XLII. New York: Association for Research in Nervous and Mental Disease.

———1971. Cultural strain, family role patterns, and intrapsychic conflict. In *Theory and practice of family psychiatry,* ed. J. G. Howells. New York: Brunner/Mazel.

Strodbeck, F. L. 1954. The family as a three-person group. *American Sociological Review* 19:23–29.

Sumner, W. G. 1940. *Folkways*. Boston: Ginn.

Sussman, M. B. 1959. The isolated nuclear family: fact or fiction. *Social Problems* 6:333–40.

Sussman, M. B., and Burchinal, L. 1962. Kin family network: unheralded structure in current conceptualizations of family functioning. *Marriage and Family Living* 24:231–40.

Tausk, V. 1933. On the origin of the "influencing machine" in schizophrenia. *Psychoanalytic Quarterly* 2:519–56.

Tharp, R. G., and Wetzel, R. J. 1969. *Behavior modification in the natural environment*. New York: Academic Press.

Thibaut, J. W., and Kelley, H. H. 1959. *The social psychology of groups*. New York: Wiley.

Vincent, C. E. 1966. Familia spongia: the adaptive function. *Journal of Marriage and the Family* 28:29–36.

―――― 1967. Mental health and the family. *Journal of Marriage and the Family* 29:18–39.

Vogel, E. F., and Bell, N. W. 1960. The emotionally disturbed child as a family scapegoat. *Psychoanalysis and the Psychoanalytic Review* 47:21–42.

Volkart, E. H., and Michael, S. T. 1957. Bereavement and mental health. In *Explorations in social psychiatry*, ed. A. Leighton, J. Clausen, and R. N. Wilson. New York: Basic Books.

Wahl, C. W. 1958. The fear of death. *Bulletin of the Menninger Clinic* 22:214–23.

Warren, R. 1971. Parent structure, children's roles, and occupational choice: variations on a theme of role congruence. Ph.D. dissertation, University of Michigan.

Watzlawick, P.; Beavin, J.; Sikorski, L.; and Mecia, B. 1970. Protection and scapegoating in pathological families. *Family Process* 9:27–39.

Weisman, A. D., and Hackett, T. P. 1961. Predilection to death. *Psychosomatic Medicine* 23:232–56.

White, R. W. 1964. *The abnormal personality*. New York: Ronald Press.

Willems, E. P. 1969. Planning a rationale for naturalistic research. In *Naturalistic viewpoints in psychological research*, ed. E. P. Willems and H. L. Raush. New York: Holt, Rinehart, and Winston.

Wolfenstein, M., and Leites, N. 1950. *Movies: a psychological study.* Glencoe, Ill.: Free Press.

Wynne, L. 1961. The study of intrafamilial alignments and splits in exploratory family therapy. In *Exploring the base for family therapy,* ed. N. Ackerman, F. Beatman and S. N. Sherman. New York: Family Service Association of America.

Wynne, L.; Ryckoff, I.; Day, J.; and Hirsch, S. 1958. Pseudomutuality in the family relations of schizophrenics. *Psychiatry* 21:205–20.

Zeilberger, J.; Sampen, S. E.; and Sloane, H. W. 1968. Modification of a child's problem behaviors in the home with the mother as therapist. *Journal of Applied Behavioral Analysis* 1:47–53.

Zelditch, M. 1955. Role differentiation in the nuclear family: a comparative study. In *Family: socialization and interaction process,* ed. T. Parsons and R. F. Bales. New York: Free Press.

Zilbourg, G. 1943. Fear of death. *Psychoanalytic Quarterly* 12:465–75.

Index

Ackerman, N. W., 283, 285, 286, 288, 300, 310
Agee, J., 249, 253
Alderstein, A., 248
Alexander, I., 248
Anthony, E. J., 33, 311

Bales, R., 48, 265, 287, 297
Bateson, G., 286, 300
Behrens, M., 300
Bell, N., 160, 163, 283, 286, 297
Benedict, R., 264, 265, 280
Bentley, A., 287
Berdyaev, N., 245
Bermann, E., 33, 313
Bernstein, A., 288, 293, 302
Blood, R., 33, 300
Borkenau, F., 246, 247, 250
Boszormenyi-Nagy, I., 288
Bowen, M., 293, 301, 315
Bowers, M., 250
Bridgman, P., 242
Buhler, C., 33, 42, 300, 327
Burchinal, L., 273
Burgess, E., 265, 297, 305
Burlingham, D., 285
Buxbaum, E., 285

Cain, A. C., 84, 289, 290, 292, 293, 295
Chadwick, M., 243
Chekov, A., 1
Clausen, J., 305
Cooley, C., 287
Cooper, D., 298

Dewey, J., 287

Ehrenwald, J., 288

Ellis, H., 251
Erikson, E. H., 1, 245, 285

Farber, B., 297, 305, 306, 310
Farberow, N. L., 309
Ferkiss, V., 273
Ferreira, A., 191
Festinger, L., 223, 245
Finch, S., 84, 289, 290, 292, 293, 295
Framo, J., 283
Freeman, R., 300, 311
Freidman, A., 296, 300
French, J. R. P., 288
Freud, A., 284
Freud, S., 112, 188, 239, 241, 242, 246, 251, 283, 284, 295
Fromm-Reichmann, F., 239, 245
Fulton, R., 117, 241, 252, 255

Gans, H., 304
Glaser, B., 255, 260
Goffman, E., 149
Goldman, E., 254
Goode, W., 267, 268, 297
Gorer, G., 248, 250, 251, 254, 259
Grosz, G., 120
Gutmann, D., 302

Hackett, T., 239, 242
Haley, J., 286, 301
Handel, G., 6, 7
Hartmann, H., 285, 288
Hawkins, R., 300
Hebb, D. O., 223, 247, 248, 249
Heidegger, M., 245
Hellman, I., 285
Henry, J., 1-4, 10, 11, 144, 145, 165, 176, 180, 182, 304, 311-13, 319, 320

355

Herzog, E., 238
Hill, R., 297, 303, 305
Hirohito, 64
Hutt, M. L., 1

Irish, D., 295

Jackson, D. D., 180, 286, 293, 300
Jackson, E., 250
Johnson, A., 285

Kalter, N., 321
Kaufmann, W., 240
Kelley, H. H., 172
Kelly, G., 245
Kent, J., 180, 294
Kerr, W., 242
Kluckhohn, C., 109, 287
Kluckhohn, F., 1, 109, 110, 124, 133, 154, 164
Knight, J., 250
Komarovsky, M., 305
Kubler-Ross, E., 239, 254, 256, 260

Lazarsfeld, P., 259
Lebby, S., 33
Lecky, P., 223, 245
Leger, F., 120
Lennard, H., 288, 293, 302
Lerner, M., 264, 265
LeShan, L., 250
Lewis, O., 9, 10, 303, 304
Lidz, T., 286, 287, 296, 300
Lindemann, E., 240
Litwak, E., 273
Locke, H., 265, 297
Lydgate, J., 255, 258

Malinowski, B., 304
McClelland, D., 245
McGuire, W., 307
Mead, M., 287
Merton, R., 259
Michael, S., 253

Miller, D. R., 1, 33, 145, 180, 223, 265, 310
Mills, T. M., 48
Mishler, E., 294, 299
Moore, B., 266, 298, 309
Murrell, S., 48

Naegle, K., 10, 11
Nelson, O., 154
Nimkoff, M. F., 297

Ogburn, W. F., 266, 297
O'Leary, K. D., 300
Opler, M., 1

Parsons, T., 265, 269, 287, 297
Peck, G., 136, 137
Peller, L., 241
Piaget, J., 245
Poe, E. A., 104
Pollak, O., 267, 268, 297

Rainwater, L., 304
Reiff, P., 188, 295
Risley, T., 300
Rodgers, R., 303
Rodman, H., 265
Rosenthal, H., 243, 244
Rosner, A., 240
Rousseau, H., 165
Russell, B., 254, 266, 298

Sartre, J. P., 245
Satir, V., 286
Schmidt, V., 33
Searles, H., 243, 244
Shneidman, E., 245
Sirjamaki, J., 265
Slater, P., 48
Speck, R., 300
Spiegel, J., 1, 109, 110, 117, 124, 133, 154, 155, 164, 283, 297
Stachowiak, J., 48
Strauss, A. L., 255, 260

Sumner, W., 309
Sussman, M., 273, 297

Tausk, V., 120
Thibaut, J., 172

Vincent, C., 267–69, 297
Vogel, E., 160, 163
Volkart, E., 253

Wahl, C., 242, 246
Warren, R., 180, 294
Warson, S., 144, 145

Waxler, N., 294, 299
Weisman, A., 239, 242
Westman, J., 33, 145, 310
Willems, E. P., 306, 307
Wolf, M., 300
Wolfenstein, M., 249
Wynne, L., 154, 280, 287, 300

Yarrow, M., 305

Zajonc, R., 288
Zeilberger, J., 300
Zilboorg, G., 239